GROWING THE GAME

Alan M. Klein

GROWING
THE GAME

THE GLOBALIZATION
OF MAJOR LEAGUE
BASEBALL

Yale University Press

New Haven and London

Para todos los angeles que custodian los portones y me ayudaron a pasar: Aida, Esther, Luz, Larry, y Luchy

Set in Galliard Old Style by SPI Publisher Services.

Printed in the United States of America.

Klein, Alan M., 1946–
    Growing the game : the globalization of major league baseball / Alan M. Klein.
        p.   cm.
    Includes bibliographical references and index.
    ISBN-13: 978-0-300-11045-6 (cloth : alk. paper)
    ISBN-10: 0-300-11045-6 (cloth : alk. paper)
        1. Baseball—Economic aspects.   2. Globalization.
    3. Sports and globalization.   I. Title.
    GV880.K54 2006
    331.88'11796357—dc22   2006001945

A catalogue record for this book is available from the British Library.

The paper in this book meets the guidelines for permanence and durability of the Committee on Production Guidelines for Book Longevity of the Council on Library Resources.

CONTENTS

ACKNOWLEDGMENTS

Work is a journey laced with acts of kindness great and small. Some barely know you but expend great effort to pave your way. More often, a word put in on your behalf opens a door; or the few moments people give you make the difference between success and failure. Each has happened in this work; and to all, my deepest gratitude.

My friends and colleagues continue to play a supportive role. Milton Jamail of the University of Texas has helped me since the beginning back in 1987 and continues to be a lifeline. Joseph Maguire, George Gmelch, Tim Wendel, Mark Melnik, and Arnie Arluke all played roles as well. I'm thankful that I could count on them to look at my work or let me pick their brains; and I hope someday to be able to reciprocate.

Closer to the home front, I'd like to thank Liz Sweet, Rosemary Thomas, and Virginia Mello for being there to tend to my kids when I was occupied or called away. Really: I couldn't have done it without you all. My gym buddies were also supportive, especially George Conduragis. And to my family—Jed, Mary, Cody, Benjy, and Jordan—my apologies for leaving in flesh and in spirit. Maybe you'll take a measure of joy in seeing the results, if not now, perhaps when I'm really, really old.

My gratitude also to Northeastern University for the generous Research Scholarship Development Fund grant awarded me that covered the lion's share of my travel.

Dan Heaton, who edited my manuscript for Yale University Press, played a very important role in making this book more focused, accurate, and, overall, better. He's quite simply the best editor I've ever worked with.

And to my baseball family: thanks to so many of you who aided me and rescued me as a traveler in foreign lands. Jim Small was on the scene in so many of the places I went that I grew to depend upon him. Clive Russell and Dan Bonanno of Major League Baseball International gave kindly of their time and set up many key meetings for me. Bob Whiting and Marty Kuehnert brokered my trip to Japan and lent me their expertise on Japanese baseball. The Kansas City Royals' Allard Baird and Luis Silverio smoothed the way for me in three countries by making certain that I had the contacts needed. They always encouraged me and provided me with open and honest opinions and analysis. Luchy Guerra of the Los Angeles Dodgers helped me maneuver the Dodgers front office. My trip to South Africa was successful because of the generosity of Edwin Bennett and Mike Randall of South African Baseball Union. And finally, thanks to a collection of baseball people who have at various times and in various ways helped me. Ralph Avila, to whom I have been grateful since the late 1980s, continues to give me invaluable insight. A slew of bright young executives in various clubs all helped guide my research with their honesty and insight: Ben Cherrington of the Boston Red Sox; Louie Eljaua of the Pittsburgh Pirates; Rafael Pérez, now with the Mets, but formerly in charge of the Commissioner's Office in the Dominican Republic; and Kris Rone, formerly with the Los Angeles Dodgers. Thanks to you all.

INTRODUCTION

Major League Baseball's efforts at globalization are not only provident for the future of the sport but also critical to its current prosperity. The ability of the game to rely upon its domestic base for fans and players has receded to the point where globalizing is imperative. This may be hard to square with the figures on attendance, which reached an all-time high in 2005, and with vigorous television ratings, but from a structural and long-term perspective the current boom is misleading. Major League Baseball must seek players and fans abroad, and indeed it is already doing so. The question is whether it will do so as a twentieth-century colonialist or as a twenty-first-century decentered global enterprise. The former strategy represents familiar ground but is doomed to slow growth and persistent resentment; the latter will at first feel uncomfortable but will aid the worldwide health of the sport.

In an effort to study this question systematically, I selected three of the game's organizations: two teams, the Los Angeles Dodgers and the Kansas City Royals, as well as the Commissioner's Office. All three are structurally representative of key dimensions of the industry, yet each is unique, and each approaches globalization in fundamentally different ways from the others. My attempt to chronicle their efforts spanned seven years (1999–2005) and covered eight countries. The core of this study looks at the political, economic, and structural arrangements of contemporary baseball on a global scale.

The Sphere of Baseball

The Commissioner's Office is much like any other multinational corporation: large, complex, guarded, and autocratic. Fortunately, one division within the office deals with international dimensions of the sport: Major League Baseball International (MLBI). At the time of my research, it was presided over by Paul Archey, with Jim Small as the vice president for international marketing and the head of the Japan office.

MLBI is responsible for generating foreign revenue for the major league franchise owners. To that end MLBI sells broadcast rights, secures corporate sponsorships, licenses products, and stages events abroad. Expanding the business opportunities of the game is critical, but within the larger framework of the industry, it is equally important to develop the game itself abroad. Major League Baseball has to deepen its roots where it already exists and engender interest where it is absent or exists only weakly: it must, in the business-inflected jargon of the organization, "grow the game." Hence MLBI is concerned with generating profits as well as with increasing the institutional popularity of the sport internationally. This requires a coherent view of the baseball world outside of the United States.

Jim Small provided me with that social mapping in my first interview. According to him, all countries are divided into three strata according to their baseball sophistication and the potential economic rewards they offer. Tier one countries are those in which "baseball is mature, it's well known. Also, there is some sort of economic activity and the ability for us to market against that love of baseball."[1] In places like the Dominican Republic, Japan, or Mexico, baseball is deeply entrenched, and the number of players signed to professional contracts is significant and consistent.

Tier two includes countries where the game is somewhat less developed. There may be leagues, but they are amateur or semiprofessional, and much less competitive than in the first tier. Nor do these countries produce numbers of major league players comparable to those coming from the first tier. Italy, Australia, and the Netherlands are examples. With a certain kind of inducement (and no one really knows just what that might be), any of these countries might move up. Currently Australia is experiencing something of a baseball renaissance. After almost a decade of decline, the sport seems poised to make significant headway. A new league is planned, and players are being signed in impressive numbers. The 2005 Minnesota Twins, for instance, had sixteen Australians under contract at various levels in their organization.

Tier three comprises those countries in which the sport has a tentative footing, where the game either has only recently been introduced or has not yet taken root in the local sporting tradition. South Africa, England, and Germany are all long-term baseball projects. Players signing contracts with major league organizations are relatively rare in tier three, and the sport itself has yet to establish itself outside of scattered pockets. Because it is a long-term prospect, tier three is not on the radar screen of many major league organizations, but MLBI has worked diligently to grow the game there. Thus far the results have been mixed, but for baseball to become a real global sport, it will have to find a way to become entrenched in Europe and Africa. Jim Small cautions, however, that "tiers are more art than science. We look at a combination of good economies, where we can sell products, and baseball acumen. It's not like we sat down and actually assigned numbers to these."[2] These are all judgment calls, but the classifications can be useful.

In countries where the game is firmly established, the primary interest of Major League Baseball International is economic: "Ultimately, we're charged with returning money to the owners."[3] The largest share of MLBI revenues is derived from the sale of broadcast rights in foreign markets. Japan is the wealthiest such market ever, at $275 million, but deals have been signed in the past few years in Venezuela, the Dominican Republic, Australia, and the United Kingdom. Foreign corporate sponsors have also begun to seek out Major League Baseball with greater frequency. The tier one areas of Asia and Latin America lead the way, as might be expected, because the game is so entrenched there. Corporate sponsorships include everything from promotions to All Star Game balloting to product lines. Licensing sales have also grown in direct proportion to the numbers of foreign players in major league organizations. The fourth leg of MLBI's revenue program comprises the events that it stages each year. They include preseason exhibition games, such as the weekend series in Valencia, Venezuela, in 2001 between the Houston Astros and the Cleveland Indians; regular-season games such as the 2004 opener between the New York Yankees and the Tampa Bay Devil Rays in Tokyo; and the biennial postseason visit of a major league all-star team to cities throughout Japan to play against stars of the Nippon Professional Baseball league.

In tier two and three countries the emphasis for MLBI is upon deepening the local involvement with the sport via a range of grassroots programs. The most fundamental program in the organization's arsenal is Pitch, Hit, and Run, a curriculum-based program administered through schools for children ages eight to twelve. Started in Australia in 1994, the program grew slowly. By 2002 more than three million children around the world had been introduced to it. Subsequent programs seek to build the base of young players until they are old enough to try out for their respective national teams.

Since these grassroots efforts are designed to change young people's minds as much as to develop the game, MLBI augments its hands-on programs with a range of televised programming. Getting youngsters to watch major league games is a major goal, along with promoting the creation of new sports heroes. Baseball Max, a weekly program filled with clips from games and interviews with stars, is produced by MLBI and disseminated around the world. By exposing young people in a lower-tier country to the game and to its colorful stars, MLBI hopes to make fans and players where few could be found before.

But while Major League Baseball International concentrates on being the game's ambassador to the world, ultimately it is the teams themselves that must be responsible for finding and grooming foreign talent. The Los Angeles Dodgers are an obvious choice for studying globalization in baseball because they pioneered it, and, while no longer alone, they continue to be among the most active in that arena. All major league teams are involved in the international hunt for talent, but big market teams like the Dodgers, the Atlanta Braves, and the New York Mets are exponentially the most involved. The cost of doing business overseas has risen considerably over the past decade. Consider that when Dominican superstars like pitcher Pedro Martínez signed with the Dodgers in 1988, almost no Latin American players signed for more than $10,000. Now a highly coveted prospect will easily get between $500,000 and $1,500,000; the record is Joel Guzmán's signing with the Dodgers for $2.25 million in 2001. It is precisely the wealth of big-market teams, combined with the rapid improvement of foreign talent, that has fueled these changes.

In certain foreign leagues owners who are concerned about losing their best players to the major leagues themselves further drive up the cost of signing their stars. A major league team seeking to sign a Japanese player, for example, must wait for ten years after his initial signing. When the player is finally posted as available to outsiders, interested teams must submit secret bids, the highest of which earns the team the right to negotiate with the player. Ichiro Suzuki cost the Seattle Mariners $13.125 million for the sealed bid, then $14 million for his contract.

The Dodgers may be representative of big-market teams, but they are also distinct in one key way: they are the pioneers in international baseball. While baseball entered the global arena in an institutional and business sense later than the National Basketball Association and the National Football League, in certain respects baseball has had a very long incubation period. The roots of its present-day efforts can be seen in the actions of Brooklyn Dodgers General Manager Branch Rickey more than sixty years ago. It was Rickey who, in 1945, flouted the barrier that had kept African Americans out of "organized baseball"—the major leagues as well as the recognized minor leagues—since late in the nineteenth century. In that monumental act, the first step toward globalization may be seen. On a social level, the Dodgers are to be credited with thinking outside of the box, showing a willingness to find players wherever they may be. This predisposed them to hurdle over national boundaries as quickly as they did racial ones.

Jackie Robinson entered a Dodger organization that was being configured to enable his ascent, and the handprint of Rickey was everywhere evident. Robinson possessed the right combination of personality traits, background, and baseball skill to make Rickey look like a genius, but Rickey planned Robinson's trajectory through three countries (Canada, Cuba, and the United States) to facilitate a smooth transition. Racial integration was a local response that had global repercussions unknown to Rickey and Robinson, but not to Dodger owner Walter O'Malley. Under O'Malley's stewardship (beginning in 1951), a foundation for a global perspective was laid. He built ties with Japan and the Caribbean and created an awareness of global possibilities when no one remotely considered such things. Schooled in proto-globalization, O'Malley's son Peter furthered these efforts when he took over at the helm. His progressive agenda included two signings with international impact: those of Fernando Valenzuela, from Mexico, and Hideo Nomo, from Japan.

While the Dodgers organization is a clear-cut choice for a study of big-market baseball's globalization, at first glance the Kansas City Royals seem anything but an obvious choice for the small-market representative. The Royals came to my attention after I read an article on their general manager, Allard Baird, who had made a grueling fact-finding trip to South Africa. He had hoped that South African baseball would be developed enough that a player might be signed with a good chance of making the majors. When Baird and his associate, Luis Silverio, began traveling about the country and holding tryouts, however, they quickly abandoned any notion of signing a prospect and launched into teaching baseball fundamentals instead. How many general managers would hold clinics for young people whom they know won't "matter" to their standings in the short term? I had to meet Baird, and promptly decided that he and the Royals were embracing a small-market mindset that had them globetrotting in advance of the big boys. Even in baseball-rich countries like the Dominican Republic, Kansas City has to adopt a different posture to sign players: they "shop without a credit card," as Baird puts it. The result is somewhat riskier, but affordable, signings. As a case study the Royals were perfect . . . plus, they always returned my phone calls.

How large- and small-market teams operate in global baseball is one of the core features of this study. I liken the small-market teams to the Portuguese sailors of the sixteenth and seventeenth centuries, who sailed fearlessly to corners of the world and wound up establishing a toehold in the business of colonialism. They did this not because they were intrepid explorers but rather because they couldn't compete directly against the big-market traders like Italy and France. Large-market teams have the option of going where talent is more costly, and when they err in judgment—which can cost millions of dollars—they have the luxury of trying again. Not so for the Milwaukees, the Tampa Bays, or the Kansas Citys of the baseball world. This is why small-market teams shop in Europe, while the behemoths head for Japan.

Baseball Globalization?

When people think of globalization and baseball, they typically conjure up cosmopolitan team rosters. The pitching staff of the 2005 New York Mets had players from Japan, the Dominican Republic, South Korea, Puerto Rico, and Venezuela, as well as from the United States. More than 29 percent of all major leaguers on opening day rosters in 2005 were foreign born. While most fans know that the Dominican Republic produces a lot of major leaguers (ninety-one of them as the season started), they may not realize that players are increasingly coming from Taiwan, Curaçao, South Korea, Australia, and Panama. The face of baseball today looks more like the United Colors of Benetton—Ichiro, Pedro, and the Rocket (Ichiro Suzuki, Pedro Martínez, and Roger Clemens)—than at any time in its past.

But baseball's globalization has many faces that we don't typically see. The face of Ho-Seong Koh, a South Korean manufacturer of sports caps, for example. Koh specializes in producing caps for U.S. teams. Just minutes after a team has won a championship, Koh may receive an order. He has succeeded because he can overnight a shipment anywhere in the United States. His factories in Vietnam, Cambodia, and Bangladesh make two sets of hats ahead of time, awaiting only that last-minute phone order. The phenomenon of Koreans producing for American markets, in factories throughout Asia, and doing so at high speed, is typical of globalization.[4]

Dominicans have become synonymous with baseball excellence. Consider that Dominicans, either native or first generation, have won the American League's Most Valuable Player award each year between 2002 and 2005 (Miguel Tejada, Alex Rodríguez twice, and Vladimir Guerrero), as well as the National League's MVP in 2004 (Albert Pujols). Dominicans' rise to dominance has been nothing short of spectacular, and while their heroics make the front page of most sports sections in newspapers around the United States, in their home country Guerrero's selection was treated as a national story. Guerrero collected his trophy in a ceremony at the Presidential Palace. "It's a celebration all over the country and in the streets," declared Jason Payano, the Dominican sports minister.[5] Dominican accomplishment in baseball has its flip side as well.

Young Dominicans—many impoverished—desperately seek to gain a toe-hold in the sport, giving rise to a host of problems that require action from MLB and the Dominican government. MLB's Commissioner's Office has made serious efforts, for instance, to regulate the way in which young players are signed and groomed to come to the United States—a less conspicuous, but equally important, component of globalizing the sport.

Globalization is found as well in the sudden appearance of an entire Japanese team in a newly formed professional league in California and Arizona. The Golden Baseball League has welcomed this Japanese cohort, the Samurai Bears, not shying away from any of the cultural or logistical issues posed by having such a foreign presence in their midst. When the Japanese players walk into the wrong bathroom or have to navigate an American menu or play their entire schedule on the road because they have no "home" field, the potential awkwardness is handled by all parties with aplomb and the requisite sense of humor.[6] Back in Japan, the mega-lithic corporation Dentsu signed a $275 million contract with MLB for the broadcast rights to games in Japan. The pact confirms the growing economic partnership between Japanese and North American baseball, as well as the parity of play that is increasingly coming within reach. One sees globalization also in the labyrinthine planning for a baseball World Cup, as the demands and concerns of the nations involved reflect their insistence on a level playing field. The politics of conceiving and produc-ing such an event has been a major learning experience for MLB. In fact, Major League Baseball has had to learn the lessons of globalization on its feet, and to its credit, has come a long way in a short time.

Baseball is globalized even in countries that don't play the game. Máribel Alezondo is Costa Rican. As a citizen of a soccer-playing coun-try, she might be expected to be ignorant of the game of baseball, but in one respect she knows quite a bit. She is one of the workers in the Rawlings sporting goods factory in Turrialba, where eleven hours a day she hand-stitches baseballs used by Major League Baseball. She earns about thirty cents per ball (MLB game balls cost $22.50 each, and regu-lar Rawlings balls retail for $15.00 at stores). Well, she used to anyway; Máribel quit on her doctor's advice, because the work was deforming her fingers and arms. She misses the work nevertheless, and while she may be resentful about the conditions she endured, she grows incredulous upon finding out what happens to the baseballs she labored over: "It's an injustice that we kill ourselves to make these balls perfect, and with one home run, they're gone."[7]

Globalization is also about building the game where it barely exists. In South Africa, where until recently hardly anyone knew what the sport was, hundreds of thousands of schoolchildren have been exposed to the game through Major League Baseball International's grassroots programs. Both MLBI and the Royals donated equipment to more than fifteen hundred schools in Black, White, and Colored (the country's three official racial categories) communities. In an unanticipated development, the government has acknowledged the race-free associations of baseball in postapartheid South Africa, proclaiming baseball as part of the "new South Africa." In a country where everything was identified by race, the government is eager to identify cultural elements that reflect new nonracial policies. Suddenly South African baseball is a part of the hoped-for future of the country. The Royals, unprompted, decided to help the game grow as well, teaching young players and holding coaching clinics. The effort has begun to pay off. Since 1999, seven South Africans have signed contracts with major league clubs, and three are still playing (fittingly, two in the Royals organization).

But What Is Globalization?

As ubiquitous as it appears, we remain unclear as to what globalization is. Is it new or old? Does it portend good things or promote bad? Will it render nations obsolete or not? Fundamentally, globalization is an economic-cultural process that has enveloped the world. It is a yet-to-be-completed system that has changed the way in which governments, businesses, and individuals relate to one another. Most students of globalization agree that it has compressed time and space and made the world more interdependent than at any previous time. With the demise of the Soviet Union, and with a bewildering string of breakthroughs in information technology, free-market capitalism has become *the* global system; but globalization taxes any conventional sense of capitalism. Success in today's commerce and politics is built on speed, flexibility, and knowledge.

The *New York Times* correspondent Tom Friedman is a proponent of globalization. He is fond of citing an African proverb that he feels captures its essence:

> Every morning in Africa, a gazelle wakes up.
> It knows it must run faster than the fastest lion or it will be killed.
> Every morning a lion wakes up.
> It knows it must outrun the slowest gazelle or it will starve to death.
> It doesn't matter whether you are a lion or a gazelle.
> When the sun comes up, you better start running.[8]

In the world of gazelles and lions, there are the quick and the dead; today's economic climate bears a similar turbo-Darwinian stamp: intense competition with success going to those who can innovate and change quickly, insolvency to the rest. Capital darts around the globe, brushing aside nations and political considerations, in search of the best economic return. Anything that can lower costs, increase productivity, integrate operations, and do so more quickly gains the attention of the "players." Manufacturing Nike's running shoes, Dell's computers, or Volkswagen's cars involves an internationally based set of facilities and staff up and running 24/7. Duplicating manufacturing sites; improving global communication between businesses, governments, and customers; and accelerating outsourcing (that is, moving pieces of the overall production away from the company) have become ubiquitous with globalization. Thus call centers in India routinely handle American's income tax returns and read X rays for our hospitals; but now cases are appearing as well in which Indian banks are outsourcing to American companies.[9]

In this brave new world, success goes to the swift, the knowledgeable, the adaptable. These prescriptions apply equally to Major League Baseball. It was the effort of several teams, rather than the Commissioner's Office, that initiated the global perspective in baseball. In part, that circumstance was the result of the tenures of strong owners and weak commissioners during the 1990s, but it also reflected the lack of any overarching view of the global dimensions of the sport. Globalization remained more or less the province of individual teams until about 2000, by which time MLB was lagging behind its rival sports.

Once it met the challenge, however, baseball moved swiftly and decisively in a number of directions. Through a rejuvenated Major League Baseball International, the Commissioner's Office engaged in a wide range of efforts to promote its global interests. While MLBI had been in existence since 1989, it turned the corner under the lead of Tim Brosnan and then Senior Vice President Archey, who, along with Vice President of International Marketing Small, vigorously cultivated the business opportunities in foreign markets and developed the game in countries where it was poorly developed. MLBI approached globalization differently than did individual teams. Teams went abroad primarily to find talent, while MLBI was the revenue-producing arm of the owners. The teams and MLBI serendipitously worked in tandem to globalize the game.

The questions to be answered have to do with whether or not Major League Baseball has embarked on a path that will promote the well-being of the game and the view of it as a socially progressive visitor in other quarters. To determine this we will have to put aside our fondness for the game and consider it as both an economic effort and a form of social engineering. At times this Janus-faced enterprise is in sync, while at other times there is a tension between the two. No matter which dominates— economic self-interest or social responsibility—MLB must always monitor its impact in other cultures. A World Series hangs in the balance.

1

THE CRISIS AT THE CORE

The worm turned late in 2003. Major League Baseball rallied as the little guys and the ne'er-do-wells remained in races throughout the season. Teams like the Florida Marlins, the Kansas City Royals, and the Chicago Cubs went into September very much in contention. The Boston Red Sox and the New York Yankees battled—literally—for the American League championship. After almost a decade in the doldrums, television ratings boomed; the fans exulted; and Commissioner Bud Selig declared, "There were no negatives the last two months. I had said before that I thought we were in the middle of a great renaissance. I think this confirms it. And we're going to do everything possible to continue it."[1]

By the All-Star break of the 2004 season, the numbers were beginning to show that Major League Baseball really had been able to "continue it." The game was headed toward a very big year indeed. Attendance at midseason was up 12 percent, and local cable ratings were robust. More than half of major league teams were within five games of first place in their divisions. By year's end, the attendance record was shattered, with more than 73 million fans having attended games. Gross revenues had increased to $4.1 billion from $1.6 billion in 1992. Concern over debt, which had risen by 90 percent among MLB teams, began to ease.[2] The postseason came on, and fans were glued to their seats as they watched the Red Sox make history twice, with an unprecedented comeback from a three-games-to-none deficit to beat the Yankees, then a sweep of the Cardinals for their first World Series championship in eighty-six years.

Even before the end of the season, though, Commissioner Selig was convinced that MLB had turned the corner on economic woes, competitive imbalance, and fan indifference: "The truth of the matter is that [by] any criteria that anybody wants to use, this sport has never been more popular. This is the Golden Era of the sport; it has never been more so."[3] This upsurge in popular interest continued through 2005, undaunted even by the steroid scandal that sullied some of the sport's brightest stars.

Selig had done a remarkable job instituting such major reforms and initiatives as meaningful revenue sharing, centralization of all club Internet assets, interleague play, and the wild card. His accomplishments prompted the columnist George Will to declare, "Baseball's golden age coincides with Bud Selig's Commissionership in no small measure because of the service he has rendered to the sport."[4] With things so rosy how can the possibility of a domestic crisis be broached? Talk of a crisis in baseball is valid only if we continue to think of the game in proprietary terms: as by and for Americans. Put differently, for Major League Baseball to continue its recent surge, it has to go global. This is as true for MLB as it was for the Roman Empire.

Built upon semiobscure economic underpinnings, empires tend to be recognizable either by a megalomaniacal optimism or by muscle-bound pessimism. In 1896 Senator Henry Cabot Lodge was euphoric over American worldwide successes. Conjuring up a self-righteous imperialism, tossed lightly with the pseudoscience of his day, eugenics, he gloated: "The great nations are rapidly absorbing for their future expansion and their present defense all the waste places of the earth. It is a movement which makes for civilization and the advancement of the race."[5] The good senator from Massachusetts had it right: the United States' ascent was fueled by its relationship with marginal areas, but the twenty-first century would mark the coming of age of these "waste places."

Progress, destiny, belief in the future—all form an optimistic core that feeds imperial efforts. At the other end of the continuum, however, one finds expansion motivated by the morbid need to fend off age and decay. Empires decline when "the vicissitudes of fortune, which spares neither man nor the proudest of his works . . . buries empires and cities in a common grave."[6] Extending life through expanding territory is an anthropological theme associated with theories of state formation and cultural diffusion.[7]

Within the world of American sport, Major League Baseball is poised at a crossroads which invites interpretations of empire both aging and rekindled with vigor. In 2001 baseball was reeling from declining interest, skyrocketing salaries, competitive imbalance, and, worst of all, the fiscal insolvency of the leagues. In the wake of Selig's claim that MLB had lost more than $500 million the year before, he announced the likelihood of jettisoning two teams. Just four years later, at midseason 2004, it seemed that all the news was good. Baseball was buoyed by television ratings that showed remarkable resurgence of fan interest. Ratings were up across the board. Of the twenty-eight teams within the United States, plus Montreal (omitting only Toronto, for which ratings were not available), nineteen had posted increased average ratings. Four clubs were flat and five posted losses.[8] The Boston Red Sox television network, NESN, recorded its highest rated telecast for its local market with a 15.1 on September 1, 2004. The 2004 season was also good from an attendance perspective. En route to setting a new record for attendance, nine teams drew more than three million fans each, and eleven others drew more than two million.[9]

Show Me the Crisis

Despite its recent gains, not only has Major League Baseball been eclipsed in popularity by the National Football League and the National Basketball Association; it also must compete for fans as merely one piece of a burgeoning leisure and entertainment industry. The sweeping ranges of alternatives, both within and outside of sport, have created a highly competitive field of options for consumers and devotees. MLB has worked hard to retain a firm grasp on its fan base, with some success. Yet as we shall see, some sectors have been allowed to atrophy, and these threaten the sport's future.

A second serious threat to baseball—as we have traditionally known it—involves the increased difficulty in maintaining our player base domestically. With expansion to thirty teams, the number of athletes it takes to adequately staff major league rosters and their minor league affiliates has swelled. For most of the twentieth century Major League Baseball consisted of sixteen teams employing a total of 400 players, with approximately 1,600 more in the minor leagues. Today thirty MLB clubs employ 750 major leaguers, with nearly 7,000 more in the minors.[10]

The overall vitality of the leagues also continues to be in question. Critics point to a dilution of talent with the proliferation of franchises and to the growing disparity between large and small markets. The competitive balance so essential to continued fan interest is—depending upon whom you believe—either buoyant or seriously jeopardized. Small-market teams labor (some would say struggle) to remain competitive in what continues to be an era of free spending for impact players.

Fan Demographics: Who's Being Taken Out to the Ball Game?

Demographic studies in marketing are annually paraded out and spun. They generally make for boring reading, but they tell us of "drifts"—and the longer the drift, the better. Who is coming to events? Who is spending, and on what? And perhaps more important, who is not? One kind of survey that gets at general trends is the longitudinal survey of the sort that Harris Poll takes annually. The following survey asked fans, "If you had to choose, which one of these sports would you say is your favorite?" They've asked this question for almost twenty years, and the trajectory is troubling for baseball (see Table 1).

Baseball has declined more than any other sport and is the only sport to have declined over the past twenty years. While all of the major sports

Table 1. Favorite Sport

	1985	1994	2003	Trend
Pro football	24%	24%	29%	+5
Baseball	23%	17%	13%	−10
Pro basketball	6%	11%	10%	+4
Auto racing	5%	5%	9%	+4
College football	10%	7%	9%	−1
College basketball	6%	8%	6%	+/−
Golf	3%	5%	5%	+2
Hockey	2%	5%	3%	+1

Source: "Harris Interactive Poll: Baseball vs. Other Sports," *Baseball America*, March 29–April 11, 2004, 22.

leagues have suffered losses of fans since the 1990s, some declines have been modest, or have been partially offset by increases elsewhere—for example, such demographic shifts as the declines in numbers of African-American fans offset by increases among women. Baseball, unfortunately, has been lagging behind its primary competitors. Whereas in 1985 pro football barely edged baseball as the United States' most popular sport, by 2003 the National Football League led easily. The pollsters noted that only bowling and horse racing have experienced popularity declines comparable to the thirteen-point drop in the percentage of interviewees declaring baseball as their preferred sport.[11] This is not good news for "the national pastime."

In their annual report, the leading business publication in sport, the *Sports-Business Journal*, validated the Harris Poll figures. In tracking the relative popularities of sports from 1998 to 2002, the publication found that MLB trailed the NFL, as pro football continued to be the nation's favorite sport. In 2002 more people identified themselves as fans of NFL football than of any other sport. Of the more than twenty-one thousand respondents, 67.2 percent claimed to be fans of the NFL. While MLB was solidly in second, at 58.8 percent, it had steadily slipped over the period, while the NFL had see-sawed. In another index, a 2005 Harris Poll on who Americans perceive as the top ten athletes mirrored these findings. Only one baseball player, Derek Jeter, was ranked among the cumulative top 10. Five NFL stars, two National Basketball Association stars (including Michael Jordan, who continues to rank first even in retirement), and golfer Tiger Woods and race car driver Dale Earnhardt Jr. round out the list.[12]

Race and Ethnicity

There are some bright spots, however, in particular the sport's success among Hispanic Americans. More modest but still heartening have been the gains among Asian Americans and among women. These gains, however, are countered by a continuing erosion of African-American presence both on the field and in the stands.

The *SportsBusiness Journal* figures in Table 2 present marketing demographics of the three leading spectator sports between 1998 and 2002. Over that five-year period the publication reports show that gains MLB made are not clear cut.

Table 2. Demographics of Sports Fandom, 1998–2002

Ethnicity	MLB	NFL	NBA
White	(73.0%) −3.1%	(71.1%) −2.7%	(61.8%) −5.6%
Black	(10.8%) −0.4%	(13.0%) 5.5%	(18.3%) 7.0%
Hispanic	(11.8%) 17.5%	(11.2%) 6.7%	(14.5%) 13.6%
Asian	(0.9%) 1.5%	(1.0%) −3.7%	(1.3%) −4.5%
Other	(3.5%) 21.7%	(3.7%) 20.6%	(4.1%) 23.0%

Source: By the Numbers 2004, 41.

Note: The first figure is the percentage that this group forms of the sport's total fans in 2002, the last year tallied. The second figure gauges the amount of growth or decline of the first figure over the previous five years.

According to MLB, their biggest gains have come among Latinos. The 17.5 percent gain for baseball is significantly larger than those of either of the other sports. Yet if we look at what percent of the sport's fan base is made up of Latinos, we see that they actually constitute a larger percentage of the NBA's overall fan base (14.5 percent, compared with baseball's 11.8) and that the NFL is almost equal to MLB in percentage of Hispanic fans. So to an extent, instead of blazing new market trails, MLB has been playing catch-up with the other two leagues.

MLB can also claim to be the only one of the three leading sports to have increased in popularity among Asian Americans. Still, while the overall numbers are quite small, the *SportsBusiness Journal* figures show that Asian fans make up a higher percentage of the constituencies of both the NFL and NBA than of MLB. Additionally, as with Latinos, the increased presence of Asian MLB fans must be interpreted against the even faster growth in numbers of Asians playing in the major leagues. One might expect gains in fans when Asians have made significant inroads in playing in North America. With the sole exception of Yao Ming—whose NBA career began at the end of the studied period—no comparable Asian base exists on the rosters of either the NFL or the NBA.

African-American Fan Base

By far, MLB's biggest marketing failure and cultural oversight has been the loss of the African-American community. After pioneering the racial integration of sports, Major League Baseball wore the mantle of

American sport's most progressive industry. By the end of 1953, six black players in the National League had won Rookie of the Year awards in a span of seven years. By 1954, twelve of the sixteen major league teams had African Americans playing for them, and the Dodgers faced the prospect of having as many as eight black players on the squad. All of Major League Baseball had become integrated by 1959, when the Boston Red Sox finally allowed outfielder Pumpsie Green to play for them. The numbers of players climbed, reaching their high point in 1975, when 25 percent of all major leaguers were African American.

Big league teams signing black players saw immediate increases in attendance and changes in the fan base, as more and more black fans showed up at games. The marketing potential was readily apparent. The historian Jules Tygiel noted that thousands of African-American fans made a special effort to attend Robinson's games, sometimes traveling long distances and chartering trains—"Jackie Robinson specials."[13] The Chicago reporter Mike Royko, who was at Robinson's first game in Chicago, later recalled, "In 1947, few blacks were seen in downtown Chicago. . . . That day they came by the thousands, pouring off the north-bound ELS [trains]. . . . They didn't wear baseball-game clothes. They had on church clothes and funeral clothes—suits, white shirts, ties, gleaming shoes, and straw hats."[14]

African-American interest in MLB increased alongside the development of black players entering the formerly white game; it did not however, translate into a permanent fan base for attendance. Bowie Kuhn, baseball commissioner from 1969 to 1984, claimed that statistics he was privy to indicated that "with rare exceptions [black] percentages are low, very low, under 5 percent."[15] In 1986 African-American attendance was 6.8 percent, growing to 9.8 percent in 1990. That figure plummeted to 4.8 percent by 1995–96.[16] MLB's failure to attract African Americans appears in an even worse light when compared with the success of other sports. Of the six sports surveyed in the *SportsBusiness Journal*'s annual *By the Numbers,* only MLB and the National Hockey League lost African-American fans by every measure between 1998 and 2001. Both the NFL and NBA experienced significant growth among these fans. The NBA has the highest percentage of African-American fans (18.3 percent in 2001)— an unsurprising circumstance, since the almost 80 percent of the players in the league are African American. Nearly as many NFL players—67 percent—are African American.[17]

With few exceptions, major sports leagues have been busier pandering to those communities that can afford their games than to those who produce its talent. The economics of professional sport is partly responsible for this trend: costs have risen so dramatically that in certain cities, with certain teams, even the middle class is being priced out of attending the games. Boston is an extreme but telling example: a family of four attending a 2005 Red Sox game—bleacher seating, parking, hot dogs, and a drink—could expect to pay more than $145.[18]

Aging Fan Base

The results of at least two studies conducted during the 1990s indicate that Major League Baseball's fan base is getting older. Marketing publications noted as early as 1993 that baseball fandom skewed older than any of the other major sports.[19] These results were confirmed by Allen St. John in 1998. Relying on an internal market research document from MLB Enterprises, St. John reported that among twelve- to eighteen-year-olds, 67 percent call themselves baseball fans. By contrast, 82 percent consider themselves basketball fans, and 78 percent are football fans.[20] The converse of that finding—that the fan base is aging—was acknowledged again by Rick Horrow, writing in 2004, for SportsLine.com. He referred to the sobering fact that 47 percent of 2003's World Series audience was fifty years of age or older.[21] The *Washington Times* writer Eric Fisher has also noted that baseball fans average more than forty years of age, "much older than [for] other leading sports."[22]

The loss of younger fans is not simply a baseball issue. In an ESPN Sports poll conducted in 2000 and 2002 to gauge fan interest in the NBA, the NFL, MLB, and Major League Soccer, two age groups were targeted: children seven to eleven years of age and those twelve to eighteen. In both age categories all sports leagues except Major League Soccer experienced declines in fan bases.[23] Immediately following the successful collective bargaining agreement between MLB and the Players Association, the Commissioner's Office began reaching out to younger fans with an ad campaign. Nonetheless, viewership for the 2003 All-Star Game continued a disturbing downward trend. The 18–34-year-old segment of the audience continued to decline, and did so at a faster clip than the 25–54-year-olds, who also continued to abandon the game.[24] Good news finally came when the hard-fought 2003 League Championship Series reversed this trend. The 2004 World Series was also considered a viewing success, with a 15.8 rating. While these figures reversed some of the losses of the past few years, and while match-ups affect the numbers in any particular year, the long-range trend indicates that such numbers constitute about half of what the ratings were in the 1980s.

Whether baseball can continue to increase its fan base remains to be seen, but MLB Executive Vice President for Business Tim Brosnan understands the depth of the problem: "Baseball is no longer the killer application for every age group. That's the big challenge we face. We're having to work harder to give kids a reason to go to the ballpark." MLB has decided to meet this historic challenge with more aggressive marketing. One recent effort was an aborted attempt to "partner" with Columbia Pictures, the maker of the film *Spiderman 2*. The film's logo was to be put on bases in parks around the league, but the initiative was dropped a day after being announced. Brosnan had backed the failed move as part of a marketing effort to respond to the threat of losing the next generation of fan. Older purists doubtless weighed in heavily on this ploy, however, and twelve-year-olds were ignored. Nonetheless, baseball's marketing effort is now clearly focused on them. "Kids are getting just bombarded with options," continued Brosnan. "There is no way we can or will rest on our laurels. Is there enough there to sell the game? Of course there is. . . . At the same time, however, we know our business spikes when there are major events to capture people's attention. So, if there's any overarching goal to our marketing, it's that we're going to event-ize the business, to turn that into a verb."[25]

Where Have All the Players Gone?

Race

The struggle to retain the fan base represents only one piece of the crisis MLB has to contend with. Another is the growing inability to generate a sufficient talent base from within its conventional borders.

According to Major League Baseball Players Association Director of Communications Greg Bouris, "Beating the bushes to shake out talent has become intense. It used to be that baseball organizations would assign scouts to bird-dog around high school sandlots in the U.S. Now you almost have to cover the four corners of the world."[26] A major source of the problem is the dwindling numbers of African Americans coming to the game. Northeastern University's Center for the Study of Sport in Society, in its 2005 annual report on race, noted that only 9.5 percent of major leaguers were African American, the lowest percentage in twenty-five years.[27] What caused this slide?

Major League Baseball, it can be argued, never really overcame its racial problems. There was and is a fundamental discomfort on the part of scouts and other baseball administrators associated with approaching the black community. That was certainly the opinion of Kansas City Royals All-Star second baseman Frank White, thinking back to his signing in the early 1970s.[28] The problem of a declining African-American player base began to be noted among some of the best sports journalists some time later. In the summer of 1991 the baseball columnist Peter Gammons commented on the declining numbers of black players in the game: "Take college baseball. It looks like it did 45 years ago (1946 at the time of the Robinson signing). . . . The Cape Cod League [an elite league for the nation's best collegiate athletes] this summer has only eight blacks."[29] Also drawing upon data from the 1990s, the sport sociologist Harry Edwards pointed to an increasingly deteriorating base of black athletes in a range of sports, not the least of which was Major League Baseball.[30] NCAA statistics document that, as of the 2003 college sports season, African-Americans account for only 4 percent of college baseball players on scholarship, compared with almost 50 percent in football and 66 percent in basketball.[31]

In black communities high school baseball programs are being eliminated due to lack of interest. At Alfred Lawless High School in New Orleans, for instance, former baseball coach Charles Searles commented that his program is "not getting the influx of young kids from the park leagues to play baseball in high school. If you travel around the city, you will see parks where baseball is being played, and Caucasian kids playing in parks from the age of 6 on. You do not see black kids out there playing at that age."[32] In an ironic sidenote related to the declining interest in baseball among African Americans, traditionally black colleges have taken to recruiting white baseball players to fill out their teams.[33]

What is it about baseball that has come to be rejected by a generation of black youth? "I grew up playing baseball," reminisces Searles. "My hero was Willie Mays. Today's heroes are basketball players who make tons of money. Football players who make tons of money."[34] For young African Americans in whose lives the athlete-hero model looms so large, the fast payoff as well as the most glamorous and visible one is more apparent in the Denver Nuggets' Carmello Anthony than in the number one pick in the baseball draft. The ability of LeBron James to move directly from high school basketball to the Cleveland Cavaliers of the NBA is only the latest in a series of such transitions to the pros. Inner-city children readily identify with the immediacy of NBA or NFL superstar status. Orsino Hill, a Colorado Rockies scout and former player, told *Denver Post* reporter Mike Klis, "It's very rare that you see African-Americans playing baseball." Klis draws a forbidding picture of minor league life: "The star college baseball player goes straight to Elmira, N.Y., for the minor leagues. On a bus. With $15 a day meal money, and an $850 a month salary. 'Baseball's just not as glamorous as the other sports,' [longtime major leaguer Tom] Goodwin said. 'In baseball, you're drafted, and you're hot stuff for a couple minutes, and the next thing you know, you're gone. A couple years later, your buddies are going, "whatever happened to that guy?" . . . Little kids see that.' "[35] The St. Louis Cardinals' field coordinator, George Kissell, echoes these sentiments: "Kids want to go right to the big leagues from college, whether it's pro basketball or football." Royce Clayton, one of the dwindling numbers of African-American major leaguers, blames basketball: "It's the era of basketball. The NBA has done a terrific job of marketing, appealing to young African-Americans. They market directly to African Americans with their hip hop genre. In the hip hop videos, they're all wearing basketball shoes. You've got basketball players rapping. At this point in time, it's more attractive for a young black man to go out and play basketball than it is to play baseball."[36]

In 1989 in South Central Los Angeles, the former big leaguer John Young knew that baseball's relationship with the black community had soured. He concocted what he envisioned as the antidote—Revitalizing

Baseball in Inner-cities (RBI)—and nursed it along with help from the city and the Los Angeles Dodgers. The organization has been working mostly through Boys and Girls Clubs of America. The Commissioner's Office took over institutional control of RBI in 1991 and likes to claim that the program has spread to two hundred inner cities. More than 120,000 children have played in the program, but until Vic Darensbourg broke in with the Marlins in 1998, no RBI product had reached the majors. Since Darensbourg, only four others have made it.

In March 2003 the city of Los Angeles's Planning Commission approved plans for MLB to build a $6 million sports academy for at-risk youth. After rejecting the possibility of building a state-of-the-art ball field on top of a landfill, MLB opted instead to move it down the road to Compton, California. This became the first domestic academy since the Kansas City Royals experimented with one in the early 1970s. A host of benefits accrue to those who attend it, including free academic, athletic, and career training on the campus and at a nearby community college. Crowed Commissioner Selig, "It is our intention to bring baseball back to urban America, and this is a major step in that direction."[37] The facility, housed on twenty acres on the Compton Community College campus, has two playing fields, a softball field, and a youth field. No one is certain whether the initiatives involving RBI can turn the tide, but the program has received active support in recent years; for example, a new facility in Harlem was unveiled in April 2005.

Age

With the recent spate of news reports about increasing childhood obesity, additional findings that youngsters are playing sports less than they used to should not be surprising. Overall participation in youth sports declined between 1985 and 2000, according to a report by the Sporting Goods Manufacturers Association.[38] The trend in the years since seems unchanged. The general inclination for children to play informal sport is offset somewhat by increased participation in organized sport. While the figures show that some children are developing very focused interests in sports—playing one to the exclusion of anything else, for example— overall time spent by children playing sports in general declined. The study shows that the largest drops were for boys; girls' programs actually increased in participation rates. Female athletes on high school varsity teams increased 40 percent in the 1990s, and soccer has made striking gains, increasing 65 percent in that decade. How did baseball fare? The biggest declines were for softball and volleyball (36 and 33 percent, respectively), but baseball was the next big loser, at 20 percent.

Little League Baseball, the signature program for organized youth baseball, lost 10 percent of its player base in the five-year span between 1997 and 2002. The number of players declined from 2.46 million to 2.23 million, causing Little League Baseball's chief spokesperson to comment, "We have never had four years in a row where our numbers have gone down. It's a real cause for concern."[39] Over a longer span of time, the drop is even more dramatic. Amateur baseball enjoyed robust participation in 1987, when fifteen million played the game. By 2004 participation had dropped 27 percent, while soccer, hockey, and lacrosse are enjoying a boom. Of the 6,400 leagues making up Little League Baseball in the United States in 1997, almost 300 have since folded. The study that Little League Baseball commissioned to figure out what can be done to stem the tide recommended that additional playing time be given to the most marginal players, "those most vulnerable to giving up the sport."[40] That solution assumes that the only problem is insufficient inclusivity. The decline is not found only among those riding the bench, however. Little League Baseball can be considered to be the sport's version of the canary in the mineshaft. Its failing health points to a host of problems from the pace of the game to the lackluster way that many MLB stars interact with the young.

Structural Weaknesses: The Economics of Competitive Balance

When the Marlins won the 2003 World Series over the heavily capitalized and favored New York Yankees, people began to speculate about whether the era of the big-market teams was passing. "Marlinization" came to be a baseball euphemism for small-market success. In the same year Michael Lewis's *Moneyball* appeared, extolling Oakland A's General Manager Billy Beane as a small-market sorcerer. With one of the lowest payrolls in the game, the Athletics were regularly contending in the American League West. The economically challenged Kansas City Royals, with a $41 million payroll, were vying for the AL Central Division lead right into August. These David-like successes, however, came amid Major League Baseball's biggest crisis. Competitive imbalance, a crisis that has been long fermenting, has the potential to be structurally debilitating to the industry. A little more than one season following "Marlinization," Beane was forced to trade two of his prize pitchers for a gaggle of prospects. Midway through the 2004 season Royals G.M. Allard Baird traded away his franchise player, Carlos Beltran, for a couple of unproven prospects as well. Early in the 2005 season both the A's and the Royals looked the way the fiscally malnourished are supposed to: bereft of the stars they cultivated and scouring the minor leagues for replacements. The A's rebounded nicely after the All-Star break, while the Royals fell just short of the American League record for most consecutive losses.

While the disparity of revenue and fortune between large- and small-market teams has always been a part of the picture, the gap grew so much in the 1990s that the well-being of the game was threatened, according to Commissioner Selig. Baseball's number two man, Executive Vice President of Baseball Operations Sandy Alderson, was often heard to warn, "The gaps are widening. . . . Without a change to the system, the competitive imbalances will get progressively worse."[41] MLB competitive imbalance is measured primarily by the differing capacity of teams to generate revenue. This economic imbalance affects a team's ability to win over time. In any given year a team like the Florida Marlins can succeed, but competitive imbalance means that with rare exceptions—the Minnesota Twins, for example, remain the poster child for small-market success—a small-market team cannot be expected to compete consistently or with predictability.

The options for small-market teams include building highly successful scouting operations capable of drafting signable players, and pushing to find talent abroad. Because large-market teams are able to sign the best players in the amateur draft, as well as free agents, small-market teams such as Kansas City find it difficult to sign the best draft picks available to them. Nor can they hold on to their players once they manage to sign them. Hence, outfielders Jermaine Dye, Johnny Damon, and Raúl

Ibañez all left the Royals when free agency kicked in, and Beltran was traded. And so it goes, as a baseball analog of the food chain: small-market clubs develop stars that play for them until such time as they can declare free agency, then big-market teams gobble them up. While not all such moves worked out for the players or their new teams, the ability to sign a player whenever it is deemed advisable gives big-market teams a leg up. Following several years of tempered bidding in the free agent market, the large-market teams seemed to throw caution to the wind in the winter of 2004. Teams spent more than $1 billion, almost all of it by such big-market teams as the Yankees and Red Sox. By contrast, the Royals spent $2.5 million, Tampa Bay $3 million, Milwaukee $9.3 million.

Just what constitutes "competitive balance" may be open to debate, but it clearly includes having resources. The absence of competitiveness dampens the ardor of fan, advertiser, and media alike. It can kill a league. As revenue becomes harder to generate, the possibility of success fades for small-market teams. In the seven years from 1994 through 2000, when there was no revenue sharing or luxury tax, fifty-one of the fifty-six major league teams, or 92 percent, that qualified for the playoffs were in the top half of player payrolls.[42] Since revenue sharing began the situation has improved some, but the franchises with the biggest payrolls still dominate. From 2001 through 2005, teams in the upper half of payroll took thirty-two of forty postseason slots, or 80 percent.

Revenue Sharing

To achieve a measure of parity and fiscal salvation, the Commissioner's Office put a revenue-sharing plan in place after the 2000 season. Its primary purpose is to enable low-revenue (usually small-market) clubs to get the capital needed to regain competitiveness by boosting payroll and signing more impact players. Under the 2002 collective bargaining agreement, each team puts 34 percent of its local operating revenue into a fund. All thirty teams share 75 percent of that pool evenly. The remaining 25 percent is split among the clubs that generated less than the major league average. In 2001, for instance, each team received at least $24.4 million. The major league average was $94.3 million in local operating revenue, so those teams earning less than that shared the final 25 percent of the pool. The result was a transfer of $169 million from high- to low-revenue clubs. Under this plan, some teams that would otherwise show losses for the year make profits instead. The Athletics lost more than $7 million in 2001 before revenue sharing, from which they received $10.5 million. Thus they came away showing some $3 million in the black. At worst, big losses shrink: the Expos lost $38.5 million before revenue sharing, $10 million after it. Under the current collective bargaining agreement (which remains in effect through 2006), the redistribution has grown to $243 million in 2004, $258 million in 2005.

The Zimbalist Critique

The foremost critic of MLB's arguments for contraction, and of its economic policies in general, is the economist Andrew Zimbalist. In *May the Best Team Win,* Zimbalist lays out his disagreement with the Commissioner's Office.[43] He takes issue with MLB on a number of points, but primarily with its claim to be creating parity. Revenue sharing, according to Zimbalist, is not being used to increase payroll. Industry insiders claim that in 2005 "low revenue clubs receive about $60 million each before the first customers arrive, from revenue sharing, national television and licensing."[44] The player agent Scott Boras concurs: "The revenue sharing funds are not being used universally to retain players and improve major league rosters. In some cases, it's just simple profit taking. The focus is not on parity."[45] Royals General Manager Baird, however, adamantly rejected this claim, saying, "Every penny goes back to the clubs' efforts to compete."[46]

Structural factors related to economics also work against MLB's efforts to promote competitive balance. Zimbalist writes that a significant disincentive exists for small-market teams to invest their share of redistributed funds in players' salaries. Zimbalist calculated the effective marginal tax rates enforced by the revenue-sharing plan, finding that the average tax rate for the top-revenue teams is 39 percent and that for the bottom teams it is actually higher, at 41 percent (rising to 47 percent by the end of the agreement in 2006). This creates an unsettling economic scenario. Using the Kansas City Royals as an example, Zimbalist shows that if the Royals played responsibly, they would be economically penalized. If, on the other hand, they cut payroll and performed with less on-field success, they would be rewarded with a greater share of the revenue-sharing plan: "For every decrease in revenues of $1, the Royals would see their transfers increase by 47 cents. So, if the decrease in payroll plus the increase in transfers exceeded the decrease in revenues, the Royals' profit-maximizing strategy would be to lower payroll."[47]

In the final analysis, the game must still be strategized and played. Shrewd acquisitions, avoidance of injury, career years by key players, and great team chemistry can make a season. The 2005 Yankees had a payroll of more than $200 million, yet as September rolled around they were struggling for wild card contention in the American League. Still, if Yankees management feels that another impact player is needed, the team has the money to go out and get him; not so for small-market teams. Since 2002 we have seen an increase in the number of teams battling for playoff spots with modest payrolls and revenue production. But when we correlate level of payroll with likelihood of getting into the playoffs from 2000 to 2004, we continue to get a sense that money still walks the walk. Among small-market teams, only Oakland and Minnesota have been consistent playoff contenders. A final index of this sort of structural imbalance was made clear following the 2004 winter meetings. As teams begin to negotiate with free agents, the *Miami Herald*'s Kevin Baxter observed that while the industry was still spending money upon free agents, it was simultaneously controlling payrolls. This development is contributing to a two-tier economic system among players. The number of players earning $12.4 million or more has doubled since 2001, but the number of players earning at least $1 million has declined for three straight years. This is only one more measure of the economic divide forming in baseball. Clearly the Twins or Royals are more likely to sign the latter players, while the large-market teams can get their share of the Carlos Beltrans and the Pedro Martínezes.[48]

There are enough signs on the horizon to give pause to the jubilation coming from MLB's quarters. Structural problems affecting the reproduction of both the fan base and player ranks exist. Whether or not they are debilitating enough to ruin the industry's health remains to be seen, but they should be addressed. MLB is doing so. Perhaps not denying issues it is facing is the most healthy reaction of all. With its myriad programs and policies concerning international development, we can examine a wide spectrum of initiatives and results around the world.

2

THE KANSAS CITY ROYALS: SHOPPING
WITHOUT A CREDIT CARD

Newt Allen, an infielder for the Kansas City Monarchs of the Negro Leagues, characterized Kansas City as "a good baseball town, if you're a winner. You've got to win, though. That's the reason the Royals and the A's had such a time. But you put a team up in first or second place, and the fans will turn up."[1] The Kansas City Royals now face the consequences of Allen's dictum, having lost consistently for most of the past fifteen years. To survive such a cold spell takes a bond between the fans and the team forged of both mutual affliction and affection. Negro League teams had a constituency, as well as a strong identity with their locales, that provided a haven for them. The Royals have the challenge of holding onto the affection of their fans in a Darwinian sport atmosphere of survival as a small-market team.

The Kansas City Royals are what many consider the classic small-market team. Compared with the large metropolitan areas of Los Angeles, New York, or Chicago, Kansas City, straddling the Missouri-Kansas line, has a small, homogenous population. Its location in the American rural heartland accentuates the small local population, making for a small television market and hence stunted revenues from local broadcast deals. As a result, the Royals' owners don't have the resources to spend lavishly on free agents. When Commissioner Selig broached the topic of major league contraction in 2003, the Royals were briefly mentioned as a possible candidate to surrender their franchise.

The team, however, has worked hard to turn its fortunes around. New ownership, a new general manager, and the creation of a set of strategies well suited to small markets enabled the Royals to compete deep into the 2003 season. Following disappointing seasons in 2004 and 2005, the team has aggressively, and at times creatively, sought to assemble a youthful core of talent for the future. Though at times people characterize the team as hapless, Royals General Manager Allard Baird has a plan to bring success back to this middle America team.

The Kauffman Years

When baseball fans think of expansion teams, they tend to have one of two scenarios in mind. One involves a lengthy building process in which both team and fans endure years of failure before becoming competitive (the New York Mets, or Seattle Mariners). The other features a wealthy owner who promptly goes out to buy the best team and competes in a hurry (the Florida Marlins). The two scenarios contrast the tribulations of the long-suffering with the instant (if empty) gratification of the rich. Kansas City fits neither mold.

The Royals were the first really cutting edge expansion team, and their first owner, Ewing Kauffman, was not cautiously frugal, extravagant, or lacking in vision. This self-made billionaire started a pharmaceutical venture in his basement that became Marion Laboratories, one of the nation's biggest. With no background in baseball, Kauffman nevertheless fashioned a successful expansion team by combining a strategy of building from the ground up with cultivation of a local sense of the team built around loyalty, stability, and reward, and a policy of hiring the best baseball advisers he could find. Nothing about this strategy is remarkable, except for how successfully it was carried out.

In just its third year of existence the club began to contend, and by the mid-1970s it became a force, winning American League West Division titles in 1976, 1977, and 1978. The Royals continued their dominance of the AL West through most of the 1980s, winning division titles in 1980, 1984, and 1985. Twice they went to the World Series, losing in 1980 to the Philadelphia Phillies and beating the St. Louis Cardinals in 1985 to become world champions.

This success may be difficult for the current generation of fans to grasp, accustomed as they are to thinking of the Royals as bottom dwelling. But for an 83–79 record in 2003, the team would have carried a string of twelve straight losing seasons into 2006. The era of muscled up payrolls, new "old" stadiums, and escalating costs, at times made the Royals look threadbare and atavistic. Their $41 million payroll in 2003 was just about the same as a decade earlier. Yet while in 1992 that was the tenth-highest payroll overall, by 2003 that figure was twenty-ninth, or the second-lowest in all of Major League Baseball.

Having been in baseball since 1954, in various scouting capacities, Art Stewart, currently senior adviser to the Royals' general manager, has observed all of the changes the Royals have faced. Before coming to the Royals, Stewart spent sixteen years with the Yankees. In reminiscing, he points out what it was about the Kauffman alternative that so appealed to him: "They sold the Yankees in 1965 to CBS . . . and the minute CBS took over you could see that the Yankees were not the Yankees anymore. The closeness, the sense that you were an important part of the front office, part of the success was gone. Then, when Lou Gorman called and told me what the Kauffman family wanted to do, I came right over. Mr. Kauffman went out and paid for the best people, but he wanted it to be like Marion Labs—a family."[2]

Using a business as a model for a ballclub, it could be argued, is as risky and fraught with corporate culture as CBS's purchase of the Yankees had been. Kauffman, however, was an owner who was the antithesis of the conventional business mogul. In most corporate takeovers, staffs are trimmed, costs are cut, and an atmosphere of fear reigns supreme. Kauffman's baseball ownership was the opposite. He created a climate of merit, security, and trust. "He'd take off his fancy, expensive coat," Stewart recalls, "roll up his sleeves, and sit [in an organizational meeting] for ten hours listening to every word. . . . And he took notes. If you produced, you were well rewarded. One of the first things he did for his employees at the Royals was institute one of the greatest profit-sharing plans that had ever been on this earth. First, he paid well. He made sure that those scouts that walked away when their time came walked away with $500,000 to $800,000 in profit sharing. Then he created a pension in addition to that!"[3]

Kauffman was able to innovate in several areas of baseball operations as well. He had all prospective draftees tested for depth perception—a notion that had never occurred to anyone. Any prospect who failed this test would have problems hitting in night games. The Royals bypassed several first-round draft picks as a result of this test.

Kauffman's most significant innovation was the creation of major league baseball's first academy. Baseball followers today know of academies in the Dominican Republic and Venezuela, but before any of these existed, the Royals instituted a little-remembered but wildly successful experiment in the United States.

The Kansas City Royals Baseball Academy began in 1970 and ended in 1974. In that brief span it produced fourteen major league players, the most notable being the Royals' five-time All-Star second baseman Frank White and outfielder U. L. Washington. Located on 120 acres outside Sarasota, Florida, the Royals Academy was, according to Stewart, who was intimately involved with its origins, a "state of the art facility."

Its origins represent an intriguing combination of factors. Ewing Kauffman conceived of the academy as a way of finding and developing talent that may have been overlooked by others. Frank White was a member of the first academy class in 1970. While he put together a brilliant major league career, he was almost bypassed. White related that Lou Gorman, then the general manager, "told me that I had been scouted but was not considered a prospect. If I hadn't gone to the academy, I probably wouldn't have made it into baseball. You're coming out of the late 1960s with lots of turmoil, with the civil rights movement. I think a lot of scouts weren't willing to go into the inner cities to scout black ballplayers. And I think that Mr. Kauffman felt that a lot of ballplayers were being overlooked, and that's why he had the idea of starting the academy."[4]

Art Stewart knew from the onset that the academy was going to tap into a talent base that was not being fully evaluated:

> I had my first tryout camp in Peoria, Illinois. Registration was at nine in the morning. I got there about a quarter to eight, and here's this long line of over a hundred kids just for this camp! And the first kid we saw in line was a big, strong kid, only sixteen years old. We find out this kid is something else! He's a catcher.

Great arm! Great left-handed batter! Now he wasn't eligible to sign, but what it did point out was that you could find [in the inner city] a top prospect that no one else had ever heard of. He was the only player in major league history to be drafted first pick out of high school. Didn't sign, though, and then taken number one out of college; his name was Danny Goodwin. That was the first kid I ever saw in these tryout camps.[5]

The idea of the academy was not at first hailed by baseball insiders, according to White: "Well, it was ridiculed quite a bit at first by other major league teams, by front-office people, and even some of our own. Mr. Kauffman bought the team in '69, and starts an academy a year later! So, he was seen as a guy who knew nothing about baseball. A pharmacist by trade, and here he was with this phenomenal new idea."[6]

The establishment of the academy was impressive, as much for its expansive nature as for the small touches—for example, Kauffman's wife, Muriel, picked out all the bed sheets and pillow cases. The physical layout of the academy took shape quickly. As a member of the first cohort, Frank White remembers, "We had two lakes on it. We had our own cafeteria, an ample locker room. The dorm housed fifty. We had a tennis court and Olympic-sized swimming pool."[7] The players who attended the academy were given free tuition at Manatee Junior College, about twenty minutes away. Kauffman made certain that the players received high-quality baseball instruction as well. "Kauffman had a slew of instructors coming all the time," according to Stewart. "Ted Williams would be there. It was an intense training program for those kids who had not played much baseball. Charlie Lau, the legendary hitting instructor who helped George Brett, would come down and work with the kids, and take 'em to watch tape frame by frame of their hitting."[8]

Ewing Kauffman's idea for an academy was well ahead of its time, and probably should have been allowed to flourish. Kauffman thought so, telling Stewart, "Art, my only regret is that I let them talk me out of the academy." Today, Major League Baseball is busy reinventing Kauffman's wheel by fashioning an academy for its Revitalizing Baseball in the Inner City (RBI) program. The goal is the same: trying to get at a wealth of minority talent within the nation's cities.

It is said that a man's character is revealed by how he dies, and Kauffman continued to illustrate what can only be described as a rare concern with philanthropy: "When Mr. K. died, the club was held in trust until new owners could be found," Stewart relates. "Where else could you find an owner of a major league team, when he passed away, have it stated in his will that his club would be donated to the charities of a city? Every penny that the Glass family paid for this franchise was divided among the charities of Kansas City. It's never happened in the history of sport!"[9]

The team began to decline in the 1990s, a trajectory that has continued into the new millennium. Royals brass believes that the team is poised to break that string. Revitalization began with the Glass family, who bought the club in 2000 and hired Allard Baird as general manager.

Allard Baird: Positively Retro

When I saw Allard Baird during spring training in 2004, he looked uncharacteristically tired. "Yeah, but it's a good tired. We're getting stuff done," he said. While ballplayers seemingly play their way into season-ready form, baseball operations people fire on all cylinders during this time of year, even if it has always been thought of as an easygoing rite of spring. A bad trade or free-agent hire can result in a lost season. Baird's security may be even more tenuous than that of most G.M.'s, since he oversees a small-market team with a recent string of losing seasons. In 2002 Baird's Royals achieved an ignominious benchmark in baseball: they had lost one hundred games in a season for the first time in club history. That fall, I secretly prayed that Allard Baird would hold on to his position long enough to have a chance at success. That turnaround happened the following year, when the Royals contended for the lead in the AL Central through most of the season. Baird was credited with the rebound, and some of his moves that had gone unnoticed or been questioned in the previous brutal season were suddenly seen as genius. "Royals Success Proves Baird's Acumen," was the headline on one story.[10] "Baird the Royal Architect," read another.[11] The baseball world was taking notice of this team again after eight straight losing seasons, and much was made of Baird's hiring of Tony Peña as manager. During the 2002 season Baird had been second-guessed for promoting minor leaguers when it was clear that the team was floundering. "Everybody was saying, 'You're going to lose a hundred games.' To me, what's the difference between ninety and a hundred? . . . I'm not satisfied with losing, but let's run the young kids up there through the last six or seven weeks, shortening the learning curve, and if we lose, we lose. There's no [other] way that we would start off the way we did [in 2003]. . . . It was a price we had to pay."[12] On the eve of the 2004 season expectations regarding the Royals rose among the faithful and throughout the league. Allard has woven together a patchwork of strategies through his passion for the job and the challenge of taking over a franchise on the ropes. He's prepared to work at any time and anywhere.

In spring 2004 I rode with Baird to a spring training game in Arizona against the Diamondbacks. Crammed in along with us was Baird's operations staff: Muzzy Johnson, assistant G.M.; Art Stewart, senior adviser to the G.M.; Joe Jones, special assistant, baseball operations; and Brian Murphy, adviser to the G.M., all of whom randomly read aloud baseball material pulled from the wires that day. Compared with A's General Manager Billy Beane—the poster boy for the new school of baseball management—Baird's staff is positively retro. Beane-ball emphasizes slick trading and an obsession with statistical criteria more than scouting for evaluating talent. Baird and his staff, irrespective of their titles, are all scouts.

Weaving in and out of traffic, Allard's staff is fashioning repartee around the material being read. The items may have to do with performance, "How could they send him down? He's batting .600." Or injury, "That's the second time he's injured that knee." Or just superficial observation, "Man, he looks a lot like his dad." They can riff off of any of these topics. Baird speaks only occasionally, usually to ask for clarification. If Howard Stern and his sidekick Robin Quivers had a baseball program, it might resemble a more ribald version of this. Hearing something that interests him, Baird comments to Johnson, and at least twice en route that was followed by a phone call to another G.M. with the particulars of a trade that one or another was proposing or had proposed. Baseball is packed with overtures and inquiries that need time to mature into actual deals. The game was uneventful. Baird has a number of other meetings waiting for him when we finally get back to the Royals offices at 6:30 in the evening. He's hardly winded from what has already been a long day.

Baird Fits in Kansas City

Allard Baird is a baseball journalist's dream. He's a general manager who actually seems to go out of his way to cultivate his relations with the press. Members of his staff say that he spends a couple of hours a day with media and in other public relations functions. Accessibility is one quality that makes it a pleasure to work with Baird, but it is scarcely the mark of the man.

In this world of slick young baseball executives, Baird is Cinderfella—though with the trim, conditioned body of a former middle infielder he looks better in his clothes than do his counterparts. More and more baseball executives these days seem to have law school credentials and a Rotisserie League mindset. Baird's selection as Royals G.M. may seem a bit outmoded. To begin with, Allard Baird lacks much of the sense of entitlement that seems branded into those who attend elite schools. Instead of using his degree as a vehicle with which to rise to the top of a major league organization, Baird just wanted to manage . . . anywhere: "I thought I was going to end up managing in the minor leagues."[13] Having played at Southern Arkansas University in 1983–1984, he went on to coach briefly at Broward Community College in 1986–1987. This was followed by a stint as hitting coach in the Royals system.

For the Baird family, "work"—any work—was vital in defining a person. Throwback? Perhaps, but nevertheless, refreshing in major league baseball these days. There were other values, equally old fashioned. Loyalty, for instance, has no place in a globalized world that places a premium on being footloose. Loyal is, however, precisely what Allard Baird is, and by extension what the Royals prize. When he was asked to interview for a senior position with the Tampa Bay Devil Rays in 1999, Baird mixed altruism with some economic tenacity, "I interviewed, but it came down to loyalty. I was born into the Royals organization, and I'm going to stay with it."[14]

The bane of the small-market team is high-priced talent. Free agency and bloated media contracts have helped drive up the market value of players to the point where teams like the Royals, Brewers, or Twins find it increasingly difficult to sign and keep players. To compete on the field, management in these small-market franchises has to find ways of getting good talent affordably. "Going shopping without a credit card" is how Baird puts it. As a result, such teams become more selective and creative. Allard Baird is neither embarrassed nor stymied by his team's comparatively poorer position, "I don't want anybody to feel bad for us. That's our challenge." When I wondered whether he ever gets frustrated by his fiscal challenge, Baird cut me short: "I never look at it that way. I think that people in our organization just look at it as, 'this is the system we work in, and these are the boundaries.' We have to make it work. I'm not saying that [frustration over limited resources] is not real. Oh, it's real, all right. We might like a player, but then we can't afford him. It is natural to think, 'Well, if you want to compete, you've got to step it up.' What do you step it up to? We know our boundaries, so we've got to work harder."[15]

Baird's notions of putting together a competitive product is less an economic theory than a series of strategies rooted in small-market economics. Small-market general managers think alike in most ways, but Baird has configured something that's a little bit different, perhaps tailored more toward Kansas City. The base of any small-market team is developing its own farm system. That is the cheapest and best way to bring talent to the team, and it begins with scouting and drafting.

Scouting, Drafting, and Risk Strategies

Developing players begins with scouting, an understanding which Baird brings to his job. All teams approach the annual draft of eligible high school and college players with an eye to signing the highest draft pick possible. Drafting in reverse order of the previous season's finish should, theoretically, benefit poorer teams, but many factors can alter the nature of first-round picks. A team may have gained or surrendered a first-round pick as compensation for a free-agent signing, or it may simply face strict economic constraints. The latter condition particularly affects teams like the Royals. They must find talent on the margins, talent overlooked; they must find talent through a sometimes complex series of transactions. Always, there is a premium on superior scouting: cleverness, keen assessment, and ability to respond quickly. Teams like the Twins, Brewers, or Royals are similar to the Portuguese explorers of the sixteenth and seventeenth centuries. All were underdogs, but by virtue of tirelessness and willingness to scour the earth for an economic leg up, all could remain competitive.

On the surface nothing could be simpler. In need of middle infielders or pitching, a team can, during its turn, draft the best prospect to answer its need. For small-market teams, however, picking the top players in the draft is not always realistic. Because top draft picks command huge signing bonuses, cash-conscious teams may have to think long and hard before committing to as yet unproven talent.

Ironically, while small-market clubs have to take risks to thrive, they are the very ones who can least afford to do so. Florida Marlins President David Samson explained this with regard to forgoing long-term signings: "When you are a team like ours, you cannot afford mistakes. Mistakes can set a franchise back for years. . . . We can't afford to be wrong."[16] With this in mind, small-market teams balance risk in deciding whether to draft high school or college players. Clearly the additional maturation of college players decreases the risk, making them more desirable, but also more costly. High school players, on the other hand, are less costly but entail greater risk, as Baird describes:

> It obviously takes a lot more time to develop a high school player than a college player, but you play the percentages. Last year I wanted a college pitcher. My scouts came back and told me, "We can get you a number 3 starter in college, but we could also get you this kid with a college pitcher's skills who's still in high school. This kid can be a number 1 starter." That [high school] kid turned out to be Zack Greinke, our promising young pitcher. If Zack were to have gone on to college, he'd have been a very high draft pick, and we'd be looking at a much bigger signing bonus, and maybe we'd have to pass on him.[17]

Yet Baird insists that overreliance upon high school draftees is also risky. Therein lies the secret to small-market success: an uneasy tension between strategies.

Some general managers will gamble that their scouts can uncover that next number one starter. This kind of thinking has fallen out of fashion in some quarters, replaced by baseball empiricism. The most famous practitioner of that empiricism, Billy Beane, general manager of the small-market Oakland Athletics, thinks of it as a system that eschews perceptions in favor of statistics. He shies away from high school pitchers, for example, because, as Michael Lewis points out, "Taking a high school pitcher in the first round—and spending 1.2 million bucks to sign him—was exactly the sort of thing that happened when you let scouts have their way. It defied the odds; it defied reason."[18] While respectful of statistics—like everyone else, he must rely upon them—Allard Baird is the Un–Billy Beane in just about every way.

Baird's scouting background merges nicely with the need to locate talent from within. He is a proponent of empowering scouting departments. "The first year I was hired we upgraded our scouting with more and better scouts. . . . You know, in our situation you take on the challenge by being supportive of your people. I've got to motivate our guys to go out and beat those large-market teams in unusual ways. So I like to give them the opportunity to pull the trigger on signings as often as possible because that keeps them looking and doing their job, and not getting down."[19]

Baseball Eugenics and the Art of Ass-Tral Projection

Signing younger players who haven't fully matured—physically or in their playing skills—is also part of the Royals small-market approach. The stakes on such players are lower, although since you know less about them, the gamble is greater. "Our approach is go younger," Baird says, "sixteen- or seventeen-year-olds. High risk, high reward. Rely on development. The failure rate will be higher, no question, but we can work with that."[20] Here, faith resides in the science of kinesiology, from which hoped for physical attributes are teased out. "Good bodies" and "bad bodies" are phrases that scouts use every day—but not in front of Billy Beane.

Small-market Bairdian economics relies upon this meta-theory of physical projection: "If you don't have money to spend, you project. And when you project, it's more dangerous because you're anticipating based on [physical] attributes: 'Well, he doesn't have a good arm right now, but he has a good body. He's got loose arm action.' You hope your conditioning staff can help him reach that potential." There is a strong element of faith in securing talent this way. The risk involved has to become part of the equation that all levels of the organization understand: "Let's face it, when you project, the percentages are against all this becoming a tool. . . . We have to take more risks, and as long as your owner understands the risk factor, it's okay. So, when you give a player $29,000, you go, 'That's our guy. I hope he makes it.'"[21]

To make sense of all this—to give it grounding—baseball people often trade in eugenics currency. They fetishize the body through pseudo-analysis, projecting (sometimes socially) what this or that type of body can do. This is especially true at the entry levels of the sport: scouting and player development. A conversation I once had with a baseball executive for a major league club illustrates this. Upon hearing that I was an anthropologist, he said to me, "You know, we have something in common." "What?" I wondered. "We both like bones. You study old bones and I study new ones, and right now I'm looking for African bones. I'm looking for players with long arms, big thighs, high butts."

Beane was one of the first to openly disparage this view of anticipating playing potential on the basis of "bodies." In *Moneyball*, Michael Lewis depicts Beane chastising his scouts for their reliance upon "bodies." Lewis portrays the scouts as troglodytes, their methods of evaluations as unreliable. "If [Beane's viewpoint] was absolutely correct," Allard points out, "teams would be slashing their scouting departments. You could save a lot by relying completely on stats. The best teams are increasing their scouting budgets, though."[22]

There is a link of sorts between physical attributes and performance. Performance is what all teams look for, but for small-market clubs the search takes on a special cast. Tony Muser, who managed the Royals for five years (1998–2002), points out that for a team with a limited payroll, "speed and the ability to play defense is probably the least expensive way to go. Everyday players, who have power, can drive in runs and steal bases, and No. 1 starters, there's where it costs you. But if we can put a group of athletes on the field and we can catch the ball, we've got a chance to win a game."[23] Limited finances, then, foster taking a chance on raw athleticism, or even more risky, the look of raw athleticism. The notion of natural "athletes" leads to discussion of what kinds of physical types are desirable. Baird likes "speed and projectible bodies"—ones that allow scouts a reasonable notion of their development in the foreseeable future. This might mean long limbs and big buttocks for pitchers or powerful legs for catchers. For small-market teams, judiciously trading in physiological futures is necessary:

Projectible bodies are very important to us. So the body is key because through a good conditioning program we can make them stronger, more durable, and hopefully into the player we'd like. We sell our foreign scouts on the conditioning and nutrition programs we use. We got this kid Alexis Gomez, nineteen-year-old, lean kid, could be a five-tool guy. When I first saw him I said, "He can't run. He's too lean." He's now an above average runner. He's got some sock [power], and it was the strength program that did this for him.[24]

Bairdian economics plays with contradictions: proponents are forced to engage in risky moves while seeking to minimize risk. Signing high school players may be risky, but small-market teams can't always wait for that player to show up as a more seasoned college draft prospect. No one realizes this to the degree that Baird and other small-market administrators do, and they guard against falling into the trap that lurks in this kind of thinking. Time represents a gamble for them—too little or too much might result in a squandered opportunity.

The Opportunity Card

When it comes to signing draft picks or other talented prospects, the cards are stacked against the fiscally constrained. Two factors, however, mitigate this general rule: not all of the good players can be signed by large-market clubs, and teams like the Royals have something to offer talented players that their richer and talent-laden counterparts might not. Their ace up the sleeve is opportunity for advancement. Frank White put it this way: "Obviously, money takes care of all your problems. The Yankees can't get all of the good players. Some will have to be available to you, if you give them the opportunity to flourish."[25]

Luis Silverio, the former head of the Dominican academy, put it more concretely: "When I have a kid who wants more than we can offer and lets me know that someone else is involved, I tell him, 'I don't have the money you're asking for, but I can promise you you'll get 150 at-bats.' They know that unless they play, they can't show their ability and they won't go anywhere. I say, 'You're not going to find three first basemen here.' That's it, and I told his people that he's our everyday first baseman.

That means something to the player and the guys who brought him in."[26]

Big-Market Gravity Pull

To some extent, small-market teams wind up having to do what more affluent teams do, only at a more modest level. In the Dominican Republic, the leading foreign producer of talent, all major league teams are actively recruiting. Whereas the going rate for talent was rarely more than five thousand U.S. dollars in 1990, a decade later stars were being offered more than $2 million. Six-figure signing bonuses are fairly common now, all of which makes it harder for clubs like the Royals or Brewers to get their share of the talent. In response, small-market clubs have had to graze more closely—that is, they have to scour the territory more thoroughly than previously. This involves a network of "bird dogs" or *buscones* that can spot players in out-of-the-way places, but it also necessitates the kind of hands-on attention that Baird is noted for. One of his most interesting innovations has been "the Caravan," in which scouts move through an area holding tryouts. Interviewed at the Royals academy, Silverio observes, "Some of the guys here, like Hanibal Figuerero, first baseman, has some tools—we found him with the caravan that Allard designed three years ago. We rent a bus. We bring all our scouts. We'll go into an area for five days; go all over the place throwing tryouts. That's one way we can beat the competition, and we don't have to deal with the 'bird dog.'"[27]

Secondly, the Royals have had to pay out more in signing bonuses than they used to. They find themselves increasingly going into the $20,000–30,000 range—an offer that pales by comparison to what well-heeled teams pay but is high by Royals standards. The Royals have intensified their efforts at finding and signing talent in the increasingly competitive Dominican Republic, and so have been drawn into the economic orbit of the big-market teams. "What we've done in the D.R. this year is add some bonus money," Baird says. "This year was the first year we paid $100,000 to a Dominican player. We've never done that before. It's usually been 3,000 to 10,000, an extreme of 12,000. So we had to become a little bit more aggressive."[28]

Even markets like Japan that are off-limits to small-market teams on occasion offer opportunities for the nimble-footed. "I'm going over there for different reasons than most of the others," Baird told me. "We went over there for ten days to look at guys [Americans] who could come back to the major leagues. We're going to announce a signing of an American who went over there to pitch and now is coming back. What's unique about this is that he made 4.5 million last year, and we got him for $350,000 plus incentives."[29] If the situation arises, Baird will reverse the process by selling players to the Japanese to expand his budget. Hence Baird's relationship with Japan differs from others in that it operates on the periphery.

Going to the Margins

"Shopping without a credit card" enables Allard Baird to do business on the margins. For instance, some big-market teams tend to view scouting Europe or South Africa as "bottom feeding," but it's a way of life for small-market teams. By far the most interesting place that the Royals have gotten involved has been South Africa. In his initial trip to South Africa, Baird decided to determine for himself what potential lay there. While the game is relatively undeveloped, the Royals have signed four young athletes out of South Africa.[30]

Baird's approach to scouting and development abroad lacks the arrogance that sometimes accompanies Western expansion, be it by Coca-Cola or Halliburton. The following examples presented by Baird illustrate the point:

> We do some things differently. We stay with our kids. When Luis [Silverio] and I went to South Africa, we said, "Let's do this right." If we go over there and take advantage of a kid, and they have a bad experience, we'll never have another chance. So we said, "We've got to make sure to get them their education." We need to sign young, as a small-market team. But when you go with those younger kids, they're still in school. We have an equal responsibility to the education of those kids. So, we told our scout, "You've got to prime the school. Then we'll allow him to leave when the Instructional League is over, go at the end of league play. And we'll pay. If he's got two years left of school, we'll pay for the two years.' We met with the parents of those

kids, many that we couldn't even sign—one was fourteen—and we told them all of this."[31]

What marks this as unique in the industry is that a relatively modest team is directing energy and resources at a place that is decades away from a payoff. Mike Randall is the Royals' scout in South Africa, and he has to spend more time teaching kids to play the game than he does evaluating them as prospects.

Baird also invited the South African Olympic team's manager to come to spring training so that he could spend time with Royals instructors. The purpose, of course, was to promote the Royals in South Africa, but also to address the absence of qualified coaching there. Baird has approached all of his foreign dealings with this considerate attitude.

Clive Russell, who heads MLBI Africa and Europe, confirms Baird's stature in South Africa: "You go into South Africa and there's tremendous loyalty. Allard has a great image down there, and South Africans will remember for a long time that Kansas City was the first group who were committed to supporting them, and answering their needs."[32]

The Dominican Academy

If we compare the Royals' academy in the Dominican Republic with that of the Dodgers, or the new complexes built by former major leaguers like Junior Noboa, the Royals would seem poverty stricken.

In looking at the Royals' academy, we get a closer view of how academies are run and how, as small-market operations, they work in contrast to the Dodgers' Campo Las Palmas, for example. The main reason most baseball academies locate in somewhat remote areas is to ensure that the rookies they house there will not be distracted. A second factor is the cost of land, cheap enough in these backwaters that even a small-market team can put together a reasonable facility. The Royals have done that quite admirably in Salcedo, a town of fifteen thousand about forty minutes outside of Santiago. In my first visit there, we wound our way out of Santiago through heavy rush-hour traffic. A torrent of transport vehicles of every kind poured out of the city, along with a flood of mopeds, the vehicle of necessity for most Dominicans. According to the newspaper *Diario Libre*, eight of every ten vehicle accidents in the

Dominican Republic involve a moped.[33] When the drivers of trucks and cars pull to within a hair's breath of a moped, the cyclist typically uses the middle of a two-lane road as a third lane, leaving only inches between the three columns of traffic. Frank White became visibly nervous at the driving, prompting Luis Silverio to quip, "Frank, you've got to do things the Dominican way. I mean what's the problem? They're [the mopeds] not going a hundred miles an hour, and they don't have insurance."

Salcedo seems connected to Moca and other towns along the route by an unending chain of farming cottages, colmados (neighborhood convenience stores), and assorted vendors. We had entered Salcedo without knowing it, and a few turns later we turned right onto a short, partially paved street with a baseball park on one side and a row of houses on the other. Squeezed between two residences was the newest neighbor on the street: the Kansas City Royals baseball academy.

While almost all major league clubs have academies in the country, most lease their facilities; only a handful of teams own their own. For owners there is a special obligation to relate well with the surrounding communities. The Salcedo ballpark is a government-owned concrete structure seating perhaps fifteen hundred. The Royals lease this facility, but they also have improved it greatly. Silverio oversaw all of the improvements to the academy.

Beneath the stands are the Royals' administrative office, the strength and conditioning room, and a shower and bathroom facility. A politic but fair description would be "utilitarian" or "Spartan." Were the building a sports jacket, I'd describe it as clean but a tad threadbare. The Royals logo is hand-painted on the wall of the strength and conditioning room. The walls of Silverio's office and the coaches' locker room are Royals blue but could use another paint job. Yet everything was clean and functional. By contrast the Royals' new dormitory–dining room building across the street is posh: crisply new and nicely built. Here the Royals logo which identifies the building complex has been painted to official specifications by a graphic artist. In comparison with the big-market facilities of the Dodgers or the Braves, this complex might still look less polished, but to truly appreciate what this complex has come to be, you must understand two things. First, the Royals built this. It's their own, not leased. The

Braves are housed in a spectacular complex in San Francisco de Macorís, and the Diamondbacks share equally plush quarters in Boca Chica, but both of these academies are privately owned, and the teams rent them. (The Diamondbacks lease their place from Noboa.) The Royals have made a relatively greater commitment by investing their more modest budget into the community and having built their own facility as part of that community.

Secondly, the Royals have built slowly and steadily, if less spectacularly. Their presence on the island dates back to the early days of big league physical presence. In 1986 only a few teams were running schools or proto-academics. Silverio recalls the humble origins and the long view of Royals owners that resulted in the present-day academy: "When we started here, [players and coaches] stayed at hotels. We cooked over there. We had to do everything there. We worked out here, and then walked back to the hotel. Did it for a couple of years. And then, Mr. Fred Draper, who used to be the Latin American coordinator, brought up the idea, 'Hey, let's build something under the bleachers.' A year later we built [the office and exercise rooms], put beds and ceiling fans, and on this side we put a kitchen and dining area."[34] The Glass family, which would buy the team in 2000, had five years earlier begun taking an interest in the Dominican Republic.

Allard Baird, whose job with the team then was crossing the country evaluating the reports of all of the Royals scouts, came through and was appalled by the conditions of the players at the academy.

"When Allard came to Salcedo for the first time he was very embarrassed," Silverio recalled. "The mattresses the kids were sleeping on were bad. All that was here before was weeds. There were mosquitoes everywhere. There were cows in the field. It was bad. But there wasn't much he could do then, because he was just a cross checker."[35]

Club leadership continued to bring about the basic working conditions that players in the United State expect. By the mid-1990s, Silverio now crows, "We have everything here. This place houses up to fifty. Enough room for players and our staff. They don't have to go and sleep somewhere else. Here the most you walk is a hundred meters." And most important for Silverio, "They don't have to go and use a moped."[36] Frank White would be relieved.

The Tryout

When I returned to Salcedo in June 2002, Silverio invited me to observe the tryout he was holding for a dozen hopefuls. After weighing and measuring them and being presented with birth documents, he led them to the field, where position players are asked to run sixty-yard sprints. Silverio clocks them and enters their times next to their names. They clustered between 6.6 and 7.2 seconds. The fastest is about five feet, eleven inches tall, while a rangier player, standing about six-foot-two and wearing an old Kansas City batting practice jersey, was in the middle of the pack. I immediately discount the latter in favor of the speedier player. Looking over their times, however, Silverio draws the opposite conclusion. The batting cage is quickly wheeled out. The "K.C." player seems to hit the ball well, sending two over the 385-foot mark in left field. But Silverio doesn't find anything exceptional or worthwhile mentioning in the drives. Yet when the smaller player, the speedier one, bats, Silverio's voice rises: "See that? When he connects, the ball explodes off of his bat." My education continues. Following Silverio's lead, I conclude that on the basis of his speed and hitting, the smaller player is clearly the more impressive. But Silverio turns around again and ignores him in favor of the "K.C." kid, "This kid is going to cost some money. He's got two brothers who already signed, so he's probably thinking seventy, eighty, even ninety thousand, U.S. We're going to try to get him for fifteen thousand, and the buscón might try for ten thousand." When I ask him how he can ignore the observed data of speed and power, Silverio simply explains, "The big kid over there. He runs 7.0, but look at his build. We like that build for the outfield. We can work on his speed some. He reminds me of a young Vladimir Guerrero." He also explains that the "K.C." kid will only get bigger and faster, while he feels the smaller one has grown about as much as he will. Projecting bodies seems to have won the day again.

We next move over to where the pitchers have been warming up. The Royals scouts are calling for which pitch they want the kids to throw, "Recta [fastball]! Cambio [change-up]! Curva!" The pitcher of the moment responds. "What is he?" queries Silverio of his coaches, "eighty-five, eighty-six [miles per hour]?" They prefer to estimate at this juncture rather than gauge the pitches with radar. The first two pitchers reveal something of interest. Pitcher number one is reedlike, wearing a red-sleeved undershirt; the second, wearing an ordinary white undershirt, looks to be throwing uncomfortably. Pitcher number one has broad, square shoulders, a plus. Pitcher number two is not throwing as hard. Silverio prefers to stand behind and off to one side of the pitcher: "I like standing here because of the arm action and release points, which you can see better." While I feel pitcher number one is the better of the two, the other candidate impresses Silverio more. "Look, he's got a controlled body, nice tight motion. He's not jerking his head. The first guy," he says, looking at me, "What you see is what you get." Another of the pitchers, a sixteen-year-old, is there with his buscón, his bird dog. Silverio likes him as well: "Look at his arms and legs. He's got long arms, some size on his legs. Not like that last guy with the herky jerky head and skinny legs. Look at what I'm putting next to the other kid's name: 'N.P.' No prospect." The sixteen-year-old, Silverio is convinced, is in fact that age. "You look at his face and you see him with peach fuzz on his face. Some of these sixteen-year-olds coming in with freshly shaven faces—they are older, but this one is really a kid."[37]

Silverio pronounces it "a good tryout for me. I could say I saw three prospects." The staff heads to the offices under the bleachers to go over their evaluations, give candid commentary, and check the paperwork provided by the recruits. This last item is particularly important in the wake of the scandals that resulted when hundreds of players suddenly were discovered to be older than they had been reported. Silverio calls in the buscón who brought the sixteen-year-old pitcher, warning him that he must do a better job of verifying the ages of the boys he brings in. One of the nine young men he previously had brought in and gotten signed had provided faulty birth records, claiming to be younger than he was.

Finally, the "K.C." kid comes in alone, and Silverio indicates that he'll be talking to his parents about an offer the next day. Silverio is on the phone to Kansas City within minutes of the boy's departure, asking Derek Lanier, director of scouting, to make some money available beyond the $15,000 the Royals generally offer someone they're interested in. "Derek, I'd like to have you save some money for me. It's going to take about twenty-five thousand. His family is probably looking for fifty thousand to seventy-five. He's got a 50 arm [in the 50th percentile], 2 power, 7.0 running. I don't love him, but I like him. He's got the build—shoulders, legs, and projects well." Lanier promises to call back, and Silverio, hanging up, turns to me and says matter-of-factly, "Paying this kid twenty-five thousand is nothing. He would be a third-round [draft pick] in the U.S., getting $500,000 out of high school."[38]

Silverio's quest on the phone for another $10,000 should be put in context. Many other teams operating in the Dominican Republic routinely pay six figures. The Red Sox, Dodgers, Braves, and Cubs—all of the big-market clubs—can do this, and they have driven the cost of doing business into the stratosphere in the past decade. Silverio will be hard-pressed to make this deal happen.

If You Love Someone, Let Him Go

During his tenure as Royals manager, Tony Muser calculates, "something like $119 million worth of players . . . became free agents and left us and we really got nothing in return." Jermaine Dye, Johnny Damon, Rey Sanchez all grew up in the organization and then became too costly to keep. Small-market clubs have to determine whether they want to be proactive or not. "We knew we probably got burned letting these guys walk to free agency, but Johnny Damon mentioned a $110 million, 10-year deal at one point. . . . We had to trade those guys," explained Muser.[39] Anticipating the departure of a free agent, a club can opt to trade him in the hopes of getting someone in return. When Damon left the Royals in 2001 for Oakland, the team got Angel Berroa (who was originally signed by the Royals) and two others. Berroa blossomed into an impact player when he took Rookie of the Year honors in 2003. Yet if he continues to shine, he too will likely leave when free agency kicks in.

Letting a free agent walk in his final year nets the team a draft pick, but those picks must still be signed and developed. As Muser points out, "Draft picks take time—five years, six years, especially pitchers. Some of them get hurt, some of them don't pan out."[40] The other option involves trading the player, but other teams routinely attempt to take advantage of the initiator, knowing that time works against a team trying to move a free agent. Do you keep the player or attempt to trade him for others who might help the club beyond one year? The rising star Carlos Beltran was in the last year of his Royals contract, earning $9 million in 2004. Baird opted to give him more money rather than trade him. "I need to be able to help my ballclub right now," he explained.[41] As the Royals floundered in 2004, the Beltran decision began to look untenable. Thus, midway through the season Baird traded him to the Houston Astros for two unproven but promising players. Again, he opted to lock the new players up with contracts for as long as possible.

While he is forever alert to the good deal, Baird is also a proponent of signing strategic players to long-term contracts. In signing first baseman Mike Sweeney to such a pact, the Royals showed a willingness to invest heavily in a key player. For Baird, the Sweeney signing helped build a psychological foundation for the team. The operative word is *strategic*, by which Baird means specific things: "Not only do they have to be the right guy, performance-wise, they also have to fit your program. If you just get your marquee player, and he's not happy with life, it can backfire on you."[42]

Bairdian economics involves a habit of coupon cutting mixed in with an occasional spending spree. The former makes the latter possible, and with any success momentum takes over. Hence Allard Baird will scour the earth to find a bargain or three, then use his savings to fund a big-ticket item. When the team succeeds, as it did in 2003, Baird is better able to convince key players either to stay and re-sign or, in the case of the slugger Juan González, a two-time Most Valuable Player, to sign for less than market value. "It's a domino effect. Guys believe we can win. They take a little less. You go down the line and it gives me maybe $2 million more to try and add an outfield or a catcher."[43] In the end the purse strings are loosened only a tiny bit, because Baird knows that ownership is treating the Royals as a business at least as much as a calling. While the Glass family has the civic-mindedness of the Kauffmans, the owners insist on accountability. Baird accepts this as part of his charge, and shares the challenge.

Allard Baird likes to insist that he's not all that different from Beane in his approach to fielding a competitive team. He relies upon statistics; he will seek out college players rather than automatically draft high schoolers; but when all is said and done, he and Beane view the world differently. Baird is hands-on; a scout lurks in his mind, and he is as intuitive as Beane is rational.

Returning to Earth: 2004–2005

"The expectations of our club were real high, and I think everyone felt it. I know Berroa did, and he pressed; but we all felt it." This was Allard Baird's take on the plunge that the Royals took in 2004. To be sure, there were key injuries, but as far as he was concerned, "We just didn't play good baseball. We didn't execute when we should've. There were quite a few games where we had the lead going into the eighth, and we couldn't complete it."[44] Playing poorly or losing one or two key players to injury exposes one of the key weaknesses of small-market teams: their lack of player depth. They depend, more than others, on not only playing well, but having everyone healthy.

The downward cycle continued for the Royals. By June the club was clearly going nowhere, and Baird exercised his key move. His prize player, Carlos Beltran, was in his last year before becoming a free agent. Baird had opted to keep him rather than trade him because they felt as if the team would compete for the division title. When it became clear that wasn't going to happen, he decided to trade Beltran early, rather than wait until the trade deadline: "I knew it was better for us to trade then when I could maximize the value of Beltran." Baird was keying in on a trade that would net him a core of young players around whom he might build. Baird was excited to end the trade flurry with John Buck, a catcher; Mark Teahan, a third baseman; and Mike Wood, a pitcher. He now had a large cadre of young talent: "We're finally at a point where seven of his [Manager Tony Peña's] regulars are not arbitration-eligible until 2008. These guys are going to be here a while. You know, if we'd have competed again last year and wound up only one game out of first place, we would have not had our catcher, two pitchers, our third baseman, and a utility player. The process I'm working on would have been stalled another year."[45]

Allard Baird really has a plan: to rebuild the team around youth, and keep the young players coming so that when the Royals finally lose one to free agency or trade, they will have more in the pipeline. After the extremely disappointing 2005 season, with more than one hundred losses, Baird remained unbowed, "If anything, I insist that we stick with the youth program. We've had a string of good drafts. Quite frankly, that's the only way it's going to work here. The only regret I have is that I didn't start the rebuilding mode sooner. The majority of these young players are going to be good, but I can't tell you exactly when. That core of young guys that we got through trades and draft going into 2006— the second phase of our rebuilding mode—is essential, and they'll be able to support some of the young guys we'll have coming up from AA. Over 50 percent of our roster will now be those young guys."[46] Baird has his team right where he wants it.

3

THE LOS ANGELES DODGERS: BRIGHT LIGHTS, BIG MARKET

When Los Angeles Dodgers owner Peter O'Malley sold his club to Fox News Corporation in 1998 for $311 million, he effectively ended the reign of the Dodgers as baseball's most successful franchise—successful in the sense not only of competitiveness on the playing field but of social progressiveness. However bitter the people of Flatbush may have been over the Dodgers' departure, the team pioneered international baseball, treated its own with consideration, and had the courage to operate with a social conscience. Peter O'Malley had read the economic tea leaves, realizing that he could no longer remain competitive operating in the country's second-largest market according to the principles he held most dear. Under his family's ownership, the Dodgers had won six World Series, and equally important, had three times been named to the *Fortune* magazine list of the hundred best companies to work for—the only sports franchise to be so named. This blend of competitive success fused with a socially progressive philosophy marked the Dodgers as special. "Being a Dodger was," according to Dodger legend Maury Wills, "as big as life. It was life itself."[1] When on the road, any Dodger could bring his family along for free. Ice cream was served—family style—when the club moved into first place or added to its league lead. Players often stayed with the organization in some capacity after their playing days. The club was a baseball Gibraltar. Between 1954 and 1996, the Dodgers had only two managers while the Yankees had gone through twenty-five changes. Even the equipment managers counted their time in decades.

Most important, the team operated without ethnic or racial boundaries at a time when few other franchises were colorblind.

Fox News Corporation purchased the team, and almost immediately baseball's Gibraltar began breaking up. Peter O'Malley knew that any new ownership would make changes, but even he could not grasp how quickly the structure would crumble: "I never dreamed there would be so many changes so quickly. . . . I don't think there's another organization in base-ball that's had that turnover in so short a period of time. Ever. . . . The last couple of years have been a very difficult time for all of us who have ever cheered the Dodgers, and that surely includes me."[2] Fox's deep pockets should have enabled the Dodgers to continue producing talented teams, but the organizational lack of vision and instability resulted in a team adrift and mounting economic losses. Fox evidently had no interest in the Dodgers as an institution. Rather it wanted to short circuit Disney's efforts to establish a sports cable network in southern California. When the cor poration had accomplished this goal, it put the team up for sale again.

The new owners, Frank and Jamie McCourt, had, by February 2004 purchased the team from Fox News Corporation for $421 million. The transfer of ownership should have been seen as a valiant attempt to save a team that had been turned into a corporate pawn. Unfortunately, the McCourts were considered carpetbagging outsiders by the Los Angeles press and many fans. Their dealings in buying the team reeked of shady finances and disingenuousness. It was unsettling to find out that the McCourts had not put any of their own money into the purchase, bor-rowing all of it instead—including $196 million from the seller, Fox. How would they go after the free agents that big-market teams need to pluck out of the annual pool? With no bona fide superstars, the 2004 Dodgers nevertheless managed to win the National League West Division title, los-ing in the first round of the postseason to the St. Louis Cardinals. In the off-season the McCourts cut their payroll by some $12 million and lost their star third baseman, Adrian Beltre, to free agency. It was their approach to the organization that rankled many, however. They raised parking fees and the price children paid to join the "Blue Crew," the youth fan club. They fired stalwarts and made hires that did not sit well with Dodger faithful. The 2005 Dodgers finished with their worst record in thirteen years, placing fourth in the weakest division in baseball.

At this trying moment in club history, did the Dodgers at least retain that one trait that had separated them from all others: their global and cross-cultural philosophy?

Who and What Are the Dodgers?

The Dodgers are a big-market team. Naturally, in considering big-market teams, we think first of the New York Yankees; but the Yankees are actually more exception than rule. In 2003, before they sold a single hot dog, before they rented a parking space or a luxury suite, without a penny in ad sales or radio rights, the Yankees had already earned $145 million.[3] They did this just from season-ticket sales and television royalties. The Dodgers, the next-largest market, generated roughly $150 million total revenue (compared with the Yankees' $238 million). It is the Red Sox, Mets, Braves, Cubs, and Dodgers who are, in fact, the typical big-market teams.

The most significant structural feature of a big-market team is that it exists in a large television market, in turn built upon a substantial metropolitan population. Local television contracts reflect these demographics, so large-market clubs generate more revenue from this source. For instance, in 2001 big-market teams averaged $26.1 million annually from TV, radio, and cable broadcast rights, compared with the $10.9 million average of small-market teams.[4] That disparity only grows with time. Gate revenues also tend to reflect these demographics.

While large-market teams have the wherewithal to sign whomever they wish, most are quick to claim that there are limits. It is the perception of limits that distinguishes the Yankees (who have none) from all other big-market teams. It is also in this curious sense of limits that we see the difference between large- and small-market teams. Boston Red Sox General Manager Theo Epstein used language to that effect in describing his organization: "I'm not going to deny that we have tremendous resources, but they're limited at the same time. We can't just spend as much as we want and go get everything we want. . . . We're like a normal team, with a little bit more to work with."[5] The 2005 Red Sox had a payroll of $121 million, while the Kansas City Royals got by on $37 million. Having $84 million more to work with is greater by just a "little bit," and clearly that gap affects which and how many talented players one seeks to sign. Large-market teams may be more likely to succeed, yet simply coming from a big market doesn't mean that you get all the fans, all the revenue, all the players, and all the titles—ask the 2003 Florida Marlins, who won the World Series against the Yankees. Former Dodgers General Manager Fred Claire laid out the lopsided reality of big- and small-market teams: "It's still a matter of dollars having a relationship with wins, and that's not going to change. Still, there will also always be a team like the Twins who will show you that good judgment equals victories."[6]

In most ways, the Dodgers are a classic big-market team. They exist in one of the Western Hemisphere's largest cosmopolitan urban centers. They seem to have little trouble in annually drawing three million fans to Dodger Stadium. Sales of their licensed products (their brand) are among the industry's leaders. Down from the $116 million payroll of 2003 (when it was the third-highest in baseball) to $81 million (ranking eleventh), the Dodgers have always been in the top half of salaries. They have been able to spend liberally in the free-agent market and can locate and pay for talent wherever they may find it.

Most important, being a big-market team means that you can afford to fail while continuing to compete. Fox News Corporation claimed that it was losing $40 million annually on revenues of $147 million. The Dodgers' payroll was one reason for these losses; another was that the team was not getting enough revenue from its local television contract because Fox had undervalued it. Yet despite the book losses, the Dodgers were able to continue to go after high-priced talent. They stunned many in 1999, when they signed the pitcher Kevin Brown for $105 million over seven years. Likewise, they turned heads in 2001 when they set the record for a signing bonus to a Dominican player, giving the pitcher Joel Guzmán for $2.25 million. They didn't hesitate in bidding for and signing the Japanese pitcher Kazuhisa Ishii in 2002 for $23.46 million. In the winter of 2005–2006 they once again went after a number of free agents. Dan Evans ran the organization as general manager from 2000 to 2003, following almost two decades with the relatively fiscally constrained Chicago White Sox. He understood the big-market advantage: "I came from the White Sox, where we didn't operate internationally at all for many years. Here they have an incredible awareness of the Latin and

Asian markets. Internationally, we're far more aggressive, with far more resources than I experienced [with] the White Sox."[7]

The Dodgers also differ from many big-market teams in noneconomic terms. They have succeeded in part because not only do they do the big things, but they can also do all the little things really well. In the summer of 2003 I observed a simple, dignified ceremony commemorating a relationship that has existed between the Dodgers and Japanese baseball for almost four decades. The team's attention to such minutiae bears social fruits and serves to differentiate the Dodgers from other large clubs. The question for the future is whether the changes that have scarred the team within the past six years will result in the loss of these carefully crafted moments. "Dodger Blue" is and has been about more than just winning. Walter O'Malley, perceived in some corners as a carpetbagger when he brought the team from Brooklyn to Los Angeles, became an important part of the area's public trust. He remade the Dodgers into a Los Angeles cultural institution. Peter O'Malley furthered this effort. The Dodgers have blended social responsibility and marketing with local ownership in a subtle way that keeps attention focused upon the team and the game.

There is one way in which this franchise is unique: it is and has been—bar none—the most thoroughgoingly cosmopolitan team in the game. Dodger interest in things international goes beyond available resources to embrace a core tenet of the organization itself. Other teams may have the resources to do what the Dodgers have done around the world, but none has done it to the same extent, as early and often as have the Sons of Chavez Ravine. Characterizing the Dodger attitude toward internationalism as a "philosophy," Kris Rone, former vice president of marketing and business, concluded, "We all really believe in it. It's who we are, not an opportunistic thing. It's part of our fiber, and we do it all levels."[8] That may be, but it is also a pragmatic strategy to overcome certain weaknesses that the franchise has had to endure in recent years. While he was in charge of the Dodgers, Dan Evans immediately saw the problem. "What we encountered here was a very unproductive farm system. I think we've had a twenty-one-year period where we've had six major league players drafted in the first round come to the big leagues. You never recapture that first-round pick, so eventually what you have to do is enter the international market and replenish your system to atone for your sins in the amateur draft."[9] Fred Claire rejects this characterization of the Dodgers. Claire cites an article in *Baseball America* that named the Dodgers the number one club in producing their own talent in the 1990s, including a string of five Rookie of the Year awards, three of whom were farm products (Mike Piazza, Todd Hollandsworth, and Eric Karros). Claire adds that in 1995 there was only one player on the club who had not come out of the Dodgers system, but by 2005 there was not a single one produced by the system.[10]

While other clubs are also active internationally, and some have done very well in certain areas (the Seattle Mariners in Japan, for example), no one matches the Dodgers for their historical commitment to going global, their range, and the depth of their internationalism.

Key Moments in Dodger Internationalism

The formidable presence of the Dodgers around the world sprang from the team's pathbreaking effort to end racial segregation in the sport. The signing of Jackie Robinson to a Dodgers contract in 1946 marked the formal declaration that this franchise was committed to pioneering social diversity. Bill Veeck, owner of the Cleveland Indians, had wanted to sign a Negro Leaguer, but it was Branch Rickey who took that momentous first step. Nor should we think that Dodgers leadership (first Branch Rickey, and then Walter and Peter O'Malley) was operating purely out of altruism and a desire for racial equality. They ran businesses, and were just as motivated as any of their peers by the competitive advantages of getting the best talent wherever it existed, as well as by the marketing bonanza that comes with finding a player that reflects the local constituency. So powerful was the imperative to find ballplayers, that some, like Calvin Griffith, owner of the Washington Senators and Minneapolis Twins, suppressed their racist views for the sake of finding cheap talent. For Griffith it was Latin American, primarily Cuban, talent that motivated him. What the Dodgers understood was that sending scouts to locate and extract talent is not the same as building relationships, and only the Dodgers seemed open to building policy and an organization that mirrored their heterogeneous worldview.

The determination to integrate baseball was only the domestic side to Rickey's cosmopolitan view. He also fostered movement abroad. According to Fred Claire, "When Al Campanis was working for the Dodgers as a scout in the mid-1940s, he would spend a lot of time in Cuba and the Dominican. He didn't do that on his own. That was [Rickey's] policy, and Al furthered that when he became general manager." Claire gives most of the credit to Walter O'Malley for globalizing the team: "This man was one of the great visionaries of the game, and he never really received the credit he deserved for making the game so international. I can remember years ago when he had been asked about the future of baseball, and he saw Tokyo as a major league city. . . . [The journalist] Jim Core asked him, 'Mr. O'Malley, what do you want to be remembered for?' Walter spun that cigar and said, 'I want to be remembered for planting a tree.'"[11] That "tree" was the Dodgers' push into an international arena when others were content to leave baseball as it was.

Dodger Manias

Jackiemania

It would become known as "Fernandomania": the synergistic electricity between fans, front office, and players that occurred when the Mexican pitcher Fernando Valenzuela landed on the baseball scene in the early 1980s, introducing a novel cultural presence that in turn created a social whirlwind. The "otherness" of the five players discussed below reveals the commitment of the team's front office to a world built purely upon merit—in short, a philosophy of internationalism. It all began with breaking the stranglehold of Jim Crow segregation. When Branch Rickey boldly signed Jackie Robinson to play in the Brooklyn Dodgers organization, black players had been barred from playing professionally with whites for more than a half-century. The notion that baseball integration was forged only (or even primarily) by two men—Branch Rickey and Jackie Robinson—is a popular oversimplification. The social context in which the Robinson signing took place is highlighted in Jules Tygiel's excellent history of the integration of the game.[12] Social progress made during the Second World War served as the most important springboard for integration. The demand for labor at defense plants set into motion a population shift by blacks to northern cities. Protests of Jim Crow segregation at army bases followed, and the black labor leader A. Phillip Randolph and others strove to promote integration. New York, with its multiracial, ethnic hue was a more likely place to introduce integration than southern cities like Baltimore, Washington, or St. Louis—where Rickey had spent almost two decades as manager and then a front-office executive for the Cardinals before coming to Brooklyn. The Northeast was also the home of a vanguard cadre of black and liberal white journalists who gave voice to integrationist sentiment, as did the Communist Party. That was the context in which Rickey and Robinson became the faces of integration, the courageous fighters who took on segregation.

Rickey also understood the economic impact of introducing a new constituency to Ebbets Field—although some claimed that integration could hurt attendance by alienating white fans. The degree of risk involved in integrating the game seems to suggest that Rickey's primary motivation was moral. The lack of encouragement from his peers—"None of Rickey's fellow executives showed any inclination to follow his lead in recruiting blacks," Tygiel writes—also underscores his moral commitment to the project.[13]

The selection of Robinson as the pioneering figure in sports integration was made with great care. Satchel Paige and Josh Gibson were better Negro Leagues players, but Robinson had the right blend of talent, intelligence, and experience in an integrated environment. Having attended UCLA and served in World War II as an army officer, Robinson was familiar with white institutions and thus thought to be less prone to buckle under intense scrutiny and harassment. He was temperate in his personal habits; he didn't smoke, drink, or carouse. While capable of restraint, Robinson was also passionate enough to stand up against injustice. During his stint in the service, he had proved this steadfastness when he defied a bus driver in Fort Hood, Texas, who ordered him to the back of the bus.[14] Most important, Rickey sensed that Robinson had the intelligence and presence of mind to channel the rage he would inevitably feel into his game. He signed Robinson first, then quickly signed the Negro Leaguers Roy Campanella, Don Newcombe, John Wright, and Roy Parlow.

The integration of Robinson into the game had to be an orchestrated affair. Giving him his first playing assignment at the Dodgers' Montreal affiliate was a key move. In Canada, and in this cosmopolitan city, Robinson could play his first season in an accepting environment. The problem was that as a rookie in the Dodger organization, Robinson would have to go to spring training in Daytona Beach, Florida. All of Branch Rickey's efforts to the contrary, the incidents that marred spring training in 1946 could not be prevented. Following cancellations and threats in Jacksonville and elsewhere, the Montreal Royals managed to begin play in Sanford, Florida. The game was stopped in the third inning as the chief of police came out on the field demanding that Robinson and John Wright be removed from the ballpark. The Dodgers organization responded firmly. Montreal General Manager Mel Jones declared, "We don't care if we fail to play another single exhibition game. If they don't want to play us with our full team, they can pull out of the games." The Royals' president, Hector Racine, added, "Jackie Robinson and John Wright go with the team, or there's no game."[15] This was the proverbial line in the sand, and the Dodgers publicly declared that they would back integration no matter where it went and what was required.

The season opened with a stretch of games in Jersey City, Newark, Syracuse, and Baltimore, the International League's southernmost city. There Rachel Robinson, who had married Jackie in February, later recalled "the worst kind of name calling and attacks on Jackie that I had to sit through."[16] She feared for his life, but the following night he responded by going 3 for 3 and scoring four runs. Paced by Robinson, the Montreal Royals easily won the International League's pennant in 1946 and beat Louisville of the American Association in the Little World Series. Robinson led the league in batting average, .349, and runs scored, 113. He was second in the league in runs batted in and in stolen bases.

Robinson's promotion to the Brooklyn Dodgers in 1947 was assumed, but it still required Rickey's social engineering. The season began amid rumors and rumblings of resistance to Robinson's presence. First, Rickey let it be known in the clubhouse that any Dodger who felt uncomfortable with his decision to integrate could request a trade; several did. Despite the institutional support for Robinson, the tension surrounding him was excruciating. The Dodgers' first series of the year was played against the Philadelphia Phillies and their race-baiting manager, Ben Chapman. Chapman was accustomed to launching racial tirades with impunity. Now he homed in on Robinson. Harold Parrott, the team's traveling secretary, recalls, "Chapman mentioned everything from thick lips to the supposedly extra-thick Negro skull . . . [and] the repulsive sores and diseases he said Robinson's teammates would become infected with if they touched the towels or the combs he used."[17] This abuse was endured, with difficulty. As the season wore on, however, Robinson's teammates, players from around the league, and many fans began if not to accept him at least to mute their feelings. He even began to receive endorsement offers and requests for speaking engagements. Robinson's stats for the season were respectable enough to win the newly created Rookie of the Year award: a .297 batting average and an on-base percentage of .383, with 31 doubles, 5 triples, 12 home runs, 48 runs batted in, and 29 stolen bases. In the context of the travails that Robinson and his family went through, the meaning of these statistics should be doubled.

By 1954 the Dodgers were able to field a team with five black players, as they did on July 17. That day Robinson, Junior Gilliam, Campanella, the Cuban Sandy Amoros, and pitcher Newcombe started, in another baseball first. Also on the squad was pitcher Joe Black, the 1952 Rookie of the Year—Newcombe had won the award in 1949, and Gilliam in 1953. These outsiders played their way into the major leagues, depending upon the hard-nosed support of Dodgers brass and the acceptance of many of its players. This cadre of black players would soon reciprocate the kindness when yet another outsider entered their midst. The racial integration of baseball was built upon the same principles that globalization relies upon: expansion of boundaries, a relatively high degree of merit, and social openness.

Sandymania: The Jew Ace

By the time that Walter O'Malley took over the Dodgers in 1950, African Americans were appearing on rosters throughout baseball. In the next decade the Dodgers had five African-American impact players: Robinson, Campanella, Newcombe, Black, and Gilliam, not to mention Maury Wills, who became a Dodger in 1959, but didn't make an impact until the 1960s. The desire to attract minorities did not start or end with

African Americans, however. In New York, Jewish players had long been sought to drive marketing. A 1935 headline, for instance, declared, "McGraw Spent Years Hunting Jew Ace," suggesting that such gems were hard to find.[18] O'Malley also searched for Jewish stars, but, ironically, those he signed did not develop until the team had left Brooklyn. Buzzie Bavasi, Dodgers general manager from 1951 to 1968, recalls, "In Brooklyn, we were looking for a young player of the Jewish faith who would attract the fans. Brooklyn was a borough of churches and temples. Cal Abrams was the closest we came to a Jewish hero, but just didn't get the job done. . . . When we came out west in 1958, we were blessed with two fine Jewish athletes, [Sandy] Koufax and Larry Sherry."[19] In fact, in addition to those two pitchers, catcher Norm Sherry also played for the Dodgers from 1959 through 1962, giving them three Jewish players. Another first.

Jane Leavy's biography of Sandy Koufax details the anti-Semitism that Jewish players have had to face in major league baseball. Unlike Robinson, Koufax was not the first of his minority group to play in the twentieth century, but there had been so few that the critical mass needed to defuse anti-Semitic sentiments had never been reached. That Koufax was a bonus baby did not help him gain acceptance. Koufax was signed in 1954 for the then-hefty sum of $20,000 (the major league minimum salary was $6,000), and the rules stated that anyone receiving a bonus of more than $4,000 had to remain on the major league club's roster for two years or risk being drafted by another team—a disincentive against the impulse for big-market teams to purchase any and all talented players. Sandy Koufax was a youngster, a relatively rich one, and a psychologically vulnerable one on a roster filled with players making less than he. Leavy refers to an "unspoken calculus": the association of Jews and money. Players and administrators all knew the prevailing attitudes. Hank Aaron recalls the view that others had of Koufax: "Sandy Koufax, being a little Jewish boy, didn't know anything about baseball. Everybody thought, Hey, he needs to be somewhere off in school, counting money or doing whatever *they* do."[20]

Unlike other young players, Koufax didn't have the benefit of a cohort of mutually supportive rookies who had moved up through the farm system together. In the minor leagues, players, besides having the opportunity to develop alongside others who are roughly at their level, learn the culture of their franchise: what is expected, the lore. Koufax, in contrast, had to prove himself immediately, and that was hard because while talented, he was not a consensus "can't miss" prospect. He was not even particularly smitten with baseball. The scholarship he had won from the University of Cincinnati was in basketball, his first choice.

Nor had Koufax impressed hordes of baseball scouts, coaches, and fans with his extraordinary abilities. Even in his own Brooklyn neighborhood he was not considered a standout. Mike Napoli was the big man in Koufax's world. So were the Torre brothers, Frank and Joe. In his only year of college baseball, Koufax won three and lost one for Cincinnati. The few scouts who happened upon him, however, noted his fifty-two strikeouts in twenty-eight innings.

He was wild, too, even for a left-handed pitcher, and that frightened off some teams. Al Campanis was not at all intimidated. As Dodgers coach and general manager, Campanis brought Koufax to Ebbets Field to throw. Campanis stood in the batter's box, as he liked to get a feel for prospects. The fledgling Brooklyn *Eagle* reporter Dave Anderson saw what transpired: "Koufax started to steam the fastball in on him. Al Campanis said—and I'll never forget this—'The hair on my arms rose, and the only other time that happened was the first time I saw the Sistine Chapel.'" Campanis wasn't the only one impressed by what he saw. Rube Walker was catching Koufax. He looked up at Campanis from his crouch and said, "Whatever he wants, give it to him. I wouldn't let him get out of the clubhouse."[21]

The Koufax story is an amazing one, not only because of how dominant he was as a pitcher for his last—and best—five seasons, but because his early wildness almost prevented him from having a career at all. It all shifted on a dime, sort of. His catcher, Norm Sherry, finally managed to get through to him, convincing him to take something off of his fastball. Amazingly, the adjustment not only improved his control but made the pitch faster, and the rest of the National League would pay for that epiphany.

In 1955 Koufax was not yet Koufax, but just an uncomfortable (Jewish) rookie resented in the clubhouse. While Branch Rickey had micromanaged Jackie Robinson's early days as a Dodgers rookie to ensure his well-being, Koufax was left to his own devices. According to Leavy, "When [Joe] Black discovered Koufax wandering around the infield wondering what to do next, he said, 'Just follow me.' "[22] That act of kindness was only the latest in a reciprocal chain that began with Hank Greenberg, the first Jewish superstar. He too, had endured a torrent of abuse early in his career, as well as in 1938, during his run at Babe Ruth's single-season home run record. Upon first encountering Robinson, whose first year was Greenberg's last, the rookie received some badly needed encouragement from the veteran. So when Koufax became the butt of anti-Semitic barbs, the black Dodgers rallied around him. Don Newcombe commented at length on the common bonds that led to minorities defending one another:

> We had our reasons [for defending Koufax]. . . . One reason . . . was because he was a Jew. Some of the players did not like him because he was a Jew. They vilified him because he was a bonus baby and had to stay on the roster. It wasn't his fault. He wanted to go to the minors. I couldn't understand the narrow-mindedness of these players when they would come to us and talk about Sandy as "this kike" and "this Jew bastard" or "Jew sonofabitch that's gonna take my job." . . . You think of crackers as being from the South but a lot of those crackers they were from California and other places.

The bigots, Newcombe recalled, "hated Jews as much as they hated blacks. I don't know if Sandy ever knew that, but that's why we took care of Sandy."[23]

If he did know what was going on, he was quiet about it, focusing instead on becoming Sandy Koufax, Hall of Famer. He pitched in a time when pitchers did not rely upon bullpens to protect their statistics. Between 1961 and 1966, he pitched fewer than 223 innings in only one year, when he was injured. He pitched more than three hundred innings three times in that stretch. In each of his final two years, pitching with a painfully arthritic elbow, Koufax threw twenty-seven complete games. Koufax had a six-year run that was unlike anything ever seen. It included 119 victories, an unprecedented four no-hitters, thirty-five shutouts, and of course, the strikeouts—an average of 285 per season.

Citing Pee Wee Reese's public on-the-field welcome of Robinson early in 1947, Leavy characterizes the timely protection of vulnerable players as "the Dodger way." Strictly speaking, it was the black players who defended Koufax, not the Dodgers front office, but such occurrences could take place because the team had become the site of baseball's progressive consciousness. In short order this most socially tolerant of organizations took their show on the road . . . outside our national borders.

Fernandomania

The arrival of Fernando Valenzuela had one of the greatest social impacts in the history of the sport because it ushered in the sport's self-awareness of having entered an international era. The Dodgers are regarded as having modernized player development in Latin America, but it must be acknowledged that the Senators, Giants, and Pirates preceded them. The Giants in the 1960s quickly developed Juan Marichal and the three Alou brothers (Felipe, Mateo, and Jesús), all from the Dominican Republic, and Rico Carty and Orlando Cepeda, from Puerto Rico. During that period the best Latin player on the Dodgers was the Cuban Sandy Amaro. Despite their tardy start in exploring the Latin American market, by the 1980s the Dodgers were the most aggressive team in the international market. The first impact signing came from an unlikely source—Mexico.

While the sport of baseball has been played in Mexico since the 1880s, Mexico has never been a significant source of major league players. Milton Jamail, an expert in Latin American baseball, says that Major League Baseball has typically viewed players (either Anglo or Mexican) in Mexico as "suspects, not prospects." Most scouting directors and general managers evade the topic, as did the following: "Mexico is a place that hasn't developed as many players as people anticipated. There just haven't been very many impact players out of Mexico since Fernando. . . . I just don't know if there are that many solid prospects there, with soccer as the big sport there."[24]

Because of the close proximity of Los Angeles to Mexico, the Dodgers have long paid attention to scouting players south of the border. Mike Brito, their main scout in the area, was alerted by one of his scouts, Corito Varona, that a young pitcher named Valenzuela was an exciting prospect. Brito followed up the report in 1978 and went to

Silao, Guanajuanto, spending the night stretched across two folding chairs in the local bus station, so that he could see Valenzuela. Only seventeen years old, Valenzuela was pitching like a wizened old pro: hitting corners, changing speeds, and, when in trouble, showing composure to get out of potentially damaging innings. As tired as Brito was, he stayed to watch and grew more impressed with each inning. Following the game, he ventured into the Guanajuanto clubhouse to speak with this phenom:

> "My name is Mike Brito."
> Valenzuela nodded.
> "I scout for the Dodgers."
> Another nod.
> "I like the way you pitch."
> "Gracias."
> "How old are you?"
> "Seventeen."
> "Where are you from?"
> "Sonora."[25]

Valenzuela is a stoic. Whether it is a function of his cultural background or of his birth order, he appears unexpressive and unruffled. Even those who knew him as a child described him as quiet and serious.

Brito sent in a gushing report, eventually getting Dodgers G.M. Al Campanis to fly down and take a look. Both men came away convinced that Valenzuela would pitch in the majors. Even the steep $120,000 price tag that his Puebla team placed on Valenzuela's contract did not deter the Dodgers. In the Arizona Instructional League Valenzuela quickly mastered the screwball, which would become his signature pitch. Brito marvels, "Within a week, he was throwing the screwball better than [Robert "Babo"] Castillo [who taught it to him]. . . . He was throwing it with two velocities."[26] At Class AA San Antonio, Valenzuela spent the 1980 season learning such techniques as how to set up a hitter with his fastball and change locations to increase the effectiveness of his out pitch. By the end of the season, he was brought to Los Angeles, where he pitched eighteen innings out of the bullpen, going 2–0.

As successful as he had been so far, the Dodgers decided that Valenzuela would compete the following spring for the last slot in the team's five-man rotation of starting pitchers. Through a series of injuries and other unexpected events, however, Valenzuela became the first rookie to start an opening day game in Dodger history. The rest *is* history. He pitched a five-hit shutout against the Houston Astros in his major league debut as a starter, prompting the Dodgers broadcaster Vin Scully to comment as a grinning Valenzuela walked off the mound at the end, "And a little child shall lead them."[27] Fernando Valenzuela went on to have one of the most remarkable rookie seasons in major league history. He opened the season with a jaw-dropping string of eight straight victories (ten in a row overall, going back to the previous September), a string that matched the major league record. Of those eight wins, five were complete-game shutouts (he would have eight for the season). Valenzuela became the only player ever to win the Rookie of the Year and Cy Young awards in the same year. In the 1981 All-Star Game he struck out five straight batters. Through it all, he appeared unconcerned about the buzz that grew around him. "He acted like he was going to pitch a game in the Mexican League," commented an incredulous Mike Brito. In the clubhouse, however, Fernando was very playful. Most of his teammates described him as a "joker."

The buzz around Valenzuela was quickly dubbed "Fernandomania," an outpouring of attention by fans and media that, in some places, bordered on frenzy. Fernandomania was a nationwide phenomenon that surrounded the entire team. Gone was the pall of intolerance that had hung over Robinson's and Koufax's entry into the league. "People just wanted to look at him, touch him, shake his hand," recalls his manager, Tommy Lasorda. "Fernando set the baseball world on fire in 1981 like something you'd never believe in your life."[28]

The legendary Dodgers broadcaster Jaime Jarrín notes that Fernando's stature in Los Angeles escaped the confines of the Dodgers faithful, spilling over into new areas: "People here in the United States grew up with baseball, they played at school and knew about the sport. But for three or four million Hispanics in Southern California, most of them grew up with soccer and were indifferent to baseball. But thanks to Fernando, they became baseball followers."[29] And it wasn't just Mexican

Americans in Los Angeles who started coming to the Park. "Walk-ups"—spectators who buy their tickets on game day at the stadium—started coming from Mexico with regularity, extending Fernandomania across the border.

Within the large Mexican-American community in Los Angeles, the outpouring of pride in "someone who speaks our language, and eats our food" was a baseball and cultural second coming. Diego Rivera–like murals of Fernando pitching, surrounded with Mexican and Dodger iconography, graced walls. *Corridos* (ballads) of Fernando were composed, recorded, and sung by new fans. Feeling kinship with his cultural compatriots, Valenzuela would go in disguise to local parks on Sundays in order to play ball with the youths who were now beginning to play the game in large numbers. Fernando sightings of this nature took on a religious quality, since any stranger who showed up to play could be none other than the baby-faced wonder. If you attended a Dodger game when Valenzuela pitched, you might think you were attending a World Cup event, as Mexican flags waved around Dodger Stadium. He galvanized the Mexican and Mexican-American communities and presented the Dodgers with a new, wildly enthusiastic fan base that they have cultivated ever since.

Wherever the nationwide phenomenon pitched, media mobbed him, and soon Valenzuela was even the subject of a special report on Swedish television. Commenting on the media attention Valenzuela received outside of Los Angeles, the outfielder Ken Landreaux likened his teammate to a pop icon: "It was like following a famous musician or artist. When you hear of someone famous coming to town, people flock to the theater. That's how it was. A lot of people would come to the stadium, hoping it was Fernando's turn to pitch."[30]

That Valenzuela did not fit any of the basic criteria for an icon only added to his mystique. Being quiet in public made it easy to shun the media frenzy swirling around him. Speaking very little English reinforced this distance. He was uncomfortable doing interviews in English, speaking instead through Jaime Jarrín. Linguistic challenges aside, he simply didn't look or behave like most baseball aces. He was round-bodied in an era when pitchers were becoming increasingly tall. His roly-poly presence on the mound did not engender great confidence, and when fans first watched him wind up, it only increased his exoticism. His catcher, Mike Scioscia, observing Valenzuela's ability to make acrobatic catches, summed him up as "great athlete, bad body." And he could hit as well, leading Scioscia to marvel, "This is like Ruth, but now he's going to finish his pitching career."[31] In trademark fashion, Valenzuela would suddenly roll his eyeballs up to the heavens before fixing his gaze on the catcher's target, a sight more appropriate to a ritual healer than to a major league pitcher.

For Dodgers fans in Southern California and elsewhere, Fernando Valenzuela opened up an era of Latin American signings that have become a staple of both the franchise and the industry. He also served to build a large Mexican-American fan base that has been the staple of Dodgers marketing ever since. Valenzuela's astounding success fostered a high level of expectation and interest in players coming out of Latin America. The team's front office was quick to invest in the Dominican Republic, Venezuela, and elsewhere, in anticipation of the quality of players coming out of Latin America, but to date none has surpassed the impact of Fernando Valenzuela.

Nomomania

For the Dodgers the arrival of the Japanese pitching sensation Hideo Nomo represented the ideal combination of great timing, great preparation, and a smidgen of luck. Because of his unorthodox pitching delivery, Nomo was branded by the Japanese baseball establishment as marginal at best. "Young man, with that tornado windup, you'll never make it," pronounced the manager of one of the elite baseball high schools, so essential for moving up the career ladder in Japan.[32] Thwarted, Nomo played for a small Japanese high school and was subsequently ignored by the powerhouse university teams. He wound up pitching in the Japanese industrial leagues, where he dominated. This performance, combined with his mastery of opponents in the 1988 Seoul Olympics, got him drafted by the Kintetsu Buffaloes. He signed with them on the condition that no one would tinker with his delivery—a rare level of presumption on the part of a rookie in Japan. The resentment Nomo felt was understandable and shared by many in Japanese baseball, but his defiance was unusual.

The Dodgers' signing Nomo was a freak occurrence because Japanese rules prohibit any professional from becoming a free agent until he has played for ten seasons and a minimum of 1,500 games. After encountering arm problems in 1994, just five years into his tenure process, Nomo was deemed damaged. He seized the opportunity to renege on the ten-year free-agency standard by voluntarily retiring and smoothing the way to test the international waters. Don Nomura, who would become his agent, was the man responsible for finding the legal loophole to get him out of Japan. Granted free agency, Nomo came to Major League Baseball and North American stardom.

Peter O'Malley immediately set his sights on Nomo, but he was not alone. The Giants, Mariners, Yankees, and Rockies were also preparing offers. While the money mattered, noneconomic circumstances gave the Dodgers an edge. No organization and its representatives were better known or more highly regarded than the Dodgers and Peter O'Malley. Then–scouting director Terry Reynolds pointed out, "Peter's ties go very deep. He gets his foot in the door."[33] Nomo himself pointed to the O'Malley difference: "After meeting Peter O'Malley, I wanted to join the Dodgers. . . . The difference was Peter O'Malley."[34] The Dodgers also benefited from being in the right place, on the West Coast. Nomo's agent revealed that "he went to several clubs, including the Dodgers, Mariners, and Giants. He settled on the Dodgers, partially because of their tradition and location in the country, and partially because of marketing concerns. It was a good choice. The Dodgers have a long history in Tokyo."[35] Fred Claire, the Dodgers general manager at the time, was also very impressed with Nomo's drive. Commenting on how Nomo felt about playing in the major leagues after being in Japan, Claire said, "Perhaps the most memorable thing he said to me is, 'I haven't proven anything yet. I've done nothing.' That impressed me a lot."[36]

The signing of Nomo was not viewed favorably in Japan. "In the wake of all this, the Japanese sports press went into its DEF-CON 4 mode, labeling Nomo an 'ingrate,' a 'troublemaker' and a 'traitor.'" Granted, Nomo added fuel to the fire with his confrontational style. Some in Japan even tried to squelch the deal before it happened: "A veteran baseball manager in Japan told an inquiring Dodger executive they were making a mistake. 'Nomo's arm is not that good anymore . . . and he's got a bad attitude.'"[37]

Once Nomo donned the Dodger Blue, his arm seemed plenty good: like Valenzuela, he won the Rookie of the Year award. In fact, his statistics as a rookie in 1995—a 13–6 won-lost record, a 2.54 earned run average, and 236 strikeouts—were remarkably similar to Valenzuela's 13–7, 2.48 ERA, and 180 strikeouts in 1981.

"Nomomania" was most certainly real, but it was more a product of the Japanese response to Nomo's success than it was an American event. The fascination of Nomo's quest was easy to understand in Tokyo. He was the first Japanese in thirty years, since the brief career of Masanori Murakami with the Giants, to attempt to succeed in the U.S. major leagues. Millions of Japanese fans might have watched live Dodger road telecasts just before heading off to work or when they first got there if their newfound hero played. When Nomo started the 1995 All-Star Game, an estimated fifteen million Japanese were glued to their sets at 10 A.M.[38] Sales of Dodgers licensed products at the stadium also rose as a result of Nomo's foray into major league baseball. Everything that Ichiro was to encounter was foreshadowed in the Japanese response to Nomo. Most striking perhaps was the emergence of a Japanese superfan who would fly across the Pacific to attend a game, returning shortly after its conclusion. Kenji Koshimizu, a store owner from Japan, took seven trips to see Nomo pitch in 1995. "I cannot explain it," he said. "I love Nomo. That's all I can say." Thousands of these fans made the long trek to see the first impact player from their country, consuming every bit of Nomo-related paraphernalia they could. One souvenir booth salesperson noted that business doubled on Nomo nights: "I've had people come up and buy 100 shirts, dozens of caps. They buy as much as they can carry back to Japan."[39] The numbers of Asian fans, both tourists and locals, swelled so much that the Dodgers arranged for a Japanese restaurant to provide part of their stadium offerings.

Nomo's first effort was a solid five-inning effort in which he gave up just one hit, striking out seven but walking four. He left with the score knotted at 0, the Dodgers eventually losing to the Giants in fifteen innings. In character, Nomo summed it up for reporters: "I'm really glad I was on the mound. I'm disappointed we lost the game," or "I was just glad to be on the mound. I don't care about the history."[40] Reflecting his team's woeful offense, Nomo got no decisions in his first five starts, though he pitched well, striking out forty. In June his efforts began to be rewarded: he won seven consecutive games (including a sixteen-strikeout effort) and started the All-Star Game.

The Japanese media did an about-face, abandoning their earlier calls for his head and instead extolling Nomo's virtues. His corkscrew delivery, so ridiculed earlier, was now viewed as evidence of the "superiority of the Japanese baseball techniques."[41] The same sportswriters who had only a few months earlier described Nomo's character as "sullen" now saw him as "serene." The eventual signings of Ichiro, Sasaki, and Ishii all followed this same path, as Japan slavishly followed every one of its defectors and proclaimed the end of the view of Japanese players as inferior. Nomo's response to either Japanese or American media was the same: indifference shading to abruptness. He spoke to the Japanese in an almost defiant way, and to the Americans only through an interpreter, even though he could speak English.

For his first three seasons Nomo lived up to expectations: he followed his Rookie of the Year performance with sixteen- and fourteen-victory seasons, pitching a no-hitter and becoming the fastest pitcher in major league history to reach five hundred strikeouts, doing it in 444⅔ innings. The three fat years were followed by four lean years. He went on to the New York Mets, Milwaukee, Detroit, and Boston, losing more games than he won, with ERAs of 4.50 or higher every season—though he did become only the fourth pitcher in history to throw a no-hitter in each league, turning the trick for the Red Sox in 2001. He then returned in 2002 to Los Angeles, where he had two solid seasons. In his second tour with the Dodgers he teamed up with countryman Kazuhisa Ishii, making the Dodgers the first team to have two Japanese starters. Not only were the Dodgers farsighted enough to forge the Asian connection, they knew how to market it as well.

One small thing that did go unnoticed by most casual observers was the clubhouse climate of internationalism that the Dodgers had created earlier than other clubs. I do not mean having foreign players on their roster; and I certainly do not refer to the Benetton atmosphere in the clubhouse, where everyone reveled in one another's culture. Rather the Dodgers wound up collecting players of diverse backgrounds, and that in turn fashioned a cultural sink in which some players—out of necessity—forged bonds, if for no other reason than to overcome cultural dislocation. Ismael Valdés, then a second-year pitcher from Mexico, could empathize with Nomo's coming to America: "Hideo doesn't know much English. I don't either, but at least I can ask for things myself. So, that's how we became friends. We run together between starts, we talk about things. I'll tell him something in Spanish and he'll translate to Japanese. I'll tell him how it translates to English. . . . It's good because we're teammates and we wear the same uniform."[42] It is noteworthy that the Dodgers' climate was so culturally diverse so early.

The Dodgers' International Presence

The Dodgers in Latin America

Although the Dodgers can list their first Latino player as early as 1930, when the Cuban Dolf Luque briefly pitched for them, they had not originally signed him, and they didn't have another Latino starter until Sandy Amoros in 1952. They are, in fact, latecomers to Latin America. Their serious presence in the Dominican Republic, the richest source of foreign talent, dates back only to the 1970s, when they scouted the island as part of their evolving interest in Latin players. They were far behind the San Francisco Giants and the Pittsburgh Pirates. By the late 1970s the Dodgers' Dominican efforts had managed to develop only Rafael Landestoy (debuted in 1977) and Pedro Guerrero (1978). In Puerto Rico they fared only slightly better, developing five journeymen players before 1980. Their biggest opportunity slipped ignominiously through their clutches. It is little known that the Dodgers were the club that signed future Hall of Fame outfielder Roberto Clemente in 1954. They paid the then-princely sum of $10,000 to sign him, but when they neglected to place him on their major league roster, he was quickly snapped up by the Pirates.[43] The Dodgers fared only slightly better in Cuba, where they signed Sandy Amoros in 1952 and shortstop Chico Fernández in 1956. By contrast, during those same years the Washington Senators (later the Minnesota Twins) had forty-two Cubans play for their organization.

Transforming the Dodgers into a Latin American powerhouse was a matter of finding someone who could serve as an innovator in the region, and then using the team's considerable resources.

The Avila Difference

In the late 1970s, Dodgers President Peter O'Malley and General Manager Al Campanis began to turn increasingly to Latin America, but it was Ralph Avila who is credited with turning the Dodgers' program in the region around. Avila fostered something new: a full-time presence in the Dominican Republic. Avila altered the Dominican baseball landscape when he engineered, along with Epy Guerrero of the Toronto Blue Jays, the first baseball academies there.[44] Avila was also the first to link major league baseball with local sport establishments. Before his efforts, the only major league presence was the scout, who, like everyone from Christopher Columbus to the legions of pirates, came to the island, took what he wanted, and left. Ralph Avila was assigned to the Dominican Republic and quickly immersed himself in the Dominican baseball scene, coaching the national team in addition to his duties for the Dodgers. Because of his outsider status as a Cuban American, he provided the institutional link between U.S. and Dominican traditions. In due course he reinvented the way things were done. It was fitting that early in 2004 Ralph Avila was knighted by the president of the Dominican Republic.

Avila had taken on the position as Latin American scout (including south Florida) at Campanis's urging in 1970. Campanis may have liked Latin America, but he certainly had not put his energy there. All of that changed as Avila established a "working relationship" between the Dodgers and the Dominican professional club Licey, a move that put him in the center of the Dominican baseball scene. He periodically managed the club as well in the Winter Baseball League. In the early 1980s Avila was already deep into his grand project. He began to envision the idea of the academy as early as 1974. In conjunction with Monchin Pichardo, the owner of the Licey club, Avila developed a prototype of the academy to develop players for Licey. Avila began to advocate for an academy that was exclusively for the Dodgers and began a modest one in 1981. Both the Blue Jays and the Phillies were beginning to invest heavily in academies during this time. Convincing the Dodger brass of the soundness of this kind of thing was tricky, but Peter O'Malley embraced the idea of building a state-of-the-art complex, and Campo Las Palmas was born.

Most people feel that Campo Las Palmas resembles a posh resort more than a baseball complex. Fifty acres of land that comprises two major league–quality fields, a sparkling complex of dormitories, a cafeteria, and offices framed by tropical farmland that produces much of its own food, Campo Las Palmas employs more than fifty people. When it first opened in 1987, Las Palmas was unique: the Riviera of Dominican baseball. Here as many as forty rookies—mostly Dominican, but some Venezuelans too—are tutored in Dodgers fundamentals. They play in the Dominican Summer League, an official league under the aegis of Organized Baseball. All of these players vie for a finite number of visas that the Department of Labor grants the Commissioner's Office.

With Avila and a spectacular facility, the Dodgers quickly became the most successful major league club on the island. Through the late 1980s and into the 1990s they signed and developed a string of major leaguers through the academy, brothers Ramón and Pedro Martínez, José Offerman, Raúl Móndesi, and Juan Guzmán. By the mid-1990s the rush to sign Dominicans was on, as every club scrambled to set up some sort of presence in the country. Money started flowing into both the signings and the academies. The political-economic terrain of the game was changing, and the Dodgers provided the template used by all. They were the first team to infuse their dealings in the country with a kind of big-market quality. Before them, organizations would send someone down for hastily arranged tryouts, or to follow up a tip received through a third party. The Dodgers showed their respect for Dominicans and their game by investing serious money in the country. They paid attention to the littler things as well; they were, for example, the only club to provide a bus bearing the team logo. They sought to be considered the best, the cleanest, the richest team with a presence in the country, because talent would be more likely to flow to that team. The Dodgers accelerated the big-money era in the Dominican Republic when they signed Willy Aybar for $1.4 million in 2000 and Guzmán for $2.25 million in 2001. The Dodgers vaulted to the front of the line in Latin America via a willingness to place resources and effort into the country long before it became fashionable. Furthermore, they placed innovative people there to ensure the organization's success. Most important, their efforts in Latin America were part of their larger orientation toward global development.

Enter the Dragons: Asian Impact Signings

The Asian market for ballplayers provides one of the key indexes distinguishing between large- and small-market teams. Japan, in particular, constitutes a prohibitively expensive market. Signing Ichiro Suzuki or Hideki Matsui is a major financial commitment. But it also involves establishing relationships, and here, too, the Dodgers blazed the trail. They understood the importance of respect, reciprocity, and attention to the little rituals. Ishi doro is one of those little things.

Ishi Doro

Lot 37 at Dodger Stadium has a unique gem concealed in the hilly slope that spoons the back of it. If you turn your back to the ballpark and look up the hill, you can make out the footprint created by a string of river-stone steps that lead to the top. The last of these stones escorts you away from the steamy parking lot, the Dodgers, Los Angeles, and even the Western Hemisphere. In front of you is a lovely Japanese garden, and staring at you is a solitary ten-foot-tall stone Japanese lantern—a sight sure to catch you completely off guard. It's called ishi doro, and seems far from its origins. On this hot July morning in 2002, however, it feels as if Japan is fused at the hip with the Los Angeles Dodgers.

This is a "rededication ceremony" for the stone gift given to the Dodgers back in 1962, when Dodger Stadium opened. The donor, Sotaro Suzuki, the dean of Japanese journalists, recognized the Dodgers as long-time friends of the Japanese game of yakyu, or baseball. Suzuki understood the presentation of this gift as part of an unbroken series of exchanges between Japanese baseball and the Dodgers dating back to 1956, when the Dodgers first traveled to Japan to play an exhibition series. It was then that Dodgers owner Walter O'Malley met Suzuki and, with input from O'Malley's administrative assistant Akihiro Ikuhara, they initiated an exchange program that is now fifty years old.

The old timers at this ceremony creep slowly up the stone stairs, holding on either to their young escorts or to their children. It is a small gathering of fifty people or so, quite a departure from the large-scale Japanese-American Day festivities planned later at the stadium. This is a solemn and dignified ceremony of remembrance, meaningful only to those who have crafted the relationship in the first place. The Dodgers brass lauds their Japanese partners both locally and in Japan. The congregation includes Dodgers President Bob Graziano, former manager Tommy Lasorda, and longtime University of Southern California and U.S. Olympic coach Rod Dedeaux. Among the Japanese entourage, representatives from the Chamber of Commerce, leading banks, and tourism and media companies stand before the ishi doro. Yet for all the mutual admiration on display, the three key figures in the creation of this relationship are not present: Sotaro Suzuki and Akihiro Ikuhara have passed away, and Peter O'Malley had a previous engagement that took him out of town. To know those three is to understand the bond that formed which is unlike anything else in baseball.

Sotaro Suzuki rose to a position of prominence at Japan's premier newspaper, *Yomiuri Shimbun,* in the 1930s. Suzuki was involved in all of the early negotiations for the Dodgers' first Japanese tour, through the course of which he developed his relationship with O'Malley. He was invited to be Walter O'Malley's special guest to mark the official opening of Dodger Stadium in 1962, and to commemorate that event Suzuki commissioned the ishi doro that was to discreetly grace the stadium.

Akihiro "Ike" Ikuhara was one of those rare individuals with cross-cultural savvy, energy, and honesty, the sort of person you hope to meet if you are planning something new. Something new was what Peter O'Malley was planning in 1965. He hired Ikuhara as his administrative assistant to set about implementing the Dodgers' second exhibition tour to Japan. Ikuhara went on to wear a number of hats on both sides of the Pacific Rim. He wrote baseball books and telecast games for his Japanese compatriots; at the same time he helped to communicate and negotiate the intricacies of Dodgers baseball interests on both sides of the Pacific. Ikuhara was instrumental in paving the way for the Dodgers in other Asian countries as well—for example, he helped Peter O'Malley build the first grass baseball field in China. Ikuhara's influence was felt even after his too-early death, when the Dodgers signed the Korean Chan Ho Park in 1994 and Nomo in 1995, and he was there in spirit on the day of the rededication ceremony behind Dodger Stadium.

Schooled by his father, Peter O'Malley ventured on his own, furthering the earlier work. He traveled to China in 1986 to foster the game there, and in 1990 he played a role in introducing professional baseball to Taiwan. It was in Japan, however, that O'Malley had the biggest impact.

Signing Players

Relationships are key—not only in Japan, but especially in Japan. It was not a big surprise that the Seattle Mariners landed Ichiro, because the team is owned by a Japanese national—Nintendo founder Hiroshi Yamauchi—but it also has its own unique and substantial ties to Japan. The Dodgers' ability to sign Hideo Nomo in 1995 and then Kazuhisa Ishii in 2001 depended on much more than their big-market willingness to spend the money. It was just as much about their use of well-established ties to influential partners in Japan. When retired Dodgers manager Tommy Lasorda ends his speech at the ishi doro with, "Just remember, the Dodgers and the Japanese love each other!" he is paying homage to a fifty-year relationship, as well as setting the tone for the next deal.

Walter O'Malley was committed to pushing the cultural margins of the game by establishing relations between the Dodgers and Asia. While still in Brooklyn, the Dodgers completed their first reciprocal exchange with Japan by making a postseason trip in 1956, and the next spring they hosted Yomiuri Giants players at Vero Beach, Florida. After Peter O'Malley succeeded his father, the Dodgers built upon these exchanges, forging a set of enduring ties to Asian baseball that resulted in the first Asian impact signings in baseball. Chan Ho Park of Korea in 1994 became the first Korean to play in the major leagues after signing a $1.2 million contract out of college. A year later Nomo became the second Japanese player in the big leagues.

The Dodgers in Asia

Walter and Peter O'Malley initiated a series of baseball cultural exchanges that became institutionalized. The Dodgers playing exhibitions in Japan in 1956, 1966, and 1993; Japanese teams trained and played in Vero Beach ten times between 1957 and 2005; and dating back to 1962, the Dodgers have repeatedly engineered exchanges with Japanese teams involving players, staff, administrators and training facilities. What Walter O'Malley initiated Peter O'Malley developed and modernized. From the Dodgers perspective, the signings of Chan Ho Park in 1994, Hideo

Nomo in 1995, and Kazuhisa Ishii in 2002 resulted from a half-century of relationships with friends in Asia.

The remarkable success of Ichiro—both as player and icon—was precisely what the Dodgers hoped to experience in signing the left-handed pitcher Kazuhisa Ishii in 2002. Free-agent signing in Japan is somewhat of a misnomer. The whole concept of free agency is—on a practical level—nonexistent in Japan. Nevertheless, through sometimes delicate negotiations, the Dodgers eventually signed Ishii to a six-year, $23.6 million deal. His record in Japan, while good, was not remarkable; hence the Dodgers risked a considerable sum on a pitcher of sub-superstar status. Why such an exorbitant sum, and why risk it on someone less than Ichiro's stature? In the case of Ishii, almost half of money went to his Japanese team, the Yakult Swallows, for the rights to bid for him. It is called the "posting process," and it consists of sealed bids by teams with interests in signing the player. The Dodgers' bid of $11.3 million was the highest, and for that amount they received a thirty-day window of opportunity to negotiate with Ishii. Ishii eventually signed for $12.3 million.

Clearly, the size of the total package for signing Ishii is the sort of thing that separates the Dodgers—and their big-market brothers—from more fiscally challenged teams. The Dodgers had the ability to enter the expensive Japanese market, but their ability to pay was only one part of the equation. Other factors were at work. Most Japanese players would prefer signing with West Coast teams because they are closer to Japan and because these cities have sizable Japanese populations. Thus the inevitable culture shock is somewhat mitigated. In Ishii's case, cultural familiarity was an even bigger factor because his wife, Ayako Kisa, a news anchor in Japan, had lived for a time in Los Angeles and hoped to land a job in broadcasting in the area. Having one of the largest Japanese populations in the country made Los Angeles a front-runner, but the Dodgers' connections to Japan sealed the deal. "If you believe the rumors," insinuated one writer familiar with the details, "the bidding process for negotiating rights with Japanese lefthander Kazuhisa Ishii may have been tilted in the Dodgers' favor. That may not seem exactly cricket, but in the real world Major League Baseball could be forgiven for doing what it felt necessary to bring Japan's biggest stars to the States. Ichiro may not have made the move had he not been allowed to sign with the Mariners, a team with strong ties to the Pacific Rim. Similarly, there's reason to believe Ishi might have remained with the Yakult Swallows had the Dodgers not submitted the high bid of $11.3 million."[45]

The Dodgers convinced themselves that signing Ishii was necessary, and they had all of the requirements in place. They had the resources, the cultural environment most desired by Ishii, and the connections. Most important, they had the motive: a long period of bad domestic draft picks.

Marketing the International Promise

Most people close to baseball separate the game from the business. Marketing baseball is—while necessary—widely downplayed by "baseball operations" representatives on ballclubs. One general manager of whom I had asked a question related to market share responded in a slightly dismissive tone, "That's something marketing people do. Not us." Marketing people often get lost in the economics of the game: in promotions, John Powers reports for the Dodgers and MLB on demographics and creation of various sorts of opportunity. But it is the relationship between marketing, team, and the game that underwrites the ability of a team to sign the best players and successfully compete.

Major league teams, concerned as they are with player development, rarely venture into international marketing. If the Chicago Cubs or Atlanta Braves occasionally drift into this area, they do so as part of a "hyphenated" day—Hispanic-American or Japanese-American day— before one of their games. The Dodgers and one or two other teams have, on the other hand, made ethnic and racial groups the centerpiece of their marketing strategy.

Latino Marketing

Clubs that enjoy a link to local Latino and Mexican consumers owe a debt of gratitude to the Dodgers. The Dodgers blazed that trail in 1958, when they initiated the first Spanish-language radio broadcasts. Jaime Jarrín pioneered that effort, which made it that much easier for Latinos to embrace the Dodgers when Fernando Valenzuela came along. The Dodgers never dropped the ball, and have cultivated a special relationship with the Latino community of Los Angeles. That relationship has paid off handsomely. According to Kris Rone, executive vice president of business operations for the organization from 2000 through 2004, about one-third of all Dodgers fans, approximately one million, identify themselves as Latino. The synergy that existed between Valenzuela and Mexican-American and Mexican fans in Los Angeles has deepened over twenty-five years to include multigenerational families. The Valenzuela windfall turned into part of the Dodgers' economic infrastructure. Following her arrival, Rone quickly carried forward the Hispanic marketing concept:

> Having Fernando here really turned on our Hispanic customers. The effect of that has been long-lasting. Our Latino base has not abandoned us when he stopped playing. We've spent a lot of time marketing to Latino customers. They're important, and we've grown dependent upon them. When I came here four years ago, we put together a pretty cohesive plan for the Hispanic market. The first phase was simple: we were going to have a genuine and sincere message to both Spanish-speaking and English-speaking Latinos, saying, "We invite you here. You're an important part of our fan base and our history, and we really want you and your family to come out here and enjoy the game. Then we put a lot out in the Spanish-speaking media, as well as community affairs responses. Third, we decided to do a couple of big promotions each year to cement the strategy. Each year we promote Día de los Niños [children's day] and Viva los Dodgers. We do these things sincerely and secure sponsors. Last April, on Día de los Niños we did an offer—with each paid adult, two kids get in free. We did it around an Autograph Day in the parking lot. We had acts from different Latin American countries. We got our sponsors involved. That day we had twelve thousand walk-ups—the second-biggest walk-up in our history! From there, over the last five years we've added other elements. It's worked. Our statistics show that of the different ethnicities that come to Dodger Stadium, our Hispanic guests come with larger party size; they're younger—which is the lifeblood of where we're going; they spend more on food, beverage, and merchandise; and they consider themselves more loyal fans than any other.[46]

Rone and Sergio Del Prado, vice president of sales and marketing, masterminded this layered program. Billboards all over the city—250 in Hispanic neighborhoods alone—kept the Dodgers brand in everyone's eye. Large inserts in the Spanish press tout upcoming Dodger events and promotions. The Dodgers distributed 600,000 pocket schedules in Spanish. In reaching out to the Latino community, the Dodgers (in partnership with Toyota) present special awards to community leaders who have had a positive effect. They also mount a mobile unit, Dodger Blue on Wheels, which tours various neighborhoods relating the history of the franchise and of the sport. Beginning in 2002 a campaign called Creando Recuerdos con Cada Juego (Creating memories with every game) was launched, featuring the voice of Jaime Jarrín, the legendary Spanish-language announcer for the team. There are also Spanish-language versions of the popular children's Blue Crew Club in addition to Viva los Dodgers and Día de los Niños.

Under Fox News Corporation there was no Spanish-language television programming. The Spanish-language radio deal the Dodgers had with their local station remained popular and lucrative, though. At the start of the 2003 season, the Dodgers took their Spanish-language radio broadcasts in-house. Management felt that the team was missing out on a significant source of revenue, a loss made more significant by the undervalued Fox News Corporation television contract. The move quickly paid off. Two months after taking over their Spanish-language broadcasts, the Dodgers were close to $1 million in advertising sales, further underscoring the depth of Hispanic marketing in Los Angeles.[47]

Fernando Valenzuela's meteoric rise from Mexico was a surprise, but the Dodgers have been able to translate his baseball impact to a marketing impact. It was not a rank opportunistic move either: "You can't force things like that," Rone declares. "You have to be a little organic with it, let it happen on its own. When it does you can certainly capitalize on it, make it larger than life. People here wanted to create 'Ishii-mania.' Ugh! You've got to let that happen, then jump on it. But there too, it's got to be sincere. I think our relationship with the Hispanic communities is that . . . sincere."[48]

The Dodgers' marketing strategy is both cross-cultural and international. It is the site where the local and the global meet because the club has been able to find the transnational links that exist within the various ethnic and racial constituencies living both in Los Angeles and in the countries the players represent. When Valenzuela first broke into the national spotlight in 1981, Mexican nationals began coming up to Los Angeles for his games, in addition to rapidly growing numbers of Hispanics in the southern California. Not much was made of it at the time, but the phenomenon showed the capacity of a team situated near the border to draw fans from the other side. The lesson was not lost upon the Arizona Diamondbacks or the San Diego Padres, who now seek to pull in fans from the Mexican side. Marketing efforts don't have to be complex, as many Mexicans have a deep attachment to the game through the Mexican League. Rich Saenz, director of Hispanic marketing for the Diamondbacks, outlines their position:

> Ownership wanted this team to appeal to Phoenix, Arizona, and Mexico. That was part of the plan, and I wanted to make this a regional team—across the border. In northern Mexico baseball is number one, along with boxing. We wanted to make a commitment to the people of Mexico, so we put together a program that would go at least five years. We went down during the Caribbean Series and put up a big banner saying, "The Arizona Diamondbacks Welcome the People of Mexico." We invested in the building of a baseball complex in Hermosillo that cost $1.2 million. We committed to playing exhibitions in Hermosillo for five years.[49]

Asian Marketing

While marketing to Asia and marketing to Asian Americans are linked, they require different approaches. Only a few teams have anything resembling a cohesive Asian marketing program. This requires a significant local Asian population, and so it is generally limited to West Coast cities—Seattle, San Francisco, Los Angeles, and San Diego. In addition, while baseball is popular in countries like Japan and Korea, the Asian American has not yet been a significant presence in major league ballparks. A major leaguer representing the group can trigger significant interest. For the Dodgers, Nomo-mania garnered a mass following.

"We've always had Japanese-American fans and promotions, like Japan-American Community Day," Rone remarks. "We partner with Rafi Sempu and different broadcasting stations around L.A. I can't tell you the actual numbers because they're still so small that statistically they aren't significant, and with a limited budget we picked the areas and constituencies which had the most upside [Hispanic], but the Asian-American fan base is growing, and we're encouraged by it."[50] So where is the incentive for the Dodgers to find new ways to market to Asians? Oddly enough, it comes from the possibility of building direct links to Asia and then, through those links, to Asian Americans. For instance, the buzz created by Nomo in 1995, Ichiro since 2001, and Hideki Matsui of the Yankees since 2004 has extended far beyond marketing to local Japanese Americans. Back in Japan, the players' following has grown to the point of being a national obsession. The media saturation of Ichiro, Matsui, and Nomo, and to a lesser extent, other Japanese players, means that virtually anything they do is reported, furthering the national obsession with them. Television games in which they appear are watched in real time, even if that means 8 A.M. Ichiro's record-breaking run in 2004, when he set the major league mark for hits in a season, was followed around the clock throughout Japan.

Of more import is the Japanese tourist boom for Seattle, Los Angeles, and New York as a result of Japanese stars on their teams' rosters. With Nomo and Ishii as Dodger starting pitchers in 2004, when the team paraded out its roster in spring training, there were more than forty Japanese tour operators, in addition to the usual gaggle of Japanese reporters and fans.[51] California is heavily dependent upon Japanese tourism, which contributes about $1.2 billion to local economies through the one million yearly visitors. Nomo merchandise jumped off the shelves at Dodger Stadium in his first year. One visiting Japanese fan bought almost $4,000 worth of Nomo-related items in one day.[52] Los Angeles's Japanese community, known as Little Tokyo, was particularly excited about the Dodgers pitchers, anticipating increased Japanese tourism. Kris Rone points out that tour operators were also trying to deal directly with the players: "The tour operators who descended on Dodger Stadium two weeks ago wanted to meet Ishii and formulate package deals for Japanese visitors that include one or two Dodger games in Los Angeles and a swing through San Francisco or San Diego." She recalls, "When Ishii and Nomo came, we worked with the tourism board, and we sent Ishii and the mayor of L.A. on a trip to Japan."[53] Similar efforts have been reported to capitalize on the presence of other Japanese stars in Seattle and New York.[54]

A newer development in the economic boom that trails these Japanese stars is the advertising that Japanese companies are doing on televised Dodger games—in real time. This is noteworthy in that the time difference between Japan and the United States ranges from seven hours (West Coast) to ten hours (East Coast) and one would suppose that advertising in real time would reach a negligible audience in the middle of the workday in Japan. That is not the case, however. Because of the numbers of Japanese watching games live, Japanese companies understand that they can get to two markets simultaneously when they advertise during a Dodgers game with Nomo pitching: consumers at home and an Asian-American market in Los Angeles.

Teams that can control their own television broadcasting—the Red Sox, the Dodgers, and the Cubs, for example—stand to see impressive revenue from such advertisers, as Rone acknowledges: "It's amazing when those dollars come in! [Japanese companies] are really happy to spend money and see their logo back in Japan. It's status. We've had several partners in Japan: Kuboto Tires did it last year. We've had others who advertise here to get the message there. What teams can do is limited because we don't own the right to Japan, so it's kind of incidental contact, but it's great."[55]

Walter O'Malley's work pioneered international baseball. The disruption of the community that had to suffer the building of Dodger Stadium is a black spot on O'Malley's legacy, but he and his son Peter have also given much back to the city of Los Angeles. Whether the Dodgers remain at the cutting edge of globalizing baseball, or even Los Angeles's favorite team, is now in question.

The damage inflicted on the Dodgers reputation and operations that began with the Murdoch ownership has, unfortunately, not abated under the McCourts. Replacing many key people in the organization; trading away popular players; trying out a general manager only to release him before he had time to prove himself—these moves have made the team look rudderless, and invoking hallowed Dodger traditions has done nothing to mitigate the damage. Institutionally, many of the international components—foreign scouting, signing, and marketing—may be continuing, but they are pale reflections of the original global strategy.

Dodgers hegemony is even being challenged at home. As we have seen, the idea of marketing global-local connections was something the Dodgers began twenty years ago. Taking their cue from the Fernando Valenzuela signing, the Dodgers fashioned a strong set of programs that tied the Latino community to them. The Dodgers became Hispanic Los Angeles's team. With the recent purchase of the Anaheim Angels, Greater Los Angeles's other team, by Arte Moreno, the first Hispanic owner of a major league team, Dodgers dominance of the Hispanic market is being challenged. The Angels now have a heavily Latinized team, with a number of superstars like Vladimir Guerrero and Bartolo Colón, and a Hispanic owner who has energized the team with fan-friendly moves—lower ticket prices, a new scoreboard—and marketing optimism. Just before the onset of the 2005 season, Moreno fired a salvo in what is emerging as a test of Dodgers brand loyalty. The Anaheim Angels changed their name to reflect their intent to become identified with Los Angeles. They would henceforth be the Los Angeles Angels of Anaheim. Despite a threatened lawsuit, the Angels blanketed southern California—and Los Angeles in particular—with five hundred billboards announcing their new image. Two teams with recent success—the Dodgers won their division in 2004, and the Angels have won three divisional titles in four years, plus the World Series in 2002—share the nation's second largest market. Determined new owners on both sides could join an epic battle of the brands. At least one late-2005 survey suggests that the battle is over, and so are the Dodgers. A poll of 1,529 sports fans selected nationwide were asked to rank professional teams on a range of variables: fan relations, ownership, stadium experience, players, coaches, and so on. The Angels ranked fifth, the highest of any baseball team. The Dodgers placed eighty-second out of ninety-one teams.[56]

Whatever the future brings, the Dodgers will always be known as the organization that built the template for ethnic-racial marketing in sports.

They did so on the field and off, globally and locally. They understood the importance of crafting relations with constituencies. They did it, as Rone said, "sincerely and genuinely." We saw this in the little things that they do, like the ishi doro ceremony, as well as the big things that they do, like breaking decades-old social barriers.

4

THE DOMINICAN REPUBLIC: FISHING WHERE THE FISH ARE

"The best government we ever had was Pedro Martínez."—resident of Manoguayabo

To qualify as a tier one country in the eyes of Major League Baseball, the Dominican Republic has to be so clearly the epicenter of foreign talent that its economic underdevelopment is overlooked. And that is the case. At the outset of the 2005 baseball season, 242 players (29 percent of all major leaguers) were foreign born. Of the fourteen countries that are represented in this figure, no country even comes close to matching the Dominican Republic's contribution. Ninety-one Dominicans were on those rosters. From a trickle a half-century ago, the numbers of Dominicans playing in the major leagues has dramatically increased in every decade: 2 in the 1950s, 22 in the 1960s, 38 in the 1970s, 65 in the 1980s, 133 in the 1990s.[1] Dominican major leaguers are only the tip of the baseball iceberg. In 2004 there were 1,325 Dominicans in the minor leagues and tens of thousands trying to get signed. It may look like a game, but baseball in the Dominican Republic has become an industry. It is subsidized by the government, receives international investment, directly and indirectly includes a significant segment of the population, and wields considerable cultural clout. Dominican stars—and there are at least a dozen—are national figures à la Michael Jordan.

In a country with as much poverty as is found in the Dominican Republic, virtually every Dominican player understands what is expected of him. After becoming a superstar, Pedro Martínez has provided for his town of Manoguayabo. He does so quietly, as a hometown kid. "I know where I'm from," declared Pedro several years ago, "a poor family from a poor country."[2] And because of his concern, humility, and help, the people of Manoguayabo love him: "He doesn't realize what he's done for this community. We hope that God preserves him, helps him, and keeps him."[3]

In contrast to Japan, the Dominican Republic offers little opportunity to "grow the business" of baseball. Few big Dominican corporate sponsors have affiliated themselves with Major League Baseball or individual teams. Despite real growth, television broadcasting deals, so lucrative in Japan, are comparatively small in the Dominican. Ironically, it is precisely because of the country's palsied economy that the game means so much more to Dominicans than it does to the Japanese or Americans. It is what they do better than anyone else, what they most rely upon and derive the most pride from. At the government level, Dominican stars like Vladimir Guerrero, Miguel Tejada, and Sammy Sosa are accorded the highest status, even made honorary ambassadors.[4] No less a personage than the president of the country flies to the United States to attend baseball "firsts" or the awarding of the game's highest honors if a Dominican is involved. When Tony Peña and Luis Pujols became the first two Dominicans to manage against each other in a major league game, President Hipolito Mejia flew to Kansas City to be present. When Miguel Tejada won the American League 2003 Most Valuable Player award and Vladimir Guerrero did the same in 2004, they were honored in ceremonies at the palace by the president personally. Drive around the capital, Santo Domingo, and you will see enormous government posters of these stars admonishing young people to work hard and study. "The government is strongly linked to the sport of baseball. What our baseball stars do to uphold and promote the country's image, if we had to pay for that, the price would be immeasurable," proclaims César Cedeño, the cabinet-level secretary of sports.[5] The government also subsidizes the building of stadiums, local fields, and the salaries of youth coaches.

The dominance of this country in the international baseball world is indisputable. The reasons for it are both immediately apparent and somewhat cloaked. Most think the key is rooted in the poverty of the country, and that is certainly largely correct. Other factors, however, also play an important role. One fundamental principle to grasp is not simply that poverty motivates, but *how* it motivates. It acts like a windblown fire, driving all wildlife ahead of it. In this instance, poverty drives the best talent in the direction of a baseball career as one of the few hopes for escape. Players are willing to endure just about anything for the possibility of not only getting to the United States but also, even if they ultimately fail, getting at least a hiatus from poverty. When a single sport has direct and relatively unlimited access to the best talent, any country is capable of producing success in the sport. So on one level Dominican dominance is a function of economic privation. Pittsburgh Pirates Special Assistant to the General Manager Louis Eljaua succinctly articulates this principle, making an even more fundamental point: "This [the Dominican Republic] is definitely the hotbed. Baseball is the only way out. They may play basketball, but baseball is known to get you out. There's poverty here, hunger here, and baseball is the ticket. Here you've got the best athletes in the country playing baseball. You can't say that in the U.S."[6] But if poverty, by itself, were the fount of this incredible success, we would expect to find comparable instances in other baseball-loving Latin American countries. On the contrary, to date—with the possible exception of Cuba—no country has matched this excellence. The reasons for Dominican baseball success must be sought in the relationship between history, economics, and culture.

The Early Game

Dominicans and Cubans were the first players from outside the United States to make the game their own. This is not to say that they were the first to play the game. Rather, Dominicans were the first to own it so completely. A unique blend of factors has helped the Dominicans to thrive on the diamond: exceptional talent proven at the highest level in great numbers, a lengthy tradition of elite competition, proximity to Cuba and to the United States, and a cultural preoccupation with the game that has only grown over the past century.

The country that most influenced the Dominican Republic early on was Cuba. The slave revolts of 1868 threatened the Cuban planter class to the point that some of them relocated their businesses next door to the Dominican Republic. In doing so, they brought with them their technology in sugar refining, their capital, their entrepreneurial drive—and baseball.[7]

Dominican baseball historians attribute the game's arrival on the island to two brothers, Ignacio and Ubaldo Aloma, who immigrated to Santo Domingo in 1880.[8] The formal inauguration of the game is claimed to have taken place eleven years later in 1891, when the brothers formed two clubs, el Cauto and Cervecería.[9] Presumably, the game was being played earlier, however.[10]

What marks the period as much as its amateurism is the speed with which Dominicans took to the sport. *Béisbol romantico* is a sobriquet given to this early period of baseball in the Dominican Republic, when the game was played out of passion, rather than for money.[11] Rob Ruck points out, however, that by the 1920s players were passing the hat at games and being compensated in one way or another for their efforts.[12] The era of semiprofessional baseball hit the Dominican Republic fairly quickly. Rather than look at baseball as "romantico," we are better served calling the decade of the 1920s a transition between early growth of the game and an era in which Dominican baseball took on a more professional appearance.

The teams that define current Dominican pro baseball were formed quite early. Licey, the most storied and oldest of these teams, was started in 1907 by a group of young men from the capital's "better families."[13] It is noteworthy that the game was taking root early in the capital and via the elite, a trajectory detailed by the historian William Beezley in his study of the diffusion of sport in Mexico.[14] Santiago, the home of the country's traditional elite, also fielded a team early on (1912), as did San Pedro de Macorís. By 1915 these three cities were tangled up in rivalries that last to the present. The final piece of the puzzle, Escogido, came into existence in 1921. Escogido was also in Santo Domingo, and the competition between it and Licey was fierce from the start.

The formation of Dominican teams coincided with an increased presence of the best clubs of Cuba, Puerto Rico, and Venezuela, as well as Americans affiliated with the military—first on casual visits, then as part of the U.S. Marines' occupation of the country from 1916 to 1924.[15] In the 1920s foreign teams, impressed by the play of Dominicans, began to hire them to play abroad. Dominican teams reciprocated by signing foreigners to play. The steadily growing sophistication of the Dominican game culminated in the 1937 season, a season that has never been equaled in the intensity of competition, caliber of talent, and outlay of money. San Pedro de Macorís had won the championship the previous year with a roster consisting mostly of Cubans. Facing a political test from restive elements, President Molina Trujillo, via his brother José, craved the luster of a baseball championship for Ciudad Trujillo, as Santo Domingo was then being called.[16] Trujillo and other owners decided to raid the Negro Leagues for the likes of pitcher Satchel Paige and slugging catcher Josh Gibson. José Trujillo preempted the other owners by traveling to Pittsburgh to sign Paige for more than $1,000 a month.

Stacked with the likes of Paige, Gibson, the speedy outfielder Cool Papa Bell, the Cubans Martin Dihigo and Ramón Bragana, and Dominican stars like Tetelo Vargas and Horacio Martínez, Ciudad Trujillo, San Pedro de Macorís, and Santiago put on an exhibition of baseball that ranks among the best series ever played anywhere. After Ciudad Trujillo won, crowds in the capital danced all night long, but in the aftermath, the game slid into an abyss. "All those players like Paige, [catcher Cy] Perkins—they received more money to play here than in the U.S. It was crazy, but at the same time we had what we felt were the best teams in the world," concludes Córdova. That source of pride in having the best, however, came at a real cost. "We wound up killing professional baseball here. Although we continued to play amateur ball, we spent many years without professional baseball after 1937."[17]

The Modern Era

That fatigue lasted until 1950, when a group of sportsmen in conjunction with the government helped to resuscitate professional play. The period from 1951 to 1954 served as a transition to modern Dominican baseball, which took shape in 1955.

While Jackie Robinson broke the major leagues' color line in 1947, most teams didn't integrate until the early 1950s. With race no longer an impediment, the door was open for players of color from outside of the United States as well, and some teams had already established relationships with Latin organizations or individuals. The New York Giants were one such club. Giants utilityman Ozzie Virgil, whose family had moved to New York while he was still young, is credited with being the first Dominican to play in the major leagues. Felipe Alou was the first Dominican to come directly from the island to play in the major leagues. Players coming from one culture to play in another faced immediate challenges.[18] Alou signed with the Giants for $200 and three years later played on the parent club, by now in San Francisco. Juan Marichal joined the Giants in 1960, the start of a sixteen-year career, almost all of it with the Giants, that made him the first—and so far only—Dominican Hall of Fame pitcher. The Giants quickly signed Felipe Alou's two brothers as well. Mateo was in the Giants lineup by 1960, Jesús by 1963.[19]

The Dominican game had already taken a more serious turn by 1955, when its relationship with Major League Baseball became formalized. First, Dominicans forged "working relationships" whereby U.S. teams lent their administrative expertise to Dominican organizations while the latter provided players and a fertile environment for player development. Second, the Dominicans shifted their play from summer to winter so as not to conflict with playing time in the States.

The idea of signing impact players out of Latin America was slow to develop, however. Initially, the authors Marcos Bretón and José Luis Villegas write,

> The purpose [signings] served was to fill out minor league ros-
> ters and thereby help train other, more talented players.
> Hamstrung by tighter budgets than more prosperous teams, the
> Athletics were looking for bargains. Ron Plaza, [Oakland] A's
> instructor, recalls why Dominicans in the A's system weren't
> making it: "When we first went in there, we had a bunch of kids
> we signed that we knew weren't going to be prospects. But when
> you fill up a ball club you have to sign a lot of players."[20]

As with so many shortsighted or socially retrograde practices, such as racially tracking players into certain positions and away from others, this system broke down only when the numbers of the disenfranchised grew to critical mass.[21] Talented superscouts Epy Guerrero of the Toronto Blue Jays and Ralph Avila of the Los Angeles Dodgers were largely responsible for getting a better caliber of player to their organizations during the 1970s. They independently developed the academy and systematized scouting on the island. By the late 1980s Latino players had regularly become impact players. Pedro Guerrero, George Bell, José Rijo, Joaquín Andujar, and Tony Fernández were typical of the kind of player signed out of the Dominican Republic. Today, Latino players are synonymous with excellence. Sosa, Martínez, Ramírez, Guerrero are household names across both the Dominican Republic and the United States.

The Academy

Academies were begun in the Dominican Republic to serve three basic and vital functions. First, they allowed major league teams to get closer to the source of talent. Teams could station scouts in the country and regularly spot and sign promising players. The academy also allowed teams to refine that talent. With a facility on the island, they could more effectively control the play and training of all their Dominican charges. Finally, the academy acted as a reservoir for foreign players until they could be brought to the United States. Assigning a player to a U.S. rookie league is dependent not only upon maturing skills; it also requires an H-2B visa, and these are parceled out on a limited basis. Each of these three functions is critical to the flow of Dominican talent that major league teams have come to depend upon. Recently legal restriction against entry to the United States has become a hot-button issue.

While all foreign players in the major and minor leagues require a visa, there are two basic types. Major league players get the P-1 visa, granted by the U.S. government to anyone considered "outstanding" in his or her profession. This is self-explanatory: a visa for those exceptionally skilled who add luster by performing or working in the United States. For minor leaguers, who have yet to prove that they are "outstanding"—though an argument could be made that, relative to the multitude playing the sport, even minor leaguers are outstanding—there is the H-2B visa. This visa is issued to a range of workers in industries that include agriculture, hotels, and service occupations. These are temporary workers, returning to their countries at the end of a season. The H-2B visa can be granted only after determination that the applicant's employment has no adverse impact on American laborers—that is, that the applicant is not taking a job from an American. Moreover, as the baseball writer Jesse Sanchez has pointed out, this category is finite; as of March 2004,

Congress allowed a maximum of sixty-six thousand such visas. The allotment to Major League Baseball had been around 1,400 visas; divided among the thirty teams, that gives each about forty-seven visas to use on foreign minor league players. If a player was injured or released, that slot was held for another player to be called up. Sanchez notes, "That's not the case anymore. In 2004, 1,236 H-2B visas were issued to Major League teams, and those 'slots' cannot be interchanged."[22] Congress, concerned about "homeland security," apparently views the H-2B visa as a quick and easy way for terrorists to enter the country; thus it has mandated that such visas be carefully limited and all applicants scrutinized.

By the beginning of the 2005 season this congressional ruling was having a deleterious effect on how teams apportion their H-2B visas. Foreign rookies playing in the Dominican Summer League, who typically went north for a part of spring training or minor league seasons, could no longer do so. The restriction is placing downward pressure upon the system, forcing players to stay longer in their respective countries or play in a country like Canada, which has no such restrictions. Finally, by mid-2005 President Bush—a former owner of the Texas Rangers—signed into law the Save Our Small and Seasonal Businesses Act, which added some thirty-five thousand visas to the national system and eased the bottleneck in the minor leagues.

Until recently there were two basic kinds of academies: full-service facilities and halfway houses. The complete academies, those equipped to deal with all of a rookie's needs, must have more than excellent playing fields. They must also have dormitories, a kitchen and cafeteria, laundry facilities, exercise facilities, administrative offices, and leisure areas for the staff and rookies. The pensión arrangement meant that a team leased a playing field and in a completely separate area, arranged for room and board to be provided. This type of academy was typical of the early presence of major league teams in the country. Not only was it costly, but the players' movements were harder to control, resulting in more problems.

The purpose of the academy is to develop the young prospect to his fullest. In the Dominican Republic this involves playing in the Dominican Summer League, an official rookie league. The academy also gives the organization the opportunity to physically regulate just about every dimension of the player's life. His diet is controlled, as are his rising and sleep times. His exercise regimen is carefully administered through a strength coach, and practices and games are all choreographed. Free time is also controlled. Oakland Athletics instructor Ron Plaza, interviewed by Marcos Bretón, was relieved when the A's finally committed to building their academy in the Dominican Republic in the mid-1990s: "Getting the complex was important because we never had control of these kids before. The only time we had them was on the field. Then they would go home and we'd have a lot of problems. We had a couple of kids walking around Santo Domingo one night and they ended up in jail. We couldn't control what they ate, how much they slept. But once we got them at the complex they were ours."[23]

The young Dominican who signs a pro contract and is sent to the academy is officially a rookie in the North American Professional Baseball system. There are real differences, however, between him and his mainland counterpart. When we hear various accounts of Dominican ballplayers, the first thing that seems to be mentioned is the impoverished background of these players. This background has a dramatic effect on how the academy must be run, because the directors are charged not only with talent development but with remedial social training as well. Ralph Avila, formerly the Los Angeles Dodgers' vice president of Latin American player development, weighs in: "Before [the academies] a lot of players were signed in this country, taken to the U.S. and released—nine, ten, maybe more in a day—because the kids weren't ready. That wasn't fair."[24] Avila emphasizes the adjustments demanded of such players: "On average, the Latin players are signed at a critical age when they are evolving from adolescence to manhood. These adjustments have to be made without the help of their parents, in a strange country, where they are not familiar with the environment, and where the language, food, and customs are different. . . . Most come from poor families . . . and have never seen the average American city."[25] Still, despite the odds, Avila says, "We had only five or six problems in all the thousands we've looked at."[26]

That success ratio reflects the discipline that Avila insists upon. Similarly, the Kansas City Royals' academy is based on a system that emphasizes building self-esteem via pride and professionalism: "Because so many of these guys have had no education, we know it's tough for them to learn English," observes Luis Silverio, who used to run the team's academy. "The Royals have these kids in all kinds of classes: psychology, reading, writing in Spanish. Classes in English come later. They don't even know their own language! We teach them about culture, such as eating, personal hygiene. I lecture these kids all of the time about rules are rules in the U.S."[27]

Signing talent is a fairly straightforward decision built around advance notice from scouts or buscones who fan out through the country in search of promising recruits. The tryout is a relatively short showcase in which the young hopeful is asked to run, hit, and field, or to throw if he's a pitcher. Signings are often the product of one of these tryouts, although for larger bonuses the prospect is examined under game conditions. Louie Eljaua notes that "a Dominican prospect has played a lot fewer games than an American kid."[28] To compensate for this shortcoming, academies must provide structure, discipline, and playing experience.

Teaching baseball is often the easiest of the tasks facing the instructors at these academies. Other skills players learn reflect the organization's particular emphasis. Small-market teams like the Royals, who often sign a prospect based on a disproportionate degree of potential rather than demonstrated skill, must devote more energy to remedial training. Silverio spends much of his time working his rookies on baseball fundamentals: developing arm speed, building up bodies, learning game skills. These are issues that affect all teams but are critical for small-market teams. Big-market teams like the Red Sox, who sign rookies with more developed tools and bodies, can assume a degree of baseball competence and demonstrated skills—"tools," in baseball parlance—that small-market teams can't take for granted.

One way for these initiates to handle the adjustment to life at the academy is to bond together. The well-run academy seeks to foster that kind of mutual dependency even as these rookies compete for limited opportunities. There are countercurrents at work also. Because so many of the rookies come from difficult backgrounds, tensions inevitably arise. Teams deal with such conflicts by leveling differences as much as possible. The rookie with a swelled head becomes the peg that sticks up from the others and must be hammered back down. At Campo Las Palmas, one Dodgers rookie talked about the chastening process: "The new [arrivals] are taught by those who have been here. If they have an attitude—well, that's a different story. We turn our backs on them, the hot dogs. We have a new guy, D___, and he is that way. Last week we played and the umps called him out twice sliding into second. Afterward, the ump explained that he thought it was close, but that the guy was a jerk, so he called him out. We all agreed and laughed. He needs it."[29] Of course, if the group has no effect, the organization will step in with coaches and instructors. Tejada dominated the Dominican Summer League during his stint in the Athletics' academy, hitting a league-leading eighteen home runs. His over-the-top strutting was too much for the team to bear, however, and the coaches began to level him, often singling him out for ridicule.[30]

The Dodgers' Avila used his authoritarian style to inculcate his players with a sense of professionalism and self-discipline that they had never possessed. Sometimes a psychologist trained in cross-cultural issues is added to a staff to get through to young players. Bretón and Villegas recount the Athletics' hiring of a Dominican psychologist to work with the cultural and socioeconomic difficulties common to many of their young players.[31] Teams often find it necessary to take on remedial work, sociopsychological evaluation, and intervention.

Middle Passage: Maneuvering Through the Minor Leagues

A successful academy program prepares rookies for the U.S. minor leagues, but it also teaches them to culturally wend their way through small-town America. Too many Latin American rookies fail to grasp that they are going not to New York or Los Angeles or Chicago, but rather Great Falls, Montana, or Wilmington, Delaware. These are places that know little of Dominican life, where the potential for culture shock is all but certain. Marcos Bretón and José Luis Villegas have compiled a poignant portrait of the cultural dislocation that awaits Dominican players first entering the United States. Clearly, signing a professional contract and receiving a large sum as a bonus—large by Dominican standards, and sometimes even by the megabucks standards of the major league market—goes a long way toward eradicating the economic hardships that young Dominicans may have faced. Compared to the harshness of life to that point, coming to the United States might be thought to pose little difficulty, but poverty is not life's only obstacle. In one particularly telling instance, Bretón and Villegas describe the transformation of a group of Dominican prospects heading to the United States for a season in minor league baseball. Whereas the day before, secure in their barrios, they had been effusive and buoyant, they grew somber as they approached U.S. customs at the airport. There, they were upbraided, in English, by an airlines employee for not having filled out the proper paperwork. Suddenly the cultural chasm they faced hit them head on. "From Miami to Dallas, Dallas to Phoenix, the players began to droop, to grow increasingly silent. Their razor-sharp wits were abandoning them here. Suddenly they were introverted, shy, and tentative."[32]

Playing in the United States poses triangulated challenges in handling culture, language, and food. Players sometimes realize that they have taken the off-field training they received in the academies too lightly, as something one is required to do after the important—baseball—part of the day. It is a rare player, like Pedro Martínez, who takes the opportunity to learn English and study American culture seriously before entering the United States. Just about every Latin player can recount the difficulty he encountered in doing even the simplest things, such as eating. The Dodgers minor leaguers I spoke with remember this in hindsight with pained smiles, as if remembering an old wound. One recalls eating nothing but fried chicken and French fries for months because he felt too embarrassed to try ordering anything else.

In fact, food offers an excellent forum for considering the differences between the United States and the Dominican Republic. As Americans, we spend more time eating food (and eat more of it) than people almost anyplace else on earth, but despite the time and energy we devote to it, food has no significant symbolic power for most of us. People who have had to struggle to get food view it differently. Mario Soto, a pitcher for the Cincinnati Reds from 1977 to 1988, commented, "Americans grow up eating cheeseburgers, but it's not that way for us. So, once you start eating that good food, you don't want to lose that good food. That's not an exaggeration. It's reality."[33] While many disparage the nutritional value of a cheeseburger, from the Third World perspective it constitutes prestige food: it symbolizes America, and it is priced out of most people's range.

Not coincidentally, the language of competition for positions and opportunities reflects the centrality of nourishment; when one player beats out another for a position, he is "quitando les la comida"—taking away food—from the other. Eating signifies success. It is never taken for granted; wasting food or treating it with disdain is considered an abomination, and those who do so are loathsome. The Dominican pitching star Juan Marichal recounted a memorable instance from his playing days on the San Francisco Giants of the 1960s, when his fellow Dominican Felipe Alou was a teammate and Alvin Dark, a bigot of classic proportions, was their manager:

> I have always thought that food is a great thing in life. With the Giants, Alvin Dark would sometimes come into the clubhouse after a loss and kick the spread of food set out for the players onto the floor. It was as if he couldn't stand the sight of us eating after we had been defeated. I remember Felipe Alou bending over after Dark did this one night, picking up some of the food off of the floor, and eating it while looking Dark right in the eye. . . . [Dark] couldn't understand that for us, even if you lose, you don't kick food on the floor. You just don't do that.[34]

In this instance, food symbolizes defiance, and becomes part of the many differences between First and Third World people.

Cultural difficulties for young Dominicans just entering minor league ball in this country go beyond their unfamiliarity with the language and cultural culinary differences. A background in poverty puts a young player behaviorally at risk. Some Dominican rookies are considered to be *tigres*, rough street urchins. For them, discipline, professionalism, and responsibility are foreign notions. On the Dodgers rookie league team, one young Dominican illustrated this temperament when he grabbed a bat to defend his turf after the manager, learning of a theft, demanded to inspect all of the lockers. The player was not guilty, but he viewed the episode as a direct threat, and the street response was the only one available to him. The staff eventually decoded the cultural problem, but the episode illustrates the lack of awareness in some organizations with the socioeconomic backgrounds of their Dominican players, a blind spot that could jeopardize the teams' investments and the young players' futures.[35]

The Dominican academies have changed quite a bit in the past decade. Prospects can occasionally be found and signed for the old rate of five thousand U.S. dollars, but most bonuses are at least five or ten times that sum. Unacceptable facilities have been replaced by state-of-the-art academies. The academy system is going through an evolutionary process: vague and ill-defined institutions are becoming uniformly regulated. In the process, Dominican rookies are benefiting. Major League Baseball is actively seeking to ensure that players' experiences are comparable to those of minor leaguers on the mainland, and that they can expect similar policy as their U.S. counterparts. Since 1990, significant shifts in these policies have been as much the product of MLB's efforts as of structural changes in Dominican baseball.

Buscones: Noxious Presence or Dominican Saviors?

By the time that Albert Pujols won the 2005 National League Most Valuable Player award, Dominicans were no strangers to baseball's top honors. There have been other MVPs (American Leaguers George Bell in 1987, Miguel Tejada in 2002, Alex Rodríguez in 2003 and 2005, and Vladimir Guerrero in 2004, and National Leaguer Sammy Sosa in 1998); batting champions (Matty Alou in 1966, Rico Carty in 1970, and Pujols in 2002, all in the NL, and Julio Franco in 1991 and Manny Ramírez in 2002 in the AL); Cy Young winners (Pedro Martínez in 1997 in the NL and 1999 and 2000 in the AL, and Bartolo Colón in 2005 in the AL); and Rookies of the Year (Alfredo Griffin in 1979, Carlos Beltran in 1999, and Angel Berroa in 2003 in the AL, Raúl Mondesi in 1994, C Rafael Furcal in 2000, and Pujols in 2001 in the NL). By 2003 more than a quarter of all minor leaguers, some 1,500, were Dominican. How have these numbers grown so?

The most important development in Dominican baseball over the past decade has been the *buscón,* a word derived from the Spanish verb *buscar,* to find. The buscón (pronounced boo-SCONE)—also known by the English term "bird dog"—locates talent for major league teams. Buscones are either directly or indirectly responsible for all of the changes that have taken place in the world of Dominican baseball, from the role of Major League Baseball as a regulatory agency on the island to the efforts of Dominicans to wrest some degree of political and economic control of their game.

The bird dog is not a Dominican creation, however. Bird dogs were significant in American baseball until the introduction of the draft. Dominican buscones, however, are more than talent trackers. Jim Salisbury of the *Philadelphia Inquirer*, one of the first to write about the buscón, defined the calling as a baseball cocktail: "Throw a scout, a coach and an entrepreneur into a blender, then mix, and you have a *buscone*."[36] Buscones find and hone the talent, running mini-academies in the process. When a player is ready, the buscón makes the connections with major league teams, and takes a commission, often a large one.

The buscón's role in player development has been controversial, to say the least. Many in baseball consider buscones to be reprehensible. One director of international scouting for a major league club, who wished to remain anonymous, admonished me, "Trust me. Some of these guys you wouldn't want over for dinner. It's a whole other element. I don't let them in the dugout." Another echoed these sentiments, again anonymously: "These are not people we want to deal with. There's some real sleaze there, but they are a fact of life down there." Stories of buscones stealing money and getting kickbacks are common. Sullying the 2004 season early on was the claim (still unproven in 2006) that Arizona Diamondbacks Director of Latin American Development Junior Noboa had been involved with the signing of a highly touted prospect by his organization through his brother, a buscón who had developed the young prospect. It appears that the Dodgers had actually outbid the Diamondbacks, but Noboa's brother allegedly suppressed that information so that the Diamondbacks might sign him. Although the case has not gone beyond an initial investigation, it is instructive because it illustrates both the unstructured way business is handled in the Dominican Republic and the view of buscones as corrupt held by many affiliated with MLB.

Many Dominicans, however, feel that buscones have been beneficial to the game. Jesús Alou, one of the trio of legendary brothers who played outfield for the San Francisco Giants, argues in their favor. As director of the Boston Red Sox academy outside of Santo Domingo, Alou sees buscones as "a very important part of what's going on in baseball in this country."[37] Because buscones are so central to Dominican baseball, and because views of them vary so radically, they merit close examination.

Buscón Beginnings

Sometime in the mid-1990s, buscones emerged in real numbers; most were former scouts. Previously there may have been individuals here and there entrepreneurial enough to try to gain a commission for bringing in a prospect, but until the 1990s such efforts were haphazard. Louie Eljaua, a special assistant to Pittsburgh Pirates general manager Dave Littlefield, contends that buscones are an outgrowth of the rush into the country of major league clubs: "In the 1990s more Dominicans started getting into the majors. They were helping win championships, and you could find them for a fraction of the cost of the U.S. Then the competition started getting more cutthroat, and so, some scouts or agents would say, 'Okay, they gave you $250, we'll give $500.' And that's how it started escalating."[38]

Luis Silverio sees this from the small-market perspective: "I think they emerged when those organizations that had big money started coming here and giving buscones and players a lot more money in signing. It sure made it tougher on small-market clubs. [Since 2000] everything is bird dogs [buscones]. Before you could tell a player, 'Hey, we're not going to deal with a buscón.' And they might say, 'Okay, deal with me,' and they would deal with the buscón on their own. Not any more."[39]

What these accounts overlook, however, is most important: a causal link between the rise of the academy and the emergence of the buscón. In examining the role of academies in the Dominican Republic in the late 1980s and early 1990s, I predicted that academies would eventually harm indigenous baseball, and in particular the amateur leagues that formed the wellspring of the sport: "The physical and organizational presence of baseball academies run by major league franchises in the Dominican Republic has fundamentally undermined the long-standing sovereignty of Dominican baseball. . . . Most important, the academies contribute to the cannibalization of the Dominican amateur leagues. By signing players at the age of seventeen and courting them even earlier, the academies are weakening the upper echelons of amateur baseball."[40]

The Ways of the Buscones

Juan Forero was among the first to chronicle the buscón as run-ning a program when, in 1998, he described Andrés James, who left scouting for the Giants to become a buscón in San Pedro de Macorís: "He cleared away the beans and asparagus and other crops he grew in front of his house. . . . The small plot that once produced food for his family is now covered in red dirt. James is now in the business of pro-ducing players, with the hope that someone he molds will wind up on a major league roster."[41]

The Royals' Silverio describes larger enterprises, which "look like little academies. They have fifty, seventy, a hundred kids working out. Boys between twelve and twenty-two, even released players. The kids will pay maybe twenty pesos a month for that bird dog to work him out. They approach the kid and move him to their program, and they feed him and house him just like we do over here. And then they say to the kid, 'I got a chance to take you somewhere.' He evaluates the kids and sets a date for a tryout."[42]

The *Washington Post* writer Steve Fainaru interprets buscones differently, characterizing them negatively as "street-level entrepreneurs," essentially hustlers (which some indeed are).[43] For Fainaru, this system of fashioning players is a chaotic marketplace where the only thing on anyone's mind is self-maximization. This view certainly made sense given his choice to study Enrique Soto, a buscón involved in illegal activities, but his blanket char-acterization of all buscones is not warranted. First of all, these men are as likely to be engineers or university professors as they are streetwise opera-tors. They are also as likely to have a well-regarded baseball pedigree as to be making a fleeting foray into the game's outermost banks.

With his shaved head and beady eyes, Samuel Herrera may look like a grown-up version of the tigres, or street urchins, that he so often recruits, but he came to the ranks of the buscones after deciding that teaching col-lege calculus was not getting him anywhere financially. He quit teach-ing to become a buscón. It's a nerve-racking business, because he is one of almost two thousand buscones scouring the country, in search of fourteen- to eighteen-year-old players with talent. His small-scale op-eration is the norm. To effectively compete he must rely on others to actually spot talent and to cue him, for a price: in this country even the buscones have buscones. At age thirty-nine, and after five years in which he has invested all of his money and his time in the business, he has a viable operation. Herrera likens it to playing the lottery, and so far he has won seven times. That's how many of his discoveries have signed. His greatest success thus far has been a 6-foot-4-inch right-handed pitcher, Mateo Aneudis, who signed with the Boston Red Sox for $400,000. Herrera's commission was $100,000, or 25 percent. The other contracts ranged from $25,000 to $100,000.

Herrera knows what I'm thinking about his commission, and so, as we're driving in his car, he reaches into the back seat and grabs a handful of nutritional supplement packets, tossing them on my lap "Do you know what these cost me?" he asks, his voice rising. "I get these from Miami. They cost five dollars each, and my boys get them every day!"

"Okay," I return. "But 25 percent? Really!"

"You came to my pensión! You saw that they had beds, a TV, a refrigerator full of food. I hire a woman to cook for them: two meals a day. Look, I know that Major League Baseball is against the buscón, but they don't know anything about what we have to do to find these boys and develop them! I have others find them, and then I talk to their parents and make them promise to stay away from drugs. 'No rum, only hard work,' I tell them. My program costs me a thousand dollars a month, and only some of these boys will get signed."

"Samuel, I believe you have costs, but," I added, "eventually there will be rules that will limit this commission of yours."

"I realize that." Herrera conceded. "That's why I have my other business." He grabbed a manila envelope off of the floor next to my feet and proceeded to show me a report from the Dominican Office of MLB on the Cleveland Indians' facility in Boca Chica, east of Santo Domingo. The report rated the facility, rather like a health department evaluation of a restaurant.

"Beds, fifteen, excellent. Mattresses, fifteen, excellent. Sheets, fifteen, excellent." He pointed to each rating and showed me the rating system.

"You have a supply company?" I deduced. "You supply them with this stuff?"

"Yes. Because being a buscón is like winning the lottery. You never know when you're going to hit."[44]

This is the way the "informal economy" operates in the Third World. Herrera is nothing if not enterprising, cobbling together a living within, as well as alongside, baseball. If he can't interest a club in the talent he's honing, well then, maybe he can provide them with sheets. Men like Herrera operate too closely to the edge to be able to specialize. If such buscones cross the bounds of legal dealings, their transgressions must be understood as products of necessity rather than willful violation of rules. The pressure is so intense to figure out one's next move in the event of failure, and the payoff so capricious, that bending rules seems a sound strategy worth the risk of apprehension. "In this country if you have money everyone is your friend, if not, bye bye," Herrera says, laughing.

If Samuel Herrera is bereft of baseball credentials, other buscones have the highest pedigrees. Former Cincinnati Reds pitcher José Rijo and other ex–major leaguers like Luis Polonia and Ramón Martínez have entered the ranks of the buscones by opening "academies." Nelson Liriano counts at least a dozen fellow former major leaguers who now work as buscones. He smiled when he hinted that he wouldn't mind becoming one himself.

I visited one of these high-end buscón operations, the newly minted academy owned and operated by Ramón Martínez. Martínez pitched fourteen seasons in the major leagues, winning 135 games and, in 1995, while with the Dodgers, throwing a no-hitter. He was born in Manoguayabo, just outside Santo Domingo, and still has a home there. The field that he uses is one built and maintained by the former Blue Jays pitcher Juan Guzmán, who also supports the Liga deportiva Juan Guzmán.

The vast majority of buscón-run programs, like Samuel Herrera's, are shoestring affairs, but Martínez's operation resembles a MLB-sanctioned baseball academy. When I visited, upward of fifty young men were going through drills in various parts of the complex. Some were being timed for running speed. Others had ground balls being hit to them. All had uniforms emblazoned on the front with "Ramón Martínez Baseball Academy" in English script. The academy has a dorm that houses eighteen; the rest of the players take cabs (paid for by the academy) from other parts of Santo Domingo.

The day I visited was not simply a workout day: scouts from the Anaheim Angels had arrived to look at the boys. The scouts pulled out their radar guns and were handed rosters of two teams while plastic lawn chairs were set up for them in the shade. The scouts were shown the routine skills exhibited in tryouts—fielding, running, throwing—but in this instance the workout was capped with a game between red and blue. Between innings one of the coaches came over to share a recorded list of the speed of the pitcher's previous inning. Today's candidates, all between the ages of sixteen and eighteen, throw between 86 and 92 miles per hour.

Nelson Gerónimo is the head coach. I commented on how well run his academy is. "Hey man. Thanks," replied Gerónimo. "We've only been open three months. And in those three months we've had four players sign. A few more will probably go this month."[45] So buscones cover a spectrum from ex–major leaguers to those with no relationship to the sport.

Balancing Buscones

Many major league academies have come to accept buscones as unavoidable, and have developed ties with them; MLB is even talking of regulating them. However one feels about them, buscones are an integral part of the Dominican baseball scene, and they perform unique functions. Luis Silverio and his Royals scouting staff regularly move through the island, but they heavily rely upon buscones they know. "This might sound nuts," Silverio says, "but they go where some of our scouts don't go. There are some dangerous areas here. There's places where you cannot throw a tryout: the facilities are not good, or it's dangerous, or maybe our cars can't get there. These buscones cover all these areas."[46]

Some observers wonder whether the scouts of today are doing their job effectively, certainly by comparison with their counterparts of the pre-buscón era. Silverio feels that scouts are as thorough as ever, but that the structural relations have changed: "Everywhere [scouts] go, every player they contact already has someone [a buscón], because everybody has programs. Ex–professional players that didn't make it, now they got programs. The guy on the street who has the energy, he'll have a program. So everywhere our scouts show up, there's already something there. So whenever they bring a kid in here, he has to have a buscón."[47]

In the final analysis, however, do buscones harm or help baseball in the country? There is no question that some—most insiders claim that they are a distinct minority—are criminally operating by taking signing bonuses from their charges far in excess of what they deserve. While working for the Florida Marlins, Louie Eljaua had occasion to deal with travesties committed by buscones: "There are a small number of people down there who are stealing money or taking it away from players. We had a kid with the Marlins who ended up leading the Dominican Summer League this year in hitting. We signed him last year and he played for the Marlins this year, but he came to us after he got his bonus [he signed for $70,000]. He had only $15,000, because he gave two buscones money, and then had to pay taxes! And this kid has a chance to be the next Adrián Beltre!"[48]

The issue of what constitutes "just" compensation for a buscón is a thorny one that is only now being taken up by the MLB Commissioner's Office in the Dominican Republic, but the buscón's take can, in some instances, be extravagant, bordering on criminal. According to Silverio, "I know academies here where it's 50–50, 50 percent to the player, 50 percent to the buscón."[49]

Still, many Dominican baseball people make the case that buscones help to develop local baseball. The Royals' Silverio details just how critical they are to baseball:

> These guys have a lot of programs. I was just in La Romana two weeks ago. Nine-thirty in the morning, Tuesday, and there were seventy players working out. But that buscón showed me three. So everybody sits until we finish our tryout. I would say that there's hundreds of these guys. Every remote rural area you might have one guy with a program. I think they have definitely become an important part of getting talent. They've hurt us [the Royals] because we've got to pay more for players, and pay the buscones, but they definitely find the players.[50]

Jesús Alou voices similar thoughts: "I think they are benefiting baseball, even if some of them are crooked. And it's not as bad as people have said. They are getting kids interested in playing. There are so many baseball programs going on in the Dominican Republic that are run by buscones. They might not know how to teach the kids the proper way to play baseball, but they've got them in a camp. They've got them interested in baseball, and that keeps them away from bad things."[51]

Baseball and the Informal Economy

There is a Dominican saying: "If the U.S. sneezes, the Dominican Republic goes to the ICU," a folksy way of pointing out the degree of Dominican dependency upon the United States. It also reflects the vulnerability of the Dominican Republic, not only to large-scale set-backs but to the simple trials of daily life. Pick almost any Dominican player and you will hear the same story of hard-pressed families, and the hope that baseball earnings will help them out of poverty. "I play because it's a career," declared one determined thirteen-year-old, who works at it every day rather than going to school.[52] The choice to gamble on a career in baseball rather than prepare for one in school seems tragic and ill conceived from the U.S. perspective, which preaches to inner-city youth that education is a vastly more reliable economic base than sports. John Hoberman compiled a score of comments and analyses by African-American public figures and scholars who have decried the overinvestment in sport among African Americans.[53] These critiques are based upon warranted assumptions: that there is a correlation between education and upward mobility (via career and earnings); and that a career in sports is likely to end in failure. But this calculus doesn't apply to the Dominican Republic. When baseball's critics shriek that these young men should be "learning trades or professions," they do so from a rarified distance. The correlation between education and employment is negligible in this country, so the preoccupation Dominican youth have with baseball is a rational response to an irrational problem.[54] Naturally, well-meaning interpreters (and readers) would like to see these young people getting educated, but until we can generate an economy that can utilize that education, baseball is more practical.

In a country where only 29 percent of elementary school students go on to high school, it is not baseball that is responsible for this depressing underachievement. As a presidential campaign slogan once put it, "It's the economy, stupid!" The many young players who dream of playing baseball, approach buscones, and try out at academies all know someone who has signed, and "made it." They don't know anyone with a law degree, or any accountants. These are children who often have to forage for a living in this poor country. The legendary Dominican scout Epy

Guerrero reiterates this point in linking poverty, education, and baseball: "The kids here are never going to have the education they need to be a professor, or doctor, or anything else. They know their only chance is baseball."[55] As long as the Dominican Republic remains in poverty, the informal economy will prevail that makes Dominicans look like ne'er-do-wells, quasi-criminals, and violators of norms and laws. The behavior that gives Dominicans access to resources often fails to meet our mainland standards of behavior, but it is what Dominicans have. If a false birth certificate allows someone to get that first contract, so be it.

The Dominican Republic has been able to produce so many players not only because of the vast numbers of talented young men playing there but also because signing these players has been so cost effective for major league teams. As in other underdeveloped countries, a chronic situation has arisen in which advanced nations do business with their poorer neighbors primarily because those neighbors offer cheap resources. Baseball is no different. Signing Dominicans is important for major league teams because, on the whole, they are able to get players with tremendous possibilities more cheaply than they can in the United States. "You have a chance to get maximum return on the dollar. Overall, we're spending less on bonuses in the Dominican than you would in other places," says Philadelphia Phillies Scouting Director Mike Arbuckle.[56] But how much more cheaply? Seizing upon older data, some conclude that Major League Baseball (and, by extension, U.S. business interests), is continuing the colonial exploitative forms that have marked "business as usual" in the Third World. The focus has been on the relatively low bonuses paid to Dominicans and Venezuelans, but that too is changing.

The average signing bonus in the Dominican Republic is now around $25,000 and climbing quickly. Red Sox head of player personnel Ben Cherington observed, "Many of these players are getting a lot more than $25,000 signing bonuses. They're getting $50,000, $80,000, and $100,000 fairly often now."[57] These higher figures, he went on to note, are in the range of what teams pay fourth-through tenth-round draft selections in the United States. While critics claim that Latinos are still signed on the cheap, the days of the $4,000 signings are over.

In his capacity of developing the young player, linking him to the team that may eventually sign him, and claiming a portion of the bonus, the buscón is involved in all of the key moments of the player's nascent career. With so much influence, the unscrupulous buscón can easily take advantage of the player and even endanger him. Instances of buscón excess are well known. Fainaru has written of one of the most egregious of these cases, in which the buscón Enrique Soto appropriated most of the $1.6 million dollar bonus given his young charge Willy Aybar.[58] Unfortunately, Soto exemplifies for many what all buscones are. Fainaru's depiction has done much to cloud a more balanced view of the buscones.

The proliferation of fraudulent birth certificates and false identities has also been laid at the door of the buscón. The Commissioner's Office has set up an office in Santo Domingo to try to halt such abuses. Age falsification is driven by the higher value placed on younger prospects. While continuing to be a problem, false documentation needs to be understood as a mechanism used to gain access to rare opportunities for upward mobility. It's part of the "informal economy," a system of strategies devised by Third World people to make the most of their opportunities.[59] Family members and the players themselves are as committed to these strategies as are their buscones.

Major League Baseball's Efforts at Regulating the Dominican Republic

The problems facing the Commissioner's Office in Major League Baseball are not limited to regulating buscones. Compared with the way baseball affairs are conducted in the United States, and even in Asia, the Dominican scene is unstructured, wide open. One agent familiar with the Dominican Republic characterized the situation as "kind of the wild, wild West of baseball right now. It's shocking, but it's not unusual to see a 16-year-old kid already on his third agent."[60] Prospective players may be fast and loose with agents, but so are agents and scouts in their handling of players. The rush to sign Dominicans has all parties caught up in a feeding frenzy. It is precisely into this baseball anomie that MLB's Commissioner's Office has stepped, taking direct responsibility for bringing order to the Dominican baseball scene. The office opened in fall of 2000, headed by Rafael Pérez.

The characterization of Dominican baseball as chaotic is hyperbolic. "Unregulated" is more accurate. With no oversight, clubs—or more accurately, scouts representing them—were free to do what they wanted. Most played by the rules, though some flagrantly violated them. In the early days it was easy for scouts and their organizations to take advantage of the impoverished, naïve young players and their families. These stories have been duly noted, and while they are the minority, their newsworthiness threatens to overwhelm the majority. Stories have made the rounds of young signees not being paid, or being paid in Dominican currency rather than in U.S. dollars. Academies were also unregulated, and their quality and usefulness to the prospect varied widely. Signing irregularities were common, and documentation provided by players of their ages was often more fiction than fact.

Rafael Pérez moves constantly from room to room, on the phone in his capacity as director of MLB's Dominican office. Issues with the Venezuelan government, the U.S. embassy, the Dominican commissioner of baseball, any of the fifty or so academies run in two countries, as well as daily conversations with the commissioner's counsel Lou Meléndez at the home office punctuate interviews and conversations. Pérez, who has since become the New York Mets' director of Latin American operations, is one of the new breed of "transnationals," cross-cultural multitaskers, able to simultaneously think, speak, and function in multiple national settings. Pérez is part of the first cohort of young Dominican players identified as future leaders. These young men have been trained by Don Odermann and his Latin Athlete Education Foundation. Born in Santo Domingo, Pérez played baseball at the University of Southern Alabama, then was signed by the Pittsburgh Pirates. He played in the minors for two years before resuming his studies at Southern Alabama, where he earned a business degree. He found his way back into baseball in 1999.

Major League Baseball formally established its presence in a residential section of Santo Domingo. In this tastefully converted white stucco house with an unobtrusive sign with a wooden MLB logo, Pérez and his staff attend to essentially all of Latin America, focusing upon his country. He divides his job into three areas: support for major league teams; overseeing the image of MLB; and regulating major league operations in the country. At first, these tasks brought him into conflict with Dominican authorities who also seek to oversee Dominican baseball. "The government, in 1994, formed an Office of the Commissioner of Professional Baseball," Pérez remembered. "That was a position that had been relegated to a corner, but with Miguel Calsada taking over [as a political appointment], he tried to become more involved. We had some friction at first. When we signed on, one of the first things we did was sign an agreement with the Junto Central Electoral for a new verification process for birth certificates. [Calsada] didn't like that he wasn't invited to take part in that."[61]

The jaundiced view that Dominicans had regarding MLB's Dominican office was also shared by major league clubs that had interests in the country. For them, having MLB in the Dominican Republic meant that they had an agency scrutinizing them; for some this signaled the end of the way they had learned to conduct their affairs in the country. According to Pérez, "I think at first I was not very well received because we basically said to them, 'Look, you've been doing this for so many years, but now you can't because you're either breaking the rules in a big way, or a little bit outside of acceptable procedure.' Little by little they saw the job I was doing, and after the first year they all saw that it was for the good of the industry as a whole. The issues that confronted us at the beginning were huge."[62]

The conduct of buscones is a topic of concern to both Dominican authorities and MLB. The issues being confronted include determination of appropriate compensation for a buscón who has developed a player, clarification and regulation of finder's fees, and protection of players' bonuses from theft. Calsada's first initiative was the formation of an organization of buscones and scouts. This effort has had limited success, as the government has found no effective way to harness them all. Having been held hostage to this system, Louie Eljaua has successfully pushed for a strategy that eliminates side checks from teams to buscones. "I see a player and put a dollar amount on him," Eljaua says. "Say a kid is trying out. Say he's worth $100,000 to me. I go to the buscón, he may ask me for $150,000: $100,000 to the player, $50,000 to him. I say I can't give you $50,000, but I'll give you $100,000 and you can work it out with the player."[63]

These alternative strategies sound reasonable but pose a myriad of obstacles. For instance, it would be in keeping with American standards of business practice to expect buscones to calculate their expenses and take a profit of 5 percent, but monitoring these expenses would pose a bookkeeping burden beyond anything MLB's offices could handle. Far from ending abuses, such a plan would doubtless usher in a new level of fraud.

Verifying Documents

As we have seen, Kansas City Royals General Manager Allard Baird, as well as other baseball executives, especially on small-market teams, pursues a strategy of "signing young." Small-market teams are more inclined to take a chance signing an eligible young player with limited tools but potential than to get into a high-stakes bidding war. Well-heeled teams also prefer to "sign young," but big-market teams can go after players with better skills. This preference for youth is interpreted creatively in some sectors of the Dominican Republic. According to Jeff Shugel, a special assistant to the general manager for the Dodgers, "Ninety-two to 93 percent of all false documents are being pushed by buscones for one simple reason: a guy sixteen is worth a lot more money than a guy nineteen."[64] Responding to the market for youth, unscrupulous buscones and some young players regularly alter the players' documents to show them to be younger than they are.

In the spring of 2002 the Los Angeles Dodgers signed a highly touted Dominican prospect. The team thought enough of Jonathan Corporán, a seventeen-year-old right-handed pitcher who threw in the low 90s, to sign him for $930,000. The Dodgers scouting staff loved his mechanics, and his build (6-foot-2, 200 pounds), and needed only to confirm his age to complete the deal. "In light of what's happened this off-season, the basic protocol for this was different from others," noted Shugel. The Dodgers spent months sifting through the documents. Their point person in such matters is a little-known dynamo named Luchy Guerra, senior manager of Latin American operations. Luchy went the extra mile—even hiring a private investigator—in an effort to verify Corporán's age. Eventually discrepancies emerged, and the U.S. embassy collected enough evidence to determine that fraud had been committed.

Seventeen-year-old Jonathan Corporán became twenty-one-year-old Reyes Soto. He still threw in the low to mid-90s, however, and that convinced the Dodgers that he was worth signing. Not for $930,000, though. Reyes Soto signed for the reduced if still tidy sum of $150,000. Shugel remarked, "It was quite an ordeal, but I'm glad we have closure. He's the same guy we thought was Jonathan Corporán. He just wasn't Jonathan Corporán."[65] Quipped General Manager Dan Evans, "He just truly is the player to be named later."[66] Corporán was one of 325 such cases discovered in the first year following the attacks of 9/11. The U.S. government began very carefully scrutinizing documents of those seeking to entrance the United States following the tragedy of the World Trade Center. In baseball, within the first few months of the overhauled verification process, that resulted in the sudden aging of fifty to one hundred players. Rafael Pérez has discovered quite a few cases:

> Before 1998 what you found was that a player who wanted to lower his age would go to a friend who worked in a government office [in the Dominican Republic] and say, "Hey, just don't put that I was born in ___." When they implemented the first verification program in 1998, suddenly there was an increase in "late declarations." They don't record the birth right away. They go to another city and come up with false supporting documents to be able to get a late declaration, two or three years later. So when you go to the books, everything seems to be in order. With 9/11 [the State Department] also clamped down and together we found that 90 percent of late declarations were false. They're using brothers' I.D.s. They're using their friend's birth certificate. We have cases of buscones going to New York graveyards looking for kids who have died around the age they're looking for, and they get the birth certificate.[67]

Pérez also knows that falsifying these documents has more severe legal consequences than those attempting to make alterations ever think of: "If you show up at the visa office and you say you are someone who you really are not, you will be ineligible for life." Most young, poor, and uneducated players do not yet understand this and continue to try such ploys. "Because of cultural issues, and being uneducated, most of the kids and their families trust buscones blindly, so unfortunately they become accomplices in this without realizing it."[68]

Curbing the widespread practice of falsifying birth certificates treats only the surface of the problem. The competition for talent fuels the frenzy. Another factor that encourages falsification is the notion, widely held by both Dominicans and Americans, that Dominican players take longer to mature." Latin players, particularly Dominican players, mature physically and mentally later than their American counterparts," Pérez asserts. "You cannot compare an eighteen-year-old American to an eighteen-year-old Dominican, but our industry is trying to."[69] By 2005 MLB had taken giant steps in curbing irregularities, and standardizing the conditions under which newly signed Dominicans play.

Is There a Dominican Response?

The picture painted of Dominican baseball has, thus far, borne the growing and overpowering imprint of Major League Baseball's interests. Is the game in the Dominican Republic simply a neocolonial outpost of mainland baseball? That was the impression I gave over a decade ago in writing *Sugarball*, but the relationship has since changed in many ways. In *Sugarball*, I discussed the nature of Dominican cultural resistance, finding it primarily in the symbolic realms: nationalism displayed in fans' preference for local over foreign hats, in deconstructed reportage in newspapers, and in foot dragging during games. Today, despite the increased presence of Major League Baseball in the country, evidence suggests that Dominicans are increasingly assuming key roles. If we look at Dominican-American baseball relations as one long commodity chain in which foreign investors are buying up raw materials with which to fashion a product that will be shipped abroad, then Dominicans are now attempting to control links of this chain. This represents a degree of control unthinkable a decade ago.

Dominicans Bankrolling Academies

The increased presence of major league academies on the island is generally taken to mean that MLB has become more entrenched; however, a number of these academies are now being built by Dominicans

and leased to major league teams. This local participation acts as a significant counterweight to MLB's hegemony. Some wealthy Dominicans,
such as Dr. Julio Hazim, have used their wealth to build academies.
Hazim's original aim was to operate the institution himself, developing
players to be sold to major league teams. He opted instead to lease it to
the Atlanta Braves. The former major leaguers José Rijo, George Bell,
Melido Pérez, and Salomón Torrez have all built academies. The former
major league journeyman Junior Noboa has been the most active in this
endeavor. He and his associates have built two academies; one is leased
to the Diamondbacks and the Rockies, the other is supersized to host
four teams. These facilities are state-of-the-art: spacious dorm rooms for
coaches and players, modern dining halls, gyms, and offices, and playing
and practice fields for each occupant. These facilities are on a par with if
not superior to those used by major league teams for spring training.
That Dominicans could finance and build such places was inconceivable
a decade ago. These academies serve to mark these developers as emerging power brokers who can exercise local influence over this valuable
resource.

Funneling Capital Back into the Country

Dominicans who play professionally in the United States funnel
considerable amounts of money back into their country, thereby contributing to a capital flow that characterizes a major form of economic
assistance. It is estimated that Dominicans in the United States collectively
send about $2 billion a year back to relatives in their homeland.[70] More
than 1,300 Dominicans play in the minor leagues, and nearly 100 play in
the majors. Dominican major leaguers earned $210 million in 2003,
according to an MLB study.[71] Minor league earnings, while not as high,
nevertheless constitute millions of dollars. MLB has estimated that baseball contributes $76 million a year to the Dominican economy, based
loosely upon salaries, economic contributions of academies, and jobs generated by MLB within the Dominican Republic: "There is a lot of money
that comes into our economy as a result of Major League Baseball. If you
can see the base of an industry contributing anywhere from $76 to $86
million a year, that is better than what a Free Zone [a commercial zone
leased by the government to a foreign company] brings in. We might not

provide as many jobs as a Free Zone, but we bring in a lot more money than one. MLB winds up leaving a lot of money in the country."[72]

What individual Dominican players funnel back is a major part of that figure, but it is next to impossible to gauge accurately. Major League Baseball estimated that roughly 20 percent of players' wages come back to family, banks, and investments. Then there are the hefty fees paid to the government by each major league team operating an academy, on top of the salaries of local employees of those academies and those involved in running of the Dominican Summer League, and the budget for MLB's office.

At times the economic contribution benefits a community in straightforward ways. Many major leaguers have built playing fields and subsidized organized leagues, in recognition of the system that was there for them, and as an investment in the future of Dominican youth. In the past several years Dominicans playing in the major leagues have attempted to buy baseball teams back home in the Winter League.[73] Dodger pitcher Odalis Pérez made an offer for the storied Estrellas Orientales of San Pedro de Macorís. In 2002 the former Dominican major leaguer Stan Javier bought the San Francisco de Macorís team.

Some, however, provide for their communities in more powerful ways. Pedro Martínez promised people in his hometown of Manoguayabo that he would never forget them. "He personally made the promise to me in front of my door," says Juana Bienvenida de Jaime Guzmán. "He said, 'If I ever get to the major leagues, I promise I will build a church,' and he did." His desire to repay this poor community extends to building homes for people as well, and "he's going to build a school for the community. We already have the grounds. We never had the land, and now we have the land because he personally bought the land."[74] Others seek to repay their country and community. After Hurricane Andrew devastated a good chunk of the island in 1998, then–Chicago Cubs superstar Sammy Sosa spearheaded the relief effort, and many other Dominicans lined up to assist. (Martínez contributed $100,000.) Still others start businesses all over the country, hiring family, friends, and others to operate them.

The Buscón as Gatekeeper

A third area of Dominican influence concerns the much-maligned buscón. At the level of cultural politics, the buscón represents both a quasi-legitimate counterpart to the Dominicans and Americans who own academies and a kind of de facto cultural resistance to American interests. Indispensable, the buscón makes certain that a requisite number of Dominican young men find their way to major league tryouts. He "grows" them, feeding and housing them, honing their skills until they are good enough to be signed. That a buscón might cut corners, that he might bend the law to get his charge a contract, then take an commission considered exorbitant by the baseball establishment—such a prospect does not deter players and their families from putting themselves in the buscón's hands. The buscón has shown he cares—this itself counts as valuable currency to parents and player.

Buscones constitute more than a fundamental conduit for Dominican talent to get to the States, however. The buscón also represents the one area that Major League Baseball and its clubs cannot control—the source of player development. Efforts to organize and eventually regulate them are framed as being in the interests of the players—and in part that is true. From another perspective, however, the regulation of this vital dimension of player development would represent a further extension of U.S. influence.

If attempts to regulate this enterprise have thus far fallen short, it is due to the nature of Dominican underdevelopment, which makes almost any organizational endeavor of this kind an adventure. Anthropologists refer to this phenomenon as life in the "informal economy." The official Dominican economy is as weak as it has been in the past quarter-century. The peso lost about half its value between 2000 and 2004, and more than 600,000 jobs vanished.[75] For a small country of eight million, that is a devastating downturn. In the Dominican Republic one typically sees a microentrepreneur with a table outside his house making jewelry, or selling sugar by the cupful in a *ventorrillo*, or small grocery store. This view of the informal economy as synonymous with subsistence-level entrepreneurship is widespread, but there are exceptions to this view. A definition of informal economy posited by sociologist Alejandro Portes allows us to include economic acts that are neither sanctioned nor proscribed by the state, enabling practitioners to earn substantial amounts of money.[76] In that he operates outside of the normative economic order, the buscón is part of the informal economy. It is noteworthy that

Dominican insiders know that the buscones are performing a vital function, and that their success has also meant that more and more Dominican youngsters are playing the game, and playing it with an eye toward making it in the professional ranks. It is also noteworthy that this is all independent of the state's efforts.

The Dominican government's role in its national game has also increased. Seizing upon its favorite sons as national icons, the Dominican government is using them as powerful emblems with which to make nonpartisan public announcements ("say no to drugs," for example), but also positions these heroes to be identified with the party in power. In return, the government has provided new fields and coaches throughout the country. It has also given MLB a tax break in return for its material contributions to the nation.

Marketing Dominican Baseball

At the outset of this chapter, I contrasted the Dominican Republic with Japan in terms of ability to generate revenue for Major League Baseball International. While the Dominican Republic lags far behind Japan economically, MLBI has, nevertheless, increased its business in the country. Major league teams have played exhibition games in the Dominican Republic. The Houston Astros and Boston Red Sox traveled to Santo Domingo in March 2000 for a two-game exhibition series. The Astros had Dominican José Lima pitching for them, while the Red Sox had Pedro and Ramón Martínez, as well as infielder José Offerman. Unfortunately, though, nearly 25 percent of the eighteen thousand seats were empty. Some blame scalpers, who are given blocks of tickets by the stadium owners and try to sell them, keeping a small commission. They may return unsold tickets at no cost to them. Pedro Martínez saw the empty seats and was moved to comment, "I think it is extremely abusive to our country. Probably 80 percent of our people here cannot afford to pay the money they were asked to pay. I think the prices should have been lower. I'm not surprised those seats were empty."[77]

In the spring of 2004 Major League Baseball a new four-year, seven-figure television deal was inked with Canal de Notícias.[78] In a separate deal, MLBI signed Grupo León Jimenes, a Dominican firm that brews Presidente beer—one of the finest in the Caribbean. While these kinds of business dealings benefit MLB, they also enhance the reputation of Dominican firms that have succeeded in putting their stamp upon the nation's favorite sport. Latin America accounts for roughly 20 percent of MLBI's annual revenue, and the Dominican Republic—primarily through its television rights deal—contributes the largest share.

Dominicans have also developed into cultural icons. Players like Vladimir Guerrero or Pedro Martínez are internationally recognized figures, admired not only in their native country but in their adopted one as well. Hence it is common to find youngsters in both Santo Domingo and Scottsdale donning a facsimile Guerrero jersey and wanting to be "like Vlad" when they grow up: a far cry from the anonymity of such Latino superstars of the 1960s as Roberto Clemente.

The newfound cultural acceptance of Latinos as role models for those outside their culture brings the possibility of commercial endorsements. Endorsements represent an even greater index of integration into the dominant society, because they mean that a mainstream corporation is willing to risk capital on Latino spokespeople. Such decisions rest upon the growing buying power of the Latino market, and on the assumption that Anglos will identify with Latino spokespeople. Contributing to this endorsement success were the sheer numbers of Latino players who had entered professional baseball, and the dawning consciousness that the Hispanic market was a large and relatively untapped treasure. As of 2003, Hispanics had become the largest minority in the United States, with a population of thirty-five million, and that figure represents some $540 billion in spending power.[79] As a result, marketing to the Hispanic community, and by Hispanic spokespersons, is gaining traction in many quarters.

When the Cuban Rafael Palmeiro became the spokesman for Viagra, it meant—among other things—that the pharmaceutical company Pfizer believed that Palmeiro could speak to multiple constituencies. After Palmeiro tested positive for steroids, he was able to withstand the cloud hanging over him, further testimony to his cultural crossover resilience. Some Dominicans joked that it was interesting to watch older white congressmen questioning Palmeiro on using performance-enhancing substances when they no doubt used Viagra—a performance enhancer of a different order . . . and touted by none other than Palmeiro. A strange symmetry.

Latinos in general have only begun to taste the endorsement dessert tray. While Pedro Martínez has become the bedrock of Mets marketing strategy, he has not had a commercial jetliner named after him, as has David Ortiz. Most Dominicans (and Latinos in general) have not fared as well. Language is a major barrier, it seems, although the Chinese NBA star Yao Ming seemed to have little trouble landing national endorsements with Apple Computers and Gatorade.

Given the numbers of players in the game, Major League Baseball should be far ahead of other sports in marketing to Latinos, but efforts thus far have been spotty at best. Some organizations, such as the Dodgers or Padres, have done very well, while others, like the Astros, have done almost nothing.

Culturally, Dominican players are no longer only a source of pride in their homeland. They have become multinational heroes and role models, to a multicultural generation of fans. This achievement represents an unprecedented level of respect and cultural integration of Latinos into the sport in the United States. Dominicans and other Latinos have been able to garner a share of the endorsement market, further evidence of the two-way flow of the game. The process may be circuitous, but Dominicans being offered endorsements in the United States can help fuel more commerce going back to the Dominican Republic. These players may be used to directly broker deals between U.S. and Dominican firms or heighten the awareness of U.S. firms looking for economic possibilities elsewhere. The changes that have been wrought in and through baseball in the Dominican Republic have been so far-reaching as to force us all to rethink the trajectory of the sport there.

5

JAPAN: EMERGING FROM THE FEUDAL ECLIPSE

As far as the Japanese are concerned, Major League Baseball is a "tar baby." They want desperately to be rid of it but can't separate from it. They want to vanquish it, yet they slavishly follow it. They invite it in the front door and toss it out the back, only to invite it in the front door again. Their impulse to eliminate foreign influences may have arisen with the Tokagawa shogunate—when the land was rid of Christian influence—but it falls prey to Freudian repression with its cloaking of seductive impulses. That structural ambivalence continues to the present, resulting in a contradictory cultural dance. In baseball, for instance, when the first Americans hired to play in the Nippon Professional Baseball (NPB) league arrived, the Japanese couldn't figure out which they wanted more: a wild display of American home run hitting or an abysmal failure on the part of these same *gaijin*, or foreigners. In fact, they wanted both: to be overwhelmed by Americans' power *and* to reduce them to baseball rubble. That tension continues. The Japanese have succeeded in making baseball their game, despite the feudal impulse to do so in isolation. Insularity has never really been possible, all the less so in a globalizing world.

Any look at contemporary Japanese baseball has to begin and end with Robert Whiting's studies.[1] Over the past quarter-century his writings have provided a rich tapestry that examines at the same time the traditional Japanese elements finding expression in the game and current corrupting cosmopolitan trends that so worry the Japanese mainstream.[2] In the case of *yakyu*, as baseball is called in Japan, the past is defined as baseball free from foreign tampering, while the future is about engaging foreign elements. In this chapter I examine, through a series of cases, the "restless torpor" that characterizes Japanese baseball's relationship to foreign influences.

The Gaijin: Can't Live with Them. Can't Live Without Them.

Perhaps the most vexing example of this cultural tension is the case of Randy Bass. Bass was twenty-eight years old in 1983, when he decided to set sail for the East. Had he stayed in the United States, Bass might have been one of those players who dominates in the minor leagues but never quite breaks through to the majors. The thirty-seven home runs he hit for the Class AAA Denver Bears in 1980, along with 143 runs batted in and a .333 batting average, should have been good enough for him to get called up for September at least. And he had been called up—five times—but he never seemed to stick.

By the time Randy Bass decided to try his luck in Japan, the Japanese had been signing foreign players for the better part of three decades. Fueled by their effort to close the gap between American baseball and their game, they were fed a steady diet of journeymen, and an occasional accomplished major leaguer (invariably past his prime) whom they signed to bloated contracts. Under the lens of intense media scrutiny, and disoriented by cultural difference, most of these players performed poorly. The gaijin unwittingly played a powerful role in inflating the Japanese national sense of self. Every failed gaijin provided further proof that the Japanese were closing the gap. From the Japanese vantage point, postseason exhibition games against major league teams were also highly pressurized contests, closely watched and painstakingly interpreted by all. No American went to Japan as an empty slate. There was an invisible fold-out in his passport, printed with the history of these two baseball-rich countries. As exchanges evolved and relations between Major League Baseball and Japan diversified, goodwill grew, less at the expense of the suspicions and distrust than in spite of it.

Bass learned quickly to shorten his swing, to accommodate slower curve balls, to hit to the opposite field. Playing for the Hanshin Tigers, Bass hit sixty-three home runs in his first two seasons, despite missing several weeks. In his third season, 1985, Bass dominated Japanese baseball, batting .350, with fifty-four home runs and 134 RBI, leading the league in all three categories—the triple crown. Most significant, he threatened the all-time single-season home run record of fifty-five, set by Sadaharu Oh. With two games left, Bass homered for the fifty-fourth time. Some weeks earlier, over breakfast with fellow traveler Warren Cromartie, Bass had predicted, "They'll never let me do it. I'll get to 54 and they'll start walking me. You'll see. They'll never let a *gaijin* break a record like that."[3] Ironically, the Tigers' final two games were against the Yomiuri Giants, managed by Oh. As he had predicted, Bass was walked twice in the first game and four times in the final game. Oh's pitchers later acknowledged that they were instructed—under penalty of a fine—to throw no strikes to the gaijin.

Even as he was being hailed as Hanshin's hero, leading the Tigers to a title, Bass's relationship with the owners was showing signs of unraveling. He was vilified by the Hanshin brass for arriving late to camp and for aggressively negotiating his contract, yet Bass managed to win another triple crown in 1986, this time batting .390, the highest batting average ever recorded in Japanese pro baseball. Whiting calls it the "least-covered record-breaking achievement in the history of Japanese sports journalism." When Bass finally left Japanese baseball two years later, one major sports paper listed his statistics and achievements without mentioning the record at all. Winning his second straight triple crown with a record-setting batting average was, however, not good enough to win the Most Outstanding Baseball Person award, which was given to the manager of the Seibu Lions, Masaaki Mori. One spokesperson for the award committee deadpanned, "There were no splendid players this year. That's why we chose Mori."[4]

The idea that a gaijin can so dominate the league is precisely why some are signed so eagerly and paid such large salaries. But when such a player exceeds all expectations, the baseball establishment grows increasingly nervous and must to find a way to level him. In Bass's case abasement was difficult because he was neither arrogant nor selfish. Quite to the contrary, he routinely praised his teammates and humbly referred to his accomplishments. Only his foreignness triggered Japanese insecurities. The attempts to hobble Bass took on a grotesque form as early as 1984, when he went home to be at his dying father's bedside. Rather than commiserate with him over his loss, the press referred to his leave as "irresponsible" and "self-centered."[5] Learning of this reaction upon his return, Bass was nearly speechless, wondering aloud, "How the hell can you put a game ahead of someone you love?" This question is lost in translation in mainstream Japanese circles, where, according to one magazine survey, 70 percent of Japanese company employees considered leaving the company or team wrong under any conditions.[6]

Following Bass's golden 1985 season, when his team won the championship and he won the league Most Valuable Player award, his stock nosedived in 1986. To begin with, he asked for (and received) a three-year contract for $3 million that included a clause that allowed him to arrive to camp two weeks later than other players. Bass's salary was interpreted as further evidence of his mercenary nature, and the late arrival at camp was proof positive of his lacking what the Japanese call *wa,* or group harmony. Every move Bass made that was not "old school" was skewered by the press. Bass grew tired of it, and in one widely read newspaper interview he retaliated against his mainstream detractors. He was made to apologize. With all of this controversy swirling around him, Bass nevertheless went on to take his second straight triple crown.

The following season, 1987, Bass suffered a bad back but continued to put up healthy numbers, batting .320, with thirty-seven home runs. The final year of his contract began well enough, but early in May, ill fortune struck the Bass family again. Randy's eight-year-old son Zachary was diagnosed with a brain tumor. Randy's play came to a grinding halt as he left (with "compassionate leave") for San Francisco, where Zachary was operated on. Bass stayed in California until he was certain that Zachary was going to be all right. As a result, he exceeded the thirty-day period of his leave. Hanshin abruptly released him. "In the corporate nation that is Japan, the company always comes first, even before a family crisis," notes Whiting.[7]

After being assured that Zachary would recover, Randy weighed his legal options. The Tigers' position was that Bass had violated their agreement with him to return within thirty days. He countered, claiming that one of the Tigers' executives, Shingo Furuya, had assured him by phone that he could stay until the boy's condition stabilized. The Tigers denied this vehemently, but Bass had taped the conversation, and the Tigers were brought up short. Bass was arguing from a contractual position, while the Japanese sought to find a harmonious middle ground in which all parties could save face. This kind of cross-cultural impasse haunts much of U.S.–Japanese relations. Bass held firm to the contract, which stipulated he was to be paid in full through his extension year, 1989, and that his entire family would have their health insurance covered by the team. The Tigers, however, had failed to take out health insurance on Bass's family.

It was a tumultuous six years that Bass spent in Japan, years in which he experienced the highest and lowest points a person might ever reach. His difficulties are sometimes thought to be reflective of cultural difference, and of course they are. But all along there were signs that the view of Bass as a selfish gaijin in need of being taken down a peg, of being controlled, was only part of the Japanese response. He was at the same time genuinely revered by various sectors of that same Japanese society. After leading the Tigers to the 1985 championship, Bass was hailed as a genuine Japanese icon. In Osaka, the home of the Tigers, traditional fan celebration includes a plunge into the Dotonbori River. Following the Tigers' 1985 victory, jubilant fans tore down a statue of Colonel Sanders in front of a Kentucky Fried Chicken and threw it into the river because the white, bearded American icon reminded them of Bass.

Those same fans were also solidly in Bass's corner as he neared Oh's home run record. When Bass was walked all four times up in his final game—thus saving the record—Hanshin fans littered the field with beer cans and bottles. "It's time to accept gaijin as equals," declared one renegade member of the media.[8] Even during the swirl of acrimony surrounding Bass's departure to be with his son, he received countless letters and cards of support.

One of the most remarkable outcomes of the Bass saga is how remarkably free of bitterness the player seems, perhaps because he understands that the rancor and resentment he encountered represented only a part of Japanese society. Unfortunately, that segment still holds power, and Bass has been repeatedly denied entry into the Japanese Baseball Hall of Fame. In 2004, his last season of regular eligibility, Randy Bass needed 207 votes, 75 percent, to get into the Hall. He received 202; five Japanese sportswriters refused to cast a vote. Meanwhile, the lone inductee was Akira Ogi, a journeyman player with a lifetime .270 batting average who had some success as a manager. Bass's fate now rests with the Hall's Veterans Committee, but that group failed to add him to the roster in 2005.

Bass's treatment by the Japanese Hall of Fame is hardly a surprise. The country's baseball establishment—owners, managers, coaches, and press—feels the need to belittle or dismiss contributions made by foreigners in the face of the most compelling evidence. Bass's response after the 2004 Hall vote was again unbelievably free of bitterness:

> I am disappointed to hear that five writers didn't vote. It is an honor and a privilege given to them. They should vote under any circumstance; in a way it is their duty. . . . Last year I heard I only missed by 10 votes, so I was kind of hoping to be elected this year. Oh, well. Maybe the Veterans Committee will elect me somewhere down the road. That would be a real honor. And I hope they don't forget Leron Lee, too. He leads Japanese ball in career average and he really should be in the Hall, too.[9]

What more can be said about the man's character? As concerned about Lee as he is about his own candidacy, Bass, now a city councilman in Lawton, Oklahoma, continues to be modest and secure. It should be noted, however, that Randy Bass is still handsomely rewarded for being "Randy Bass" in Japan. One well-placed insider estimated that Bass earns between $300,000 and $500,000 a year from old timers' games, grand openings, and other celebrity functions. With his history Bass's sincerity is never in doubt, but earning that kind of income certainly helps to assuage insults to ego. Japan cannot stop vacillating between heralding and hating this man, and can't seem to figure out which response is more legitimate. In his turn Randy Bass is riding his Japanese roller coaster for all it is worth, having long since figured out the key: it's not personal.

Major League Baseball and foreign players represent the most serious and immediate threat to Japan's baseball sovereignty. What began as an occasional major leaguer coming to play in Japan has evolved into a two-way flow of talent, and to the increased involvement of MLB in Japanese professional baseball and the promotion of the American game's business in Japan. We now turn to a series of cases involving players who left Japan, and the evolution of relations between the Japanese baseball establishment and MLB in response to these departures.

The Spirit and the Letter: Masanori Murakami and the "Working Agreement"

The nationalism of the Meiji period (1868–1912)—including the reconfiguration of the foreign sport of baseball as Japanese—fueled the vigorous growth through which Japan emerged as a modern state. That nationalism also contains within it a static response, in contrast to the dynamic system that accompanied the Meiji period, as well as Japan's postwar industrial growth. The most evident form of this stasis is Japan's recurrent use of protectionism, an attempt to preempt all foreign competition.

In Japanese baseball, protectionist policy solidified after a player first slipped out of the system in 1964. Masanori Murakami played only two seasons (1964–1965) for the San Francisco Giants, constituting only a footnote in major league history, but in Japan his case had far-reaching consequences. Thirty years before pitcher Hideo Nomo got ready to break from the Japanese system, Murakami pitched in relief for San Francisco. He emerged through a legal loophole, just as Nomo would in 1995. In both cases Japanese officials failed to fully comprehend the contract because they couldn't fathom that their players could ever be desirable to American clubs.

Murakami was part of a special pact, an early predecessor to what would evolve as a "working agreement" between the San Francisco Giants and the Nankai Hawks. The agreement allowed players from one country to train in the other. The pact contained a clause (part of the standard major league contract) that allowed San Francisco to pick up the contract of any Japanese player that made the parent club by paying the Hawks $10,000. The Hawks' general manager, Makoto Tachibana, didn't think twice about signing off on the clause because, like most in Japan, he didn't think any Japanese players were good enough to interest major league baseball.

No one, least of all the Hawks brass, anticipated Murakami's fluorescence in the California League that summer. He dominated opposing hitters, and the Giants called him up in September. He pitched fifteen innings in nine games for San Francisco, with an impressive 1.80 earned run average. "Mashi," as Murakami came to be known by his San Francisco teammates, enjoyed pitching in the United States. It was easier than Japan. "In Japan, batters only swing at strikes. Here, they try to hit everything out and they don't care if you throw a strike or not," he observed.[10] It came as no surprise, then, that the Giants offered him a contract for the 1965 season. To satisfy the option clause, the Giants sent a payment of $10,000 to the Hawks, who accepted it. But when it became clear that San Francisco expected Murakami for the 1965 season, the Japanese were incensed. What followed was the baseball equivalent of the Cold War, replete with saber rattling.

Murakami had enjoyed his season in the United States and returned to Japan with the idea of pitching for the Giants again in 1965, but the Hawks threatened him with lifetime banishment. His family chimed in as well, insisting that he remain in Japan. Murakami capitulated. The Giants had a contract with him, and as far as MLB owners were concerned, Murakami's sudden turnaround was in violation of the reserve clause, which legally bound a player to his team for as long as the team wanted him. Letters between the American and Japanese commissioners criss-crossed the Pacific, each demanding that his authority be recognized. The Hawks, for their part, claimed that they had never intended to sell Murakami; rather, he had been leased by the Giants. The $10,000 that the Giants had paid was, as far as the Hawks were concerned, a bonus payment for his services, not a termination of their claim on Murakami. The Giants pointed to the agreement signed by the Hawks as a binding document. And so it went back and forth. On February 17, 1965, relations between the two baseball organizations had deteriorated to the point where U.S. Commissioner Ford Frick suspended any further baseball dealings between the two countries.

Whiting astutely points out that the fundamental problem lay in the different ways in which the two cultures approach relationships, especially contractual ones: "The Japanese believed more in the spirit of a contract than the letter." They view contracts as mutually beneficial and subject to loose construction to allow for changing circumstances. "For Japanese, a contract did not define a relationship, it signaled the beginning of one," writes Whiting. The details of the contract should allow for changes, according to this view, and interpretation should be fluid. Frick, on the other hand, interpreted relations in an American fashion: "Sanctity of contract is the most essential feature."[11]

A compromise of sorts was eventually reached. Face was saved when the Hawks consented to allow Murakami to play for San Francisco in 1965 on the condition that he have to return to his Japanese club thereafter. "Family considerations" provided the public explanation—specifically, Murakami's father was alarmed with his son's growing Americanization. The young man's steadily growing independence—and his gaijin girlfriend—had upset the elder Murakami. Officially, the father pleaded through Japanese Commissioner Yushi Uchimura: "He's my only son. I want him here with me, not stuck in some foreign country."[12]

Working Agreement

Murakami's case resulted in the United States–Japanese Player Contract Agreement of 1967. This "treaty," known more popularly as the "working agreement," had a hard side and a soft side. On the formal side, each organization would honor the other's regulations and contractual obligations with its players. Since both MLB and Japanese baseball had a reserve clause, this agreement had the effect of protecting either side against any future desertions, although it benefited the Japanese more than the Americans. The pact was the fundamental reason why it would be another thirty years before another Japanese player became a major leaguer.

The more publicized element of the working agreement encourages cooperative efforts between Japanese and major league teams. For instance, in 2002 the Yankees and the Yomiuri Giants publicly announced a new agreement that included the exchange of information about players, as well as joint player development and treatment of injuries. The contracts of some players in the Yankees minor league system might eventually be sold to their Japanese trading partners, while the Giants agree to provide information on high school prospects whom they won't draft but who could be of interest to the Yankees. Additionally, players on the Yomiuri roster whom they deem expendable might be previewed by the Yankees before they are posted as available for all MLB teams to bid on.[13]

Ray Poitevint, a longtime scout of Asian talent, has been building relations with Japanese baseball interests for decades. He understands the long view: "Most people go to Japan and spend two weeks and twenty thousand dollars of company money and come back to report that they had good meetings. But they don't realize that those meetings have to go on for eight or nine years before they get real results." As we have seen, the Los Angeles Dodgers have known this even longer. Beginning in the early 1950s, Walter O'Malley of the Dodgers began forging relationships with several teams in Japan. This long-standing relationship, and the exchange of information that it entails, contributed to the signing of Kazuhisa Ishii in 2002. Poitevint acknowledges, "If we're working with one of our clubs, they'll help us sign a Japanese pitcher or hitter from high school. They help us quite a bit."[14]

One of the most highly visible components of the Dodgers-Kintetsu working agreement has been legendary Los Angeles manager Tom Lasorda, who has been providing coaching expertise to the Buffaloes. Lasorda feels certain that his presence has been beneficial: "That team had not won in many, many years. We brought them right into the World Series [the Japan Series]. We brought 'em good players. I scouted good players for them. We built up the farm system."[15]

In an incisive and critical revelation, Kuehnert argues that these working agreements are at best marginal to the success of the Japanese team. According to Kuehnert, a team like Kintetsu, which loses between $35 million and $40 million a year and has become a serious candidate for a merger, can ill afford costly contracts with the Dodgers. The working agreements with the Dodgers came at a steep price for the Buffaloes, he observes. They involved payments in the neighborhood of $1 million a year to Lasorda. Disputing Lasorda's claims that he was instrumental in the team's success, Kuehnert told me, "You think that the Buffaloes were successful because of what he was able to do for them? Since that Japan Series appearance they've been at the bottom of the standings and attendance has been down." Kuehnert thinks of the working agreement as incidental, relative to the serious issues plaguing Japanese professional baseball:

> In my column I noted that [Lasorda] and the Dodgers got a million dollars a year for these services, and Tommy flew first class, stayed in the best hotels, came on a regular basis, and what did it gain them? It gained them a lot more debt. A Kintetsu official wanted me to understand that it wasn't one million between Lasorda and the Dodgers; it was one million apiece. They paid

two million dollars for the honor of having dinner with Lasorda. If he really wanted to help them, Lasorda could have told them that they were paying too much to lease the stadium. They have a ten-million-dollar-a-year stadium lease. The [Orix] BlueWave are spending $600,000 a year for theirs. He could have advised them to push for revenue sharing, or a modern marketing philosophy. If Tommy wants to help them, he doesn't need to coach them. They coach very well. It cost them six to seven million dollars over three years to get all that help![16]

The working agreement arose from the dispute over whether American and Japanese management would be able to control labor in their respective locations. While the reserve system in the United States has faded into oblivion—in a major league player now must stay with his club only for the first seven years of his career—it remains in Japan. Working agreements might sound like equitable arrangements between sovereigns, but as we see from one of the actual cases, they tend to be weighted in favor of the more powerful partner—in this case, MLB.

Hideo Nomo

Hideo Nomo "has the balls and the heart of a lion."—anonymous major league executive

While Hideo Nomo was not the first Japanese to play in the major leagues, he may well have been the toughest. When baseball people discuss him, the word *warrior* comes up a lot, along with references to his gumption, his determination.[17] Nomo quickly became iconic in the United States, but in Japan acknowledgment of Nomo's talent and success was grudging at best. Japan's mixed feelings toward Nomo began with his bizarre corkscrew pitching form, which is so odd that only a kid could have manufactured it—and indeed, he developed it as a youngster. In the conformist system of Japan, one courts rejection by deviating, by becoming conspicuous. "In the U.S. the saying is, 'The squeaky wheel gets oiled.' Well, here it's the opposite; it's 'The nail that sticks out gets pounded down,'" commented Major League Baseball International's Derrick Thomas, who is the child of a Japanese-American union.[18] Nomo flouted that cultural system. As a result, he was rejected by the manager of the prestigious baseball factory Kindai High School: "With that tornado windup, you'll never make it."[19] Such negative pronouncements dogged his career but never altered Nomo's style. His school never made it to the Koshien Tournament, the national high school championships, so the scouts who swarm that event never saw him. Naturally, no university of note recruited him, so Nomo took the plebian route to professional baseball: Japan's industrial leagues. In the early 1990s thousands of companies around the country fielded teams. The bright spot for Nomo in this forlorn venue was that no one stopped him from using his unorthodox style.

His domination of team U.S.A. in the 1988 Seoul Olympics finally piqued the interest of professional clubs. The Kintetsu Buffaloes of the Pacific League signed him for a then-record $1 million bonus. Rather than accept the money without hesitation, as most would, Nomo insisted that the team not tamper with his delivery. Buffaloes execs flinched in embarrassment at this un-Japanese display of individuality—but they agreed to the clause. Kintetsu's laid-back manager Akira Ogi (who later was to manage Ichiro as well) had no problem with the pitcher's form, however, and Nomo went on to win the Rookie of the Year and Most Valuable Player awards, along with Sawamura award as Japan's best pitcher.

By 1993 Nomo had become the dominant pitcher in Japanese baseball almost despite the NPB, utilizing the full force of his abilities and supported by Ogi. In this atypical environment Nomo flourished, until Ogi was replaced by a more traditional manager, Keishi Suzuki, whose philosophy of pitching Robert Whiting characterized as "Throw until you die."[20] With such a rigid, conventional manager, Nomo's days were numbered. Suzuki quickly put an end to Nomo's supposedly lax American pitching regimen (in reality modeled on the training habits of the age-defying workaholic Nolan Ryan). No longer allowing four days' rest between pitching performances to allow the tiny tears to Nomo's arm to heal, Suzuki pushed Nomo's pitch count through the roof. Suzuki kept Nomo in one game, for example, despite his desperate struggle with control. In that marathon, Nomo walked sixteen batters and threw 191 pitches. Not long afterward, in another iron-man effort, Nomo threw 180 pitches. Suzuki's obsession hastened arm problems for Nomo, and when the pitcher voiced concerns, Suzuki characterized him to the press as "lazy." Nomo remained taciturn throughout but was keeping score, plotting how to escape this system, which had never treated him with respect.

It wasn't long before Nomo encountered the Japanese-Anglo baseball agent Don Nomura. Nomura had targeted Japan as his niche. He scrutinized the Japanese Uniform Players Contract (based on the American version), looking for loopholes that would allow him to get players out of Japan. The NPB's reserve system (like MLB's, pre–free agency) was intended to hold onto players in perpetuity; but it had one glaring fault: it underestimated the desirability of certain of its players to major league teams. A strict interpretation, Nomura argued, would allow Japanese players to circumvent the spirit and letter of the reserve system. The shortsightedness of the Japanese contract limited a team's control over a player's movements to Japan. Once a player was no longer desired by his club or physically unable to play for it, and he retired, he was free to go elsewhere. Nomo and Nomura used the latter clause—voluntary retirement—to challenge the letter of the agreement. Nomo would become a free agent by retiring. When the baseball establishment tried to thwart him, it was met by a clear-cut legal interpretation that it couldn't get around.

Nomo had endured the Japanese system without so much as a whisper, but at the same time he had exhibited a strong individualist streak, flouting Japanese convention. A Japanese player, hemmed in on all sides by rules, conventions, and norms, can exhibit rebelliousness only on a small scale. For instance, while it may not seem particularly iconoclastic to an American audience, Nomo became the first Japanese player to wear Nike—rather than Mizuno—shoes during the All-Star series. Meanwhile, he endured his manager's attempts to hammer him down and teach him humility and consensus, but Nomo was readying himself to exact a measure of revenge.

Whiting describes some of the meetings between Nomo and Kintetsu officials, in which ownership sought to morally browbeat Nomo into submission. Nomo would have none of it. "Think of what you're doing to your career. Think of the team," rebuked an executive of the Osaka club. "I am. That's why I'm leaving," retorted Nomo. Having been caught off-guard, Kintetsu went into "face-saving mode." "'Do you want permission to let you go to the States?' offered a rather desperate Buffalo official. . . . 'We can arrange to do that.'" To which Nomo testily replied, "We don't need your permission to go to the States and play."[21] This lack of deference to his superiors was completely out of character for Japanese players, including Nomo. His response clearly bore out an accumulation of resentment that had festered too long. And when his father attempted to emotionally coerce Nomo, threatening not to speak with him, Nomo—unlike Murakami—simply called his bluff.

Nomo's entry into major league baseball was spectacular. He delighted American audiences, winning awards and impressing his major league colleagues. Americans knew little, however, of the route he took to get here: a path filled with difficult personal decisions, institutional and legal challenges to the entire Japanese baseball system.

Alfonso Soriano

The Japanese reserve system extended to include foreign players that they developed as well. The case of Alfonso Soriano, star second baseman for the Texas Rangers, is striking. Soriano is a Dominican who came up through the ranks of the Dominican baseball academies. His academy, however, was the only one on the island affiliated with a non-MLB team. The Hiroshima Carp built their academy there in 1990. Soriano signed with them at sixteen years of age, playing well enough to earn his ticket to Japan by the time he was seventeen, in 1997. Dominicans signing with the Carp entered into a series of contracts that bound them to that team even longer than the nine-year free agency rule then in effect in Japan. Dominicans had to sign a bridge contract, which tied them to the Carp for an additional seven years, either in Japan or in the Dominican. The nine-year free agency clause kicked in only once a player made the big club. Given this sixteen-year obligation, a Dominican player could be forced to spend his entire career with Hiroshima.

Soriano was trapped, and the fact that the Carp continued to pay him only the minimum $45,000 was evidence of his state. Don Nomura, upon meeting Soriano, informed him that the Carp had signed him before he had reached Japan's legal age of twenty, without involving a legal guardian. Nomura persuaded Soriano to seek to void his contract and declare himself a free agent. The NPB Executive Committee, not surprisingly, sided with the Carp. Soriano voluntarily retired, but NPB countered with the claim that the league's interpretation of voluntary retirement had been expanded to preclude signing a new contract anywhere. This came as a shock to MLB, whose officers claimed that they had never been notified. A meeting between the two organizations confirmed that the Japanese had privately extended the ruling so that any player voluntarily retiring remained the property of his Japanese club. Referring to the way that the NPB conducted its affairs, one MLB representative commented, "It was a joke that these guys were representing Japanese baseball. They might as well have sent Soupy Sales."[22] Acting Commissioner Bud Selig ruled that Soriano should be placed on MLB's "voluntary retired" list—that he was legitimately retired from Japanese baseball. Japanese professional baseball did not press the issue, and a new agreement prohibited the NPB from unilaterally making changes and clarifying the player-exchange process between the organizations. Under the new system, any major league club would be allowed to bid for a chance to sign a player made available—that is, "posted"—by his club at any time. The club with the highest bid pays the Japanese team holding the player's contract for the right to sign the player during a thirty-day window of opportunity. If the U.S. team and the player agree on contract terms, the Japanese team keeps the posting money; if not, the posted bid is returned, and the player resumes his career with his Japanese team. This posting system confirms both that MLB has the institutional power to effect changes in Japan and that the Japanese players are now of a high enough caliber to attract major league interest.

Ichiro

"That little shit can really hit the ball."—Barry Bonds, on first playing against Ichiro Suzuki in Japan in 1996

The title of Robert Whiting's *The Meaning of Ichiro* connotes something unprecedented that the player brought to the game: a genuine Japanese baseball hero for an American public. Ironically, Ichiro Suzuki, widely known by his first name alone, was "our" hero before he was Japan's. He played in Japan's Pacific League, which, from a media perspective, is the equivalent of the Australian outback. He was viewed on Japanese television only a handful of times, and attendance at the Orix BlueWave's stadium was mediocre. Whiting notes that while Japanese fans certainly knew who Ichiro was, he never attained the icon status of a Hideki Matsui. Even lesser players on the Giants received more media exposure than Ichiro ever did. Coming to the United States, however, he electrified major league baseball and its fans, becoming nationally known and recognized—notoriety that in turn reverberated back in Japan. Ichiro was, as one American sportswriter confided to Whiting, "the first cool Japanese I've ever met."[23] To gain a sense of what Ichiro meant to both Americans and Japanese, we must first distinguish between the successful marketing of a player and a player's popular appeal. Hideo Nomo, Japan's first genuine success in major league baseball, back in 1995, was marketed by the Dodgers via their "Nomomania" campaign. His popularity was predictably high in the Los Angeles area, but Nomo lacked an outgoing personality; he could bring fans in with his pitching, but he couldn't become an icon. Ichiro, on the other hand, played the game with such panache that he changed the way American fans perceived the Japanese people.

Making an Ichiro

Until he came to the United States—and even immediately afterward—Ichiro's entire life was built upon the most regimented imitation of Japanese feudal tradition imaginable. In Whiting's account of Ichiro's upbringing, both the player and his father methodically forged his career as a player from age seven on; their determination was so fierce that one can easily forget what incredible natural abilities Ichiro possessed. Each day of the year was the same: long, meticulously scripted hours of throwing, fielding, and batting practice that took father and son deep into the night. It is tempting to paint the father as an overbearing, even abusive, man, determined to live his thwarted baseball dream through his son. Other children may have rebelled actively or passively, but the intense focus somehow resonated with Ichiro.

His father's stern, unyielding commitment to these practices were peppered with valuable lessons. Ichiro—originally a right-handed batter—was taught to swing from the left side so that his motion ended in a stride toward first base. He was also taught to treat his body with respect; his father massaged the boy's feet each night before bed. The care and attention Ichiro was instructed to give his glove bordered on that of a religious ritual.

By sixth grade Ichiro, sticklike in appearance, could outperform most high school players. The pitching machines he abused nightly had to be ratcheted up, eventually tweaked to pitch 93 mph. Ichiro also learned to incorporate a golf swing into his evolving batting style to enhance his weight shift from one foot to the other.

In Japan high school baseball is considered to be the most pure form of the game, and the Koshien Tournament, which takes place each summer in Nishino, is Japan's most closely followed sporting event. The fifty thousand–seat stadium is packed for each game during the two weeks when the best high school teams in the country compete, and these games are televised nationwide. Anyone standing out in this tournament is certain to be drafted by a professional team.

The Suzuki family opted for Aikodai Meiden Kokko, one of the best baseball schools, with an established record for success. There, Ichiro absorbed the systematic denigration meted out to all freshmen players, even as he went about the business of distinguishing himself. He performed menial chores but seized opportunities to sneak off and practice on his own. He was unruffled by the demands, and more important, he transcended the rituals of being Japanese to become . . . well, almost American. Obeying the rule forbidding him to touch a ball until he was deemed ready would have been the Japanese thing to do. Ichiro, however, was so focused that he would circumvent such rules to achieve his ends, even while maintaining the form and philosophy of the classic Bushido, the feudal Samurai code of behavior. Over three years at the school he batted .502, with 19 home runs, 211 runs batted in, and 131 stolen bases. In 536 official high school at-bats he struck out only 10 times, never on a swinging strike.

Going Pro

The family was certain that Ichiro would be taken very early in the draft and was disappointed when he wasn't selected until the fourth and final round, and thirty-sixth overall, by the Orix BlueWave, in the weaker Pacific League. To make matters worse, the BlueWave offered only a $43,000 signing bonus. Ichiro's diminutive size—5 feet, 9 inches, and 120 pounds—seemed to diminish the staggering numbers Ichiro had put up during his high school career.

Whatever disappointment the Suzuki family may have felt dissipated as Ichiro quickly reached the NPB. After a series of abortive efforts to change Ichiro's swing, the BlueWave hired a new manager, Akira Ogi, who promised not to tamper with the hitter's style. The young outfielder responded immediately by becoming the first Japanese player to collect two hundred hits (in a 130-game season). He also set a Pacific League record with a .385 batting average, showing power (thirteen home runs) and speed (twenty-nine stolen bases) as well. Not surprisingly he was voted the league's Most Valuable Player and was also awarded a Gold Glove for fielding excellence. That season started a string of seven batting titles and three MVP awards. Having mastered baseball in Japan, he had nothing left to prove there. While others might have been content to rule their world, Ichiro wanted to go to the next level. By 2000 everyone knew he would test his mettle in the American major leagues. All that kept Ichiro tied to Japan was loyalty to Ogi, and his manager quickly gave his consent.

Posting Ichiro

A different interpretation of Ichiro's departure emerges when viewed through the lens of political economy. Simply put, the BlueWave was already paying him $5 million, and the team's executives knew that they would never be able to meet his next salary demand, so they opted to "post" him. The Japanese baseball journalist Marty Kuehnert favors this explanation: "The posting system was pushed more by [owner] Mr. Miyachi and his G.M. at the time, Steve Ino. They knew that Ichiro would leave when he reached the free agency level, and they'd get nothing in return. He was costing them more money than any player in Japan, and there would be no end to that."[24] Posting was a path out of an untenable economic situation.

As we have seen, a 1998 agreement between the U.S. and Japanese baseball organizations allows American team to bid for the right to sign any player deemed expendable by his Japanese club. Because this system requires the successful American suitor to pay twice—once to the Japanese team, and once to the player himself—it is an expensive way to get talent, even if the players are considerably more developed than those eligible in the U.S. college draft. Most American teams think twice before entering the Japanese posting system. For small-market teams especially, the expense is usually prohibitive. When Ichiro became available, however, the Seattle Mariners were not dissuaded: their bid of $13.125 million won them the right to negotiate, and they then signed Ichiro in the winter of 2000 to a three-year, $14 million contract.

Aside from the bias against small-market teams, some suspicions have arisen about how fair the posting system is even among the better-heeled clubs. How coincidental that Ichiro would be signed by the Seattle Mariners, a Japanese-owned enterprise! While scouting Japan for the Red Sox in 2002, Ray Poitevint knew the outcome of this process in advance: "I told [Red Sox General Manager Dan] Duquette, 'For our honor, I want to put in a bid, but Seattle's going to get him.' That was a month before it got settled. There was only one team that had a chance to sign Ichiro. The reason why is because you were dealing with one Japanese-owned team in Japan, and one Japanese-owned team in Seattle. It was impossible for those two owners to allow someone else to get him."[25]

Breathless in Seattle

In his first season in Seattle (I hesitate to apply the term *rookie* to a player who had won seven batting titles in Japan), 2001, Ichiro led the American League in batting, hits, runs scored, and stolen bases. He was voted the league's Rookie of the Year and its Most Valuable Player, as well as earning a Gold Glove. His baseball accomplishments were grounded in a kind of training and preparation that Americans hadn't seen before, and in a style of play that they hadn't seen in fifty years. Ichiro was a throwback to a time when baseball was a craft, and he was completely dedicated to that craft. He slashed the ball to the left side of the diamond with the precise skill of a swordsman (59 of his 242 hits that year were infield hits). He had an arm that writers like to think of in terms of artillery, and speed often described in terms of fleet-footed animals. In short, Ichiro was the complete package. But his performance was framed by his exotic rituals and approach to the game. He rivals Dodgers infielder Nomar Garciaparra for the most idiosyncratic batter's box gyrations; before settling into his stance, he stretches, bends elbows, and performs bat manipulations that rival Busby Berkeley dance numbers.

The Mariners quickly capitalized on Ichiro's instantaneous rise to prominence. Sushi was sold at Safeco Field, and legions of white fans sported headbands bearing Japanese characters, and shouted "Gambare" (Go! or Good luck!). Ichiro merchandise became high fashion in and around the Pacific Northwest and elsewhere. Japanese tourism to Seattle grew dramatically in the wake of Ichi-mania. Marketing a star's ethnicity is often a smart business move—recall that a food company in New England quickly attached Pedro Martínez's name to a salsa line when the Dominican star first arrived in Boston—and it also can promote cosmopolitanism. Cultural awareness can in time lead to cultural tolerance and appreciation. But what happened with Ichiro went far beyond basic sociology. Ichiro came to embody "cool," along with, according to Kris Rone, a former vice president of marketing for the Los Angeles Dodgers, a seductively mysterious quality.[26]

Ironically, Ichiro's major league success was a surprise in Japan, even though he already was a superstar there. While his play was unassailable, members of the media back home considered him aloof, disdainful, and self-centered—and, worse, Westernizing. The player who had spent so much of his life emulating traditional culture now showed a penchant for hip-hop and other urban Western cultural forms. A large number of Japanese youth have embraced this "in-your-face" cultural style as an antidote to the tradition-bound past. But it would be an oversimplification to portray Ichiro as an iconoclast. As the correspondent on Japanese baseball Jim Allen observes, "Ichiro may like hip-hop and faddish things, but that's just personal taste. He longs to be ultraconservative."[27] Ichiro's spectacular success forced the Japanese media to follow him in the United States. The media then did an about-face, as if they'd always been in his corner. His record-shattering 2004 season, when his 264 hits broke the single-season record of 257 held for eighty-four years by George Sisler, was followed intensely on both sides of the Pacific, but it should be noted that he was first idolized in America.

Americans loved him for his devotion to craftsmanship, his work ethic, and, relative to the common perception of many major league stars, his lack of greed: he accepted less money to play here than he would have earned had he re-signed in Japan, and once here, he turned down about $35 million worth of endorsements. It was refreshing to fans to see a player who respected the game. But this "throwback" persona existed in an exciting tension with the image of the suave, urbane "playah" that Ichiro also brandished. He was a Samurai who appealed to Americans. At a time when the game has drifted to narcissistic power displays, Ichiro evokes an earlier time when a single could be a work of art. At a time when a youngster is as likely to know a player's salary as his on-base percentage, Ichiro sacrificed money in order to play where he wanted to play. In a time of entitled, unappreciative superstars who seem to care only for themselves, Ichiro tends to his glove and bat as if they were his children.

In sum, Ichiro embodies the Japanese conflict between reverence for the past and hunger for the future, between the culturally myopic past and the global future. Like Nomo, Ichiro came up against a tradition-bound Japanese baseball establishment that questioned his values, his commitment to his craft. His batting form, his love of urban cosmopolitanism, his sowing of wild oats all drew criticism. So he was not drafted as high as he should have been, and his first manager sought to demote him and make him conform. Unlike Nomo, Ichiro took it quietly . . . until he came to Seattle. Ichiro represents a shift in which Japan's best have begun to play part of their careers in the major leagues. The anxious question in Japan now is: How many more superstars will be lost?

Kazuhisa Ishii: Can Lightning Strike Twice?

Kazuhisa Ishii's signing with the Los Angeles Dodgers in 2002 was a widely publicized event on both sides of the Pacific. In the flurry of publicity put out by the Dodgers were photos of a smiling Ishii, even joking with the press in English, "Good weather, good golf courses, I'm a Californian." Trying to ride the wave of big-impact Japanese signings, the Dodgers' divisional rival San Francisco traded for outfielder Tsuyoshi Shinjo. Suddenly, it seemed as if everyone had to have an Asian.[28] Following the new wave of Japanese signings, Jim Allen of the *Daily*

Yomiuri noted that it was really the Dodgers who were following the Giants after seeing how popular the Shinjo trade was in San Francisco. "He is a very popular guy. He has a massive following in Japan because he is interested in image, celebrity. When the Giants got him, all of these Japanese fans wanted to see him play in San Francisco, and when the Dodgers saw that they salivated."[29] Baseball operations aside, there was a desire on the part of the Dodgers front office to uphold their image as major league baseball's Asian pioneer. The Dodgers had not experienced the economic synergy between exciting player and specialized fan base since Nomo's first years with the organization.

Ishii was to remedy that. He was a proven star in Japan, winning seventy-eight games over ten seasons and compiling an ERA of 3.38 for the Yakult Swallows. For marketing honchos like the Dodgers' Kris Rone, Ishii seemed a certain bonanza, while for General Manager Dan Evans the pitcher represented an opportunity to reconnect the rudderless, Murdoch-owned Dodgers with the O'Malley global tradition. The team's Pacific Rim connections would be revamped and luster restored. "When they signed Ishii, Dan Evans held a press conference in Japan," Allen recalled. "Ishii was signed across the Pacific, in L.A., yet they all flew to Japan for an official press conference."[30] Why? "Because," Evans said, "we know what a popular player Ishii is in Japan, and we want to appeal to the Japanese fan."[31] Evans and the Dodgers had in fact signed a pitcher who had the ability to win in the major leagues, albeit inconsistently, but they had erred in their assessment of who Ishii was in his country. "Ishii has zero popularity in Japan," states Allen, "He's a flake! He is a terrific pitcher, but a loner with no following whatsoever. He was better known for going to the mound with his fly unzipped than for his performances."[32] Either Evans was exaggerating his sense of Ishii's popularity in Japan, or he was misguided by operatives such as former manager Tommy Lasorda. Relying upon Lasorda for insight into Japan is like George Bush depending upon Bugs Bunny for advice on foreign policy: wisecracking is hardly wisdom. Particularly when the Dodgers had an "Asian Division," with such alleged experts as Acey Korogi, who should have been able to highlight the differences between Ishii and Nomo. At bottom, the signing made it clear that even clubs with a history of involvement in Japan don't always understand baseball outside of the white lines.

Ishii made it immediately apparent that he was as frivolous as Nomo was serious. Ishii didn't just ignore his body, he abused it with a three-pack-a-day cigarette habit and a penchant for junk food. Ishii considered himself a rebel, defined as someone who cares only for himself. In one remarkable scene from a documentary on Ishii shown on Japan's NHK television network in 2001, Ishii receives a gift of an autographed bat from Sammy Sosa: a welcome to the neighborhood from a reigning superstar. In the film, Ishii lays the bat down dismissively and says, "I'm only interested in myself."[33]

Forging the National Pastime

That Japan was introduced to the sport of baseball early in the Meiji Restoration (1868–1912) is not accidental. The Meiji Restoration was Japan's rapid reintroduction to Western culture after three hundred years of feudal isolation. Under the Meiji Emperor Mutsuhito, the army, government, and educational institutions were all modeled after European and American forms. Baseball was introduced as part of the physical educational system by Horace Wilson, an American missionary teacher. The first game was organized by another young American teacher, Albert Bates, who taught at Kaitaku University.[34]

Embraced as part of the American cutting-edge philosophy of physical education, and identified with the United States, the sport quickly took root in Japan. Baseball became one arena in which tensions between emerging modernism and hallowed traditions were defused. While the sport's foreign origins were acknowledged, the game was reconfigured to be Japanese by fusing it with traditional elements, and no institution did it better than Ichiko, the First Higher School of Tokyo.

Japan's leaders came from this elite school. For Ichiko, baseball became a contemporary extension of *Bushido*. Ichiko organized a baseball team almost at the inception of the school in 1886. To keep the players uncontaminated, they were housed in special dorms and lived by a code of physical discipline that would have made the Samurai proud. The team quickly became one of the best in Tokyo. Its main rival was an American-influenced school called Meiji Gakuin. In 1891 the two schools met in a clash of Japanese orientations: pro-West versus anti-West. Meiji Gakuin won the game, and tensions between the two schools grew. The loss to Meiji Gakuin inspired a determination not only to avenge the loss but to do so via the most traditional path: the Samurai code of behavior. The Ichiko team's regimen was nicknamed "Bloody Urine," because practice sessions were proudly said to last until the players were exhausted to the point of passing blood.[35] In short order, Ichiko developed a style of play called *seishin yakyu,* or spiritual baseball, which fused the game with martial arts.

Ichiko became a national phenomenon when it trounced a team of Americans from the Yokohama Athletic Club by the score of 29–4 in June 1896. The teams played two rematches, both won easily by Ichiko. In a third rematch, the Americans, augmented by sailors with extensive baseball experience, narrowly won. As news of the first Ichiko victory traveled outside of the school grounds, the media quickly elevated the victory to a sociopolitical level. Crowds gathered and chanted victory over the United States. The Japanese quickly folded these wins into their emerging international self-awareness and newfound respectability as a nation. They also came to see the game as an expression of their own culture, independent of the nation that had introduced them to baseball. "Ichiko players should ignore the American way and devise a system that suits Japanese," admonished their manager.[36]

The Political Economy of Japanese Baseball

Japanese baseball may be a study in nationalism and protectionism, but it is also a case study of the burden of some of the very elements that make it unique to Japan. Japanese baseball's strength—its tradition-bound structure—is also its weakness. What follows is an organizational look at the tension between traditional and modernizing influences in Japanese baseball.

Break Up the Giants!

From a political-economic point of view, the most fundamental difference between the major leagues and Japanese professional baseball has to do with the profit motive. In the majors teams are owned and operated to make money. All strategies are geared to that end, so that marketing the game to maximize profit is what determines success or failure. The current owners of the Boston Red Sox, for instance, bought the team in 2002 for an estimated $660 million, taking on a huge debt. With the game's second-highest payroll and a ballpark with the smallest seating capacity in the majors, they immediately set to generating new revenue streams. They added high-end seating, set up new concourses with food courts, and instituted a slew of marketing gambits to raise revenues. The Red Sox have even taken to selling and marketing MLB's online assets via a subsidiary company called Fenway Sports Group.[37] They have to, not only because the Commissioner's Office makes certain that teams keep their debt within manageable limits, but because it would be inconceivable that American owners wouldn't seek to maximize their investment.

Japanese teams, by contrast, have traditionally been owned for the purpose of advertising their corporate parent companies. Profits are nice but unnecessary. What matters in Japan is that the team's owner—the parent company—is in the public eye each day. So when the Hanshin Tigers play and the results are reported throughout the country, it is the railroad company that is being publicly paraded. It is the same for the Nippon Ham Fighters, owned by a pork manufacturer that, after buying the team, rose from Japan's fifth-largest meat company to its second-largest. In this context, the advertisement on the right field wall at Yankee Stadium for *Yomiuri Shimbun*—rather than for the newspaper's team, the Giants—makes sense. Even though the working agreement signed a few years back was between the Yomiuri Giants and the New York Yankees, it is to the benefit not of the Japanese team but of its parent firm, Yomiuri Group. National, prime-time advertising on Japanese television is so expensive that owning a team is cheaper than paying for advertising over the course of a season.

In a structural sense, these teams are somewhat in the mold of the semipro teams that used to be common in small-town America. Marty Kuehnert, who served briefly in 2005 as general manager of the new Rakuten franchise, and whose involvement with Japanese teams spans more than thirty years, argues, "Japanese baseball shouldn't really use the word *professional* in its title. They're really industrial teams, company-owned teams. Industrial teams really just publicize the company, give the employees something to do, and throw a little cash their way."[38] Consistent with that view, Robert Whiting notes that Japanese players

tend to identify themselves as company employees rather than perform-
ers or professional athletes.[39]

The Japanese team that has come to epitomize the game there is the
Yomiuri Giants. The Giants are a wildly successful team. Until quite
recently, they were led by a seventy-seven-year-old patrician, Tsuneo
Watanabe. Like all Japanese owners, Watanabe heads up a large corpora-
tion: Yomiuri Group. The crown jewel of this conglomerate is *Yomiuri
Shimbun,* the world's largest newspaper, but the group includes smaller
publishing efforts (*Daily Yomiuri, Hochi Shimbun*), television (Nippon
Television is the country's largest network, after public television), and
real estate development and leisure parks (Yomiuriland, an interest in the
Tokyo Dome).[40] For their success both on the field and off, the Yomiuri
Giants have been considered the Japanese equivalent of the New York
Yankees.

The Giants became Japan's team in part because they're located in the
largest city, and in part because they were so successful, winning twenty
championships, including nine in a row between 1965 and 1973.
According to Jim Allen, "There is an affinity for dynasties here in Japan.
Fans like a proven thing, like Chanel, the Yomiuri Giants, or the New
York Yankees. It's branding."[41]

The Giants increased their reach and popularity in the aftermath of
World War II by being televised nightly throughout Japan, becoming the
most widely followed franchise in the country. For years their ratings
topped 20; their games were sold out; they drafted the best players and
won championships. Their ability to generate revenue easily outstripped
that of any other team in Japan.[42] So dominant are the Giants that one
knowledgeable observer of the Japanese baseball scene half-jokingly contends, "The Japanese pro league was created, in one sense, as a way to
give the Giants someone to play."[43]

The Giants and Watanabe are the six hundred–pound gorilla in
Nippon Professional Baseball. Consider their domination of the televi-
sion market and its revenues. The *Daily Yomiuri*'s baseball reporter Jim
Allen estimated the revenue the team garners and its market share:

> The home team gets 100 percent of the revenue from home
> games. There's no sharing of revenues. Here is my ballpark esti-

mate: The Giants generate about 80 percent of the television revenue in Japan. They get to keep about 40 percent of that—that is, they get to keep roughly 35 percent to 40 percent of all the television revenue in Japan.

The TV revenue is per game. The amount of money a home team is going to get against the Giants is somewhere between $8 [million] and $16 million per game. Nobody will confirm this. I'm guessing $10 million per game, and it's because prime-time, nationwide advertising is so expensive in Japan. So that's $10 million a game for 140 games; that's probably 80 percent of all TV revenues. The Giants will get half of that. Of course, they don't have to pay for their home games, because they're broadcasting on their own network. So they're getting seventy games at $10 million per game, and that makes $700 million. The other Central League teams get their 10 percent of all TV revenues. The Pacific League teams get about 1.8 percent of the package. So it's 40 percent for the Giants, 10 percent [each] for the five [other] Central League teams, and 1.8 percent [each] for the six Pacific League teams.[44]

This lion's share of the wealth also explains why the Giants get their pick of players in the draft and through free agency. They can outspend anyone and have established a draft system that allows them to get any player they want. According to Kuehnert, this is a system that Watanabe protects against any changes:

No team can be competitive if the draft comes along and you have no chance for the number one pick, no chance for the number two. You're going to get the fifteenth or sixteenth player. You'll never get a decent player in this system! In Japan there's a "reverse designation system," where the guy can say where it is he wants to go. That's created by Watanabe. It applies to Industrial League or college players, and Watanabe wants to extend it to high school players. You know how you determine where you go? It's how much you get under the table. The Giants tell the number one pick, "You come with us, and you get

$10 million. And you say that it's been your lifelong dream to play for Yomiuri."[45]

The Worm Turns

In a scandal that "suddenly" surfaced in August 2004, the Yomiuri Giants were caught offering a college pitcher the equivalent of $20,000 under the table to play for them. While violating collegiate regulations, the Giants were only following a long-standing tradition of teams surreptitiously paying college players. The future Japanese Hall of Fame pitcher Tadashi Sugiura, for instance, was given an allowance by the Nankai Hawks while at Rikkyo University in the 1950s. In an audacious act of hypocrisy, the Japan Scholastic Baseball Federation decried the Giants' flagrantly illegal act. To put the matter aside, Yomiuri owner Watanabe resigned from the club—a ceremonial gesture at best, for he then handpicked his replacement, another Yomiuri executive, Takuo Takahana. The decades-long domination of the NPB by one team has, without question, harmed the development of professional baseball in Japan. Once the best and brightest began defecting to the United States, however, the crisis came into full relief.

The same recession that has gripped Japan since the early 1990s has had a dampening effect on the willingness of owners to buy and run teams only for free advertising. In a departure from the traditional approach, the president of the Osaka-based railway corporation Kintetsu, Masanori Yamaguchi, flatly stated in the summer of 2004, "It's impossible to continue putting management resources into baseball when there is no prospect of paying dividends."[46] The Kintetsu Buffaloes had been hemorrhaging losses in the neighborhood of $40 million a year for several years. Declines in attendance, rising player salaries, and a stadium lease that cost a whopping $10 million put the franchise in the position of seeking a merger with another Pacific League team, the Orix BlueWave. Kintetsu became the poster child for Japan's crisis, but a complex of factors has infected every team and weakened the game. Kintetsu didn't just single out baseball. "Baseball cannot be the only exception," noted one corporation executive, pointing to the withdrawal of the company from "unprofitable sectors such as theme parks, theaters, as well as real estate operations."[47]

When Kintetsu announced that it couldn't continue to lose money on the Buffaloes at the rate of $40 million a year, and that it was selling the naming rights to the club, the freshly minted commissioner, Yasuchika Negoro, backed by Watanabe, attempted to stop the deal. "It's against the rules of Japanese baseball," declared Watanabe. Other owners disagreed. "It's the same as selling a team," said one. Kuehnert pointed out a precedent, citing his tenure with the Nishitetsu Lions, whose owner had sold the naming rights.[48] History and precedence only get in the way of business as usual. The Kintetsu franchise's economic travails eventually led to a mid-summer 2004 announcement of merger with the Orix BlueWave (like the Buffaloes, in the weaker Pacific League).

If pro teams in Japan reject the "cheap advertising" premise for owning a team, then future owners will be more likely to demand that the teams be run profitably. For teams to turn a profit, however, some form of revenue sharing must be established, a development that would diminish Yomiuri's economic domination. The threat of ruin, however, could serve as an impetus for owners to band together against Watanabe and reform the game. The Kintetsu-Orix and serious talk in 2004 of merging the two leagues galvanized some of the owners to openly oppose Watanabe's positions on the future of the game.

Most baseball insiders in Japan realize that the first and most formidable stumbling block to reorganization is Watanabe. Kuehnert is not alone in his assessment of the impediment that Watanabe constitutes to the advancement of the league: "Whether you have one league or two leagues, as long as you have a system built around one team, and which benefits one team—a team that monopolizes the revenues, the media, and where the players go—that's an unsound system. . . . Watanabe can do whatever he wants. He told the players to go to hell yesterday. The players wanted to meet with him, and he said, 'There's nothing in the rule book that says we have to talk to the players. Players are not at the same level as us.' "[49]

The "C" Word: Contraction

The proposal to merge the Buffaloes and BlueWave sent shock waves through the Japanese baseball community. Rumors of other mergers quickly followed, setting into motion a full-blown crisis. From the owners' perspective, combining these two would create structural imbalance and a scheduling nightmare, so contraction of a second pair of clubs began to be discussed. Then came rumors that the two six-team leagues would be collapsed into a single ten-team league. The formally stated reason for contraction was an issue not of economics but of quality. "There are a lot of games now that you would be hard pressed to call 'pro caliber.' But with 10 teams, higher quality of play would attract more interest from fans," Seibu Lions owner Yoshiaki Tsutsumi said.[50]

In the midst of these revelations came the news of a buyer for the Buffaloes, someone willing to rescue the team and the league. This should have been welcome news indeed. The commissioner would be spared having to make far-reaching decisions in his first days in office. The other owners would be allowed to conduct their affairs as usual. In place of a collective sigh, however, the baseball establishment acted as if a rabid animal had been thrown in their midst. The noxious beast was a thirty-one-year-old Internet wiz, Takafumi Horie. Most owners are at least twice Horie's age and considered his youth enough to warrant his dismissal, but his enterprise—the successful Internet firm Livedoor—also caused consternation. The owners are all representatives of traditional industrial and corporate sectors. Horie represented the new and little-understood world of information technology (as of late 2005, one still could not email most Japanese teams or the Nippon Professional Baseball league). Watanabe dismissed the effort; Livedoor "was a new company that he knows nothing about and therefore he has no intention of meeting with Horie."[51] Later, a Yomiuri executive declared on television that Horie had been rejected because he never wore a tie, which showed disrespect for the old ways. The owners and league were clearly unnerved by the audaciousness of this young upstart from an exotic field.

Horie's ideas were even more unconventional than his dress. He intended to bring a venture capital outlook to the game, including the extension of stock options to fans and players, and to employ modern marketing principles, such as marketing the players over the Internet.[52] But Kintetsu officials rejected Horie's offer, and the Commissioner's Office announced that Kintetsu's future had been decided via a merger with Orix.

A second plan for contraction was quickly put on the table when Seibu Lions owner Yoshiaki Tsutsumi argued for the formation of a single league with ten teams. All of these discussions of contraction would involve the loss of jobs as well. The number of players involved in this would be in the hundreds, though ownership tried to appease the players by assuring them that that would not happen. Still the Kintetsu-Orix merger could have cost as many as thirty players their jobs. The pending disaster for players was severe enough to cause the pusillanimous players union to threaten a strike.

Building of Emotions and Resistance

Calls for reform came slowly at first, and then the movement gained momentum from disparate quarters: kill the merger, protect the players, find a buyer, keep the two-league system. The Players Association, in a bold move, began to call on fans to come to their aid. Fans responded with petition drives, but that did little to assuage the anxiety because the owners were for the most part dismissive of their concerns. At Kintetsu Buffaloes games fans were reported screaming obscenities at Watanabe. Players Association head Atsuya Furuta announced that the union's home page would make fan feedback easier. The fans were way ahead of the union. When Livedoor's Horie attended a Kintetsu game on July 4, the fans chanted slogans like "God, Buddha, Mr. Horie." Visiting the team store to assess the merchandizing of the team, Horie was mobbed by more than one thousand fans, and later he addressed thousands more. Players waved to fans to show solidarity with their shouts opposing the merger.[53]

There were even the stirrings of sentiment from other owners against Watanabe's dictatorial manner, especially with regard to contraction. On July 16 the other five Central League team owners convened a meeting in Osaka. Missing was Yomiuri's Watanabe. The owners decided to abandon the plan, favored by Watanabe, of contraction to a single league. More bad news for the Yomiuri boss followed, as Sanyo, a key sponsor of the All-Star series, announced that it would terminate its relationship with the event if it went to the East-West format that Watanabe was pushing to accommodate his single-league format. Sanyo, in essence, went on record in support of the two-league structure. Reform was in the air that day, as the Hanshin Tigers intended to propose interleague play. Other Central League owners opposed the plan because their teams would play fewer games against the Giants and lose revenue as a result. The Tigers, also a Central League team, were going against their own vested interests in what can only be understood as a snub of the Watanabe control of the game. Two months later Watanabe let it be known in an interview that he perceived a concerted effort to challenge the Yomiuri Giants.[54]

By late summer 2004 the players union had been backed into a corner. Its effort to block the Kintetsu-Orix merger had been rejected by the Tokyo District Court in late August, and the union had few options but to take a strike vote. The players voted overwhelmingly on September 9 to strike. Although the court had chastised the players union for not taking into consideration the fans of the country, public opinion polls were solidly behind the strike. In one poll conducted by the Kyodo News Service, 80 percent of the respondents backed the union. Fan support for the players was so overwhelming that the owners' option of a preemptive lockout was untenable.[55]

On September 18 and 19, 2004, the Japanese Players Association went on the first strike in league history. Their main demand was the retention of the two-league, twelve-team format in the NPB. Even in striking, the Japanese sense of "wa" was evident. The walkout, which rattled the players, was the shortest baseball strike on record. Afterward, Robert Whiting told me, "The players apologized repeatedly and held free clinics to appease fans' sense of displeasure, then returned to work on Monday. A two-day strike!"[56]

The Kintetsu-Orix merger was passed by the owners, but to appease the union and fans, a new team was added to the league. It is noteworthy that that team was also fronted by an Internet-related company. By early October, Rakuten, the nation's largest online shopping mall operator, formally announced its bid for the vacant twelfth spot in the league. Rakuten owner Hiroshi Mikitani took a page from the Livedoor deliberations. He shaved off his beard and bought a new suit, hoping to create an image that would help him avoid unnecessary obstacles. His first order of business, however, was to name Marty Kuehnert as the general manager of the new team. A third Internet firm, Softbank, made a move to buy the Daiei Hawks, owned by another financially troubled corporation.

Even with the disgrace that was to come to Horie in 2006, the reforms that began in the summer of 2004 were reminiscent of the dismantling of the Berlin Wall. Everyone but Watanabe and the Giants was giddy with anticipation of the changes, and any change seemed to be good change. The naming of Kuehnert would have been a satisfying place to end this story, but though Rakuten's youthful owner seemed to be part of a new wave, he was in fact staunchly conservative in a number of ways. When Rakuten got off to a terrible start in 2005—5 and 22 in April—Mikitani shaved his head in a traditional act of self-purification and removed Kuehnert from his post. The specter of gaijin-baiting rose, prompting one longtime sportswriter in Tokyo to muse, "When the blame game starts, the gaijin had better take cover."[57]

Japanese–MLB Relations

MLBI Comes to Tokyo

Japan's preoccupation with maintaining its sovereignty is increasingly at odds with its need to take its place among the international baseball powers. Hence working with Major League Baseball is predictably conflict-laden.

The press conference was called for 2 P.M. on July 8, 2004, at the Tokyo Dome Hotel to announce the upcoming fall All-Star series between the Nippon Professional Baseball champions and a group of major league all-stars. On the cab ride over, Jim Small, manager of the Tokyo office for MLB, half-laments his lack of preparation. He intends to deliver his part of the press conference in Japanese (which he has been busily studying a few nights a week), but he likes to rehearse such an address a few times before giving it, and there just hasn't been time.

About 120 members of the press are waiting to listen as Major League Baseball International's Small and executives from the event's sponsor, the newspaper *Mainichi Shimbun*, deliver details of the series. Small is marking his office's first full year in Japan, heading up MLBI's efforts to tend to existing business and cultivate more in Japan. And business has been good. Japan currently accounts for a bit more than 60 percent of MLBI's revenues. Record television broadcast deals, new sponsors, and licensing are all robust business indexes. Small has been busily tending to programs in both formative and final stages, as well as the day-to-day issues—banks, checks, and signature stamps, the latter very important in Japan. Four new sponsors have been signed by Small: Suntory's Magnum Dry Beer, Meiji Yasuda Life Insurance, Kagome Fruit and Vegetable Juice, and Shiseido Cosmetics. Small is an impressive blend of energy, curiosity, intelligence, and sagacity. His sense of when to be formal and when to kick back, when to bow and when to glad-hand, is unerring, and he is always MLBI's lead man in the field.

Small gets up, adjusts the mike, and addresses his audience in Japanese. He lets them know that the All-Star series is drawing keen interest on the part of MLB players, but the media want names. Is Bonds coming? Pedro Martínez? Small reluctantly dishes out one name: "Albert Pujols is interested." Good enough! (In the event, Pujols did not sign on.) Typically, the media have no questions during the question-and-answer session, reserving inquiries for after. (In an odd twist, Japanese reporters generally find the formality of the press conference too intimidating.) The press conference goes without a hitch, except that the official poster of the event had had to be changed just before the start. Says Small, "The poster that was up today said 'NPB vs. MLB.' When I saw it the other day, the MLB was in red, white, and blue. I told them, 'You can't do that. We're a league representing thirty-three countries. It's not just the U.S. versus you.'" Everyone at MLBI protects the brand and pushes the international face of MLB. Jim handles these matters diplomatically. No one at Mainichi or anywhere else lost any face.

MLBI has done so much business in Japan that it needed a permanent presence. This is led by a newly minted television contract with the Japanese advertising giant Dentsu: a six-year, $275 million deal. It is the largest international television deal negotiated by any U.S. sports league. Dentsu will lease broadcasting rights from MLB and sublease rights to various Japanese networks. The size of this broadcasting package reflects the steadily increasing number of Japanese players in North America, which in turn drives television ratings up. In 2003 there were 272 regular-season games broadcast in Japan, averaging 1.5 million viewers per game, an increase of 55 percent over 2002. There were more than 300 games televised in 2004. The first game of the 2003 World Series, featuring the

New York Yankees' Hideki Matsui, was the most-watched major league game ever in Japan.[58]

The New York Yankees and the Tampa Bay Devil Rays opened the 2004 season in Tokyo, the most significant of several cooperative events that year between the two nations' baseball organizations. That major undertaking required extensive negotiations involving everyone in MLB from the Commissioner's Office to the teams to the Players Association, as well as Japanese sponsors, airlines, hotels, legal experts—and that was before the teams arrived. Small was the point man in this effort. Having seen him function in Venezuela, I knew his freneticism could easily pull together everything needed for this kind of cross-cultural extravaganza, but the distances involved and the culture of doing business in Japan created special conditions and challenges.

The logistics of the trip were daunting. Fourteen-hour flights and a ten-hour time difference turn biological clocks upside down. MLBI could do nothing to shorten the trip, so it attempted to eliminate as much of the disruption that accompanies a trip like this as possible. It booked roomy jets and expedited service with U.S. Immigration. On the ground the players were cocooned, as Small explained: "Our goal is to eliminate the culture completely, or as much as possible, during the 2½ hours they are on the field. We want those 2½ hours to be exactly like if they were playing at Tropicana Field. But outside those 2½ hours we want them to experience and enjoy the culture."[59] Pre- and postgame food consisted of "normal food"—that is, normal American food: pizza, spaghetti, filet mignon. About 150 people on each team traveled, and the logistics involved everything from bringing ultrasound machines and a gaggle of doctors and therapists to accommodating the players' wives, three of whom were pregnant. Chuck LaMar, the Devil Rays general manager, was even given a Japanese cell phone and fax machine, and his number was sent to other GMs so that he could conduct business as if he were back in Florida. The event was widely followed on both sides of the Pacific.

In November 2004 the MLB-NPB All-Star series took place in four different cities in Japan. Roger Clemens, David Ortiz, and Manny Ramírez were among the major league stars. Los Angeles Dodgers pitcher Kazuhisa Ishii also made the trip, pitching twice. The series was won by MLB five games to three and featured some wonderful performances.

The most impressive was Ortiz's home run at the Tokyo Dome that traveled an estimated 514 feet: the Japanese do love that kind of drive. Events like this generate revenue for MLBI, but, as important, they serve to deepen the ties between baseball institutions in these countries. The nature of that relationship is oddly packed with jocularity and jostling, with solidarity and suspicion. It is neither as altruistic nor as innocent as it is portrayed in the press. It is about business and national bragging rights, as much as it is about a shared passion for the game.

MLB Domination or Reciprocal Relations?

There are those who view MLB as a colonizer, exploiting foreign players to fill out its rosters, selling itself around the world, busily generating new markets where none existed, and all with little or no concern for local concerns. This is classic dependency theory in a baseball jersey. The contrasting model of what is currently happening has MLB leading the internationalization of baseball, with other countries increasingly sharing power and finding ways to push their own national agendas. There is truth in both perspectives.

The migration of Japanese stars to major league baseball has caused consternation in certain circles. The fear that Japanese baseball would be fatally weakened and ultimately reduced to a feeder system for MLB has been on the rise since Ichiro's startling success in America. Japan's Central Research Services, a polling firm, conducted a survey for Major League Baseball International in 2004. One question asked of fans was whether they were worried that Japanese baseball would become an adjunct to MLB. Of two thousand people surveyed, 21 percent voiced that concern.[60] The fear of losing identity to the West is an old one in Japan. Mitsutoshi Koyata, a fifty-one-year-old father of two in Tokyo, fretted, "I would hate to see baseball decline in Japan—I'm concerned about its future. I feel a little sad because Japanese baseball may become a farm league for Americans."[61]

The Japanese sense of nationalism is also invoked, however, as pride in the accomplishments of emigrés to the major leagues. Hiromoto Okubo, a Tokyo sports commentator, put a positive spin on Japanese players' emigration: "The Japanese always used to feel inferior. We players were awed by American baseball. But now because our players are in America, we have changed our perspective. We're not so modest. We have more confidence."[62] "This is great for Japan," beams Nobuo Hakoyama, a fifty-two-year-old Tokyo resident. "Hopefully, with more players like [Ichiro] going abroad, it will help to narrow the gap between American and Japanese baseball."[63] However it is viewed, the movement of top Japanese players to the major leagues will have the effect of drawing the two countries into an ever-closer relationship.

Looking at marketing relations between MLB and NPB we see similar tensions. In extended discussions with Jim Small, several things grew increasingly clear about MLBI's strategy for Japan. Buoyed by its recent successes, when MLBI opened its Tokyo office, it declared its intentions: "It will take a long time for us to reach our goal here, and that goal quite frankly is to make our brand ubiquitous here, to make it the strongest brand in Japan." Small knows that MLB is viewed with some suspicion among the old-guard Japanese, and he is sensitive to that resistance, whenever possible seeking to include the Japanese as equal partners. But there is business to be done here, and Toyota had no compunctions about entering U.S. markets with the same sort of competitive zeal that Small is voicing on MLBI's part:

> My first week on the job here, I walked into a meeting with general managers of the NPB, and there were not a lot of smiling faces in there. Here I am opening up shop and they're worried that we're going to take their players, take their market, take their yen away from them. It's certainly a big issue everywhere we go. There are times when we need to bend over backwards to accommodate them, in part because we're looked at as a threat. But there are times when we need to be aggressive in a way that opens us up to being thought of as pushy foreigners.[64]

MLBI is in a position to be economically successful in Japan because of the evident gap between aggressive American marketing and Japanese baseball's lackluster efforts in that arena. Most American observers are chagrined by the minimal Japanese baseball marketing effort. Marty Kuehnert, who has dealt with NPB for decades, shakes his head in disbelief on the subject. He dismissed the most recent ad campaign of the Yomiuri Giants, built around the phrase "Fresh fight for the team." Said

Kuehnert, "I bet this new catch phrase probably cost them a hundred thousand dollars to concoct. They think that's positive change. This year their 'image girl' is this young girl singer on a television drama. These attempts are meaningless without any serious strategy or change. Is there any store in the country where a kid can go in and buy the hat of their favorite team? No. We [the Japanese] don't even have a market within our own country."[65]

While MLBI is content at present to market the Japanese players that are in America, their larger goal is to push major league baseball through the players. Sponsors are being encouraged to use all the league's logos. According to Small,

> Ichiro had a multiyear deal with Pepsi. They chose not to use him in their campaign this year. We sell team marks [a team brand in association with a player] rights so that they can put them in uniform and associate with a brand, and associate with Ichiro. We say, "Why buy Clark Kent, when you can buy Superman [in uniform]? We were able to talk them into not only buying the marks, but paying a little more and getting player marks for all the players in the MLB Players Association. . . . The reason we did that was to build the brand.[66]

In Small's argument for international marketing, however, a contradiction emerges. On the one hand, MLBI argues that it is not identified with one nation, that it has an international character. On the other hand, MLBI is very much rooted in the American corporate culture, and is effectively identified with the United States.

Two prevailing conditions inform Small's sense of baseball's marketing advantage over other competitors. First, in Japan, baseball, whether MLB or NPB, is more important than other sports. After Nippon Professional Baseball, no other sport leagues rank higher in Japanese consciousness than MLB.[67] Secondly, the Japanese claim the sport of baseball as theirs, even to the point of fabricating their own origin myth: "I've had Japanese guys tell me that baseball began here, and was exported to the States a hundred years ago," reveals Small. This cultural sense of ownership of the game makes the Japanese both willing consumers and a bit thin-skinned about Americans coming into their world, their market.

Small also understands that the Japanese sense of ownership of their game reflects other—less flattering—dimensions of their culture. For example, the Japanese historically have played the role of cultural (and sometimes military) aggressor against other Asian countries—a parallel to the way they perceive the United States bullying them. It is telling that the Chinese perceive baseball as an "Asian sport," and thus beating the Japanese in the game has a very personal edge to it. "We're optimistic about China," Small reports, "because to them baseball is an Asian sport, not an American sport. And their goal—they told me—is to beat the Japanese. They've got a whole regional geopolitical thing about it. I mean, the Chinese may know that baseball somehow came from America, but they don't care because they're interested in dealing with the Japanese."[68]

With this in mind, globalized baseball could take a giant step forward if an Intra-Pacific League were formed, including South Korea, Taiwan, China, and Australia, along with Japan. The caliber of competition and play could be greatly increased by tapping some of the nationalist antipathies that exist among this grouping.

MLB has the ability to promote its interests in subtle ways that create the impression of cooperation and mutual consent, but at times MLB acts aggressively to promote its interests, as in the case of Alfonso Soriano, for example. Kevin Millar provides another case in point. Theo Epstein, the general manager of the Boston Red Sox, considered Millar one of "the better unknown hitters in baseball" and attempted to sign him to a 2003 contract as a free agent. The Florida Marlins, for whom Millar had played in 2002, had agreed to allow Millar to negotiate a contract with Japan's Chunichi Dragons for two years and $6.2 million. Then in a rapid turnaround, Millar declared that he did not want to go to Japan with the United States on the brink of war with Iraq and the Red Sox showing an interest in signing him. Chunichi, backed by NPB, pressed its case, as did MLB. Only after MLB and the Major League Baseball Players Association threatened to cancel the proposed opening of the 2003 season by the Seattle Mariners and Oakland Athletics in Tokyo did Chunichi drop its claim on Millar. The *Boston Globe's* Gordon Edes reported, "The Marlins returned $1.2 million to Chunichi that the Dragons had paid for the rights to sign him, then sold him to the Red

Sox for the same amount."[69] What is revealing—though hardly surprising—is that MLB clearly has the authority to press its agenda in international dealings. The degree of reciprocal influence between MLB and NPB may be growing, but it remains minimal.

The Millar case represents an instance in which MLB stepped in to void a contract between an American player and a Japanese team. Do Japanese professional teams have the same degree of control over the movement of their players through those contractual loopholes that have become points of contention? The cases of Hideo Nomo and Alfonso Soriano clearly show that the NPB was unable to prevent the loss of players; the "posting" provision of their free agency system represents an effort at least to gain some sort of compensation for the losses.

Reciprocal Flow

True to the laws of physics, for every reaction there is a reaction, and while MLB's power is considerable, the Japanese have been able to exert a growing influence. Whiting reported that Japanese views of training—which some view as their paramount accomplishment in the history of the game—are being incorporated by MLB. When he managed the Seattle Mariners, Bob Melvin began to incorporate Japanese training routines for bunting, advancing the runner, base stealing, and other skills. Japanese excellence in conditioning and practice is legendary. In fact, they are so preoccupied with practice that the Japanese sportswriter Masayuki Tamaki jokes that NPB "should replace the Japan Series with a 'practice tournament' to see who can practice the most."[70]

One straightforward example of Japanese influence on Major League Baseball was the purchase of the Seattle Mariners by Hiroshi Yamauchi in 1992. After years of fielding teams with losing records and poor attendance, Mariners owner Jeff Smulyan decided to move the franchise to a warmer city. Local civic leaders spearheaded efforts to keep the team in Seattle. One of these local leaders was Yamauchi's son-in law, Minoru Arakawa, who ran U.S. Nintendo operations and who loved the Mariners. He approached his father-in-law, according to Marty Kuehnert, asking him, "We're about to lose our baseball team, and it's not good for the Pacific Northwest. Would you buy them and keep them here for the good of the State of Washington?"[71] Yamauchi readily agreed. Little did he know that this magnanimous gesture would be interpreted by MLB and team owners still edgy in the wake of the robust growth of the Japanese economy as an attempt on the part of the Japanese to "buy up" more of Americans' national heritage. Yamauchi's move to buy the team led to a minor rash of Japan-bashing, including a photograph of a group of U.S. congressmen smashing a Japanese-made car with sledgehammers. The Japanese, it should be noted, are not above their own provincial sentiments. In 2003, when the American firm Ripplewood sought to buy the Daiei Hawks, it was stymied by the Yomiuri Giants' Watanabe, who would not allow the foreign "vultures" into the fold.[72] The Commissioner's Office and MLB eventually agreed to Yamauchi's purchase of the Mariners, but only under the strictest conditions: Yamauchi could buy no more than 60 percent of the team and had to limit his voting interest to less than 50 percent. This protectionist treatment of Yamauchi makes subsequent MLB statements about Japanese protectionist impulses ring hollow. Fortunately for Seattle, Yamauchi was not a baseball-mad meddling owner (he has never even seen the team play), nor was he looking for a profitable venture (the team had perennially lost money), so he remained above the xenophobic American reaction. The Mariners, of course, went on to become contenders and acquired Ichiro, who rapidly—and without any prejudice—became a national icon. The irony is that it was Yamauchi who, in a rare role as mediator, suggested that Seattle secure Ichiro; hence this victim of MLB prejudice became instrumental in helping MLB look progressive and globally active.

There is no question that MLBI, on some level, plays an invader's role in Japan. Japanese owners might benefit from the marketing experience of Jim Small or Marty Kuehnert, but they no doubt resent the implication that U.S. interests will dictate, determine, or even guide Japanese baseball to the next level. Some of this antagonism must have filtered into the Japanese threat to forgo the upcoming baseball World Cup that MLBI was busily cobbling together for 2006.

A less publicized illustration of the reciprocal flow of U.S. and Japanese influence involves Hideo Nomo. In 2003 Nomo and his partners bought the Elmira, New York, baseball team, the Pioneers, in the independent Northeast League. Marty Kuehnert feels certain that the purchase was in part prompted by a cause Nomo is supporting back in Japan. The failure of the industrial leagues in Japan has exacerbated the shortage of venues for players who are not drafted or recruited by colleges. One of the teams that was eliminated was the very one that gave Nomo his big break. "He feels he owes something to baseball here [in Japan]," Kuehnert says. "First thing is to buy the Elmira club. He's letting a certain number of Japanese players that got cut or washed out go to Elmira to play. The roster had about three pitchers and two position players. Don Nomura [Nomo's agent] scouts guys out here, and they always have a place to play now. That's one of the biggest reasons they bought it."[73] Nomo's adventure as a baseball executive illustrates a degree of Japanese influence in North America.

The movement of players between the two countries has become more frequent and more nuanced. The one-way flow of talent changed when Cecil Fielder, trapped as a part-time player for the Toronto Blue Jays for four years, went to Japan. He signed with the Hanshin Tigers in 1989 and clubbed thirty-eight home runs in 106 games. That got the interest of the "other" Tigers, the ones in Detroit, who signed Fielder to a two-year contract. In 1990 Cecil Fielder hit fifty-one home runs for Detroit, and his major league career was finally launched. After Fielder's American success, Japan could no longer be thought of as an elephant's graveyard for over-the-hill American players. Other non-Japanese players have come to the major leagues via Japan. Julio Franco, Shane Mack, and Darryl May also played their way back, and as we have seen, Texas Rangers second baseman Alfonso Soriano launched his career in Japan as a product of the Hiroshima Carp's Dominican academy. Clearly, MLB no longer views the talent flow as one-way. Players from around the baseball world are finding their way to North American clubs at all levels.

Nor do refurbished former major leaguers and Japanese stars come only to play in the American big leagues. Increasingly, Japanese players and others are being sought for play in the U.S. minor leagues. These players come from the ranks of high school and university teams, many of them from baseball factories. Jim Allen considers this a newly contested area between the United States and Japan: "This past year there were three or four Japanese guys who were drafted in American minor league ball. They come out of high school, college, and industrial leagues. I think there's about a dozen playing in the American minor league system. That number will no doubt increase each year."[74]

In a dramatic new development, a Japanese team joined the newly minted independent Golden Baseball League. The Samurai Bears became one of the eight founding teams in this league in 2005. All of the teams are owned by the league, but the Bears are made up of Japanese players who had gone undrafted in Japan, where only eighty-five players are chosen. With about four thousand high schools and dozens of universities fielding teams in Japan, hundreds of highly skilled players never get the opportunity to play professionally. Managed by one of the most successful gaijin players to have played in Japan, Warren Cromartie, the Samurai Bears play a ninety-game schedule as, in Cromartie's words, a "farm system for Japanese ballplayers."[75] They do this all as a road team; they have no home field. Their existence is further proof of the reciprocal flow that exists between the two nations.

Talent is flowing both directions at all levels. We have entered an era in which labor is leading the way to globalization. Whereas Americans have thought of global baseball as having a major league roster that resembles a mini–United Nations, the actual developments reach more deeply. Players are being developed the world over, and they are moving in myriad directions. While becoming a major leaguer is still the ultimate goal, players move toward that goal in zigzag fashion. One player might go to Japan before landing on a major league roster. Another might be developed by a Japanese club in the Dominican Republic to play in Japan, then go on to the United States. Major leaguers—mostly, but not exclusively Americans—leave to play in Japan, throughout the Caribbean and Latin America. Tuffy Rhodes, currently a star in Japan and co-record holder, with Oh, for home runs in a season, resurrected his career after a forgettable effort with the Astros and Cubs. And Darryl May was the reason Kansas City Royals G.M. Allard Baird went to Japan. Small-market teams go to Japan in search of affordable talent, whether American or foreign.

These crises and currents all indicate that Japan is modernizing. The loss of its stars will hasten that process, but if Japanese baseball continues to cling to nationalist prejudices, it will be missing the opportunity to become a global player. Currently Japan is developing into the most important baseball presence outside of North America. Because it has both economic clout and a solid player development system, Japan is critical to international efforts and to MLB's health. Trying to defend the Japanese character of the game is in all likelihood a losing proposition; efforts should instead emphasize the possibility of locating a major league franchise in Tokyo, or building a regional league structure that would play for the Asian Cup every two years. In time, when the game has evolved in China, the formation of an Asian professional league might be advisable. This could have the effect of shifting Japan's primary focus from its relationship with the United States to its relationship with other Asian partners. For its part, MLB must allow decentralization of its power and the ascendance of other countries as equal partners; it must recognize a future of stewardship, not of empire. In the long run, imperial notions fail, because the center cannot hold.

6

ITALY, GERMANY, AND THE UNITED KINGDOM: THE EUROPEAN BACKWATER

Only in the context of baseball could Europe be considered underdeveloped. But by the standards of Major League Baseball, the continent is positively Third World. In countries like England softball is better known than baseball. Even in the two best-developed baseball countries— the Netherlands and Italy—citizens often seem surprised that the sport is played there. Not surprisingly, when a European signs a baseball contract, he generally goes unnoticed at home and becomes a quirky trivia question here—"Who was the first German player to sign a baseball contract?" Major League Baseball International is undeterred, however; borrowing a page from the U.S. Marshall Plan of 1948, MLBI has targeted Europe as a growth area, suitable for the deployment of resources.

Europe as a whole is considered a tier three area for baseball, but there is considerable variation within the continent. I have picked three countries, at different points of development, to illustrate this range. Italy is considered to be a European baseball power. It has an excellent track record in international competition, good facilities, and a fairly competitive club structure that is semiprofessional in nature. Germany is in the middle of the pack. It has a large player base but has not fared well in international competition. The United Kingdom has been showered with MLBI resources, has grassroots programs, has experienced growth in coaching and youth exposure, but has performed poorly in international competition and in producing skilled players. Compared with eastern Asia or Latin America, Europe is in its baseball infancy. As a result, its leagues lack exposure and have little chance to attract the most talented athletes from the best-developed sports in their own country. This has proven to be especially difficult in Europe because of two conditions: the overwhelming dominance of soccer and the comparative affluence of most western European societies.

Italy

It might seem contradictory to say that in Italy, where food is a religious experience, the citizens are not hungry, but where baseball is concerned, that seems to be the case. Italians are considered a European baseball power, but there have been only five major leaguers who were born in Italy, and all of them emigrated to the United States early in life. Are the reasons why to be sought in the realm of physiology—are Italians just too small? Is it because they don't have the venerable traditions of other baseball-rich countries? Or is it organizational, a function of the way the game is played in the country? I've heard knowledgeable baseball people cite all three potential reasons why the Italians "just haven't taken the game to the next level."

Baseball Origins

When Mario Ottino emigrated to the United States in 1909, at age four, he went through many changes, among them his name. Freshly minted as Max Ott, he busily assimilated to his adoptive country—as did countless other immigrants—by falling in love with baseball. Reminiscent of the lengths to which Dominican boys go to play the game, Mario/Max and his friends would stitch together balls made from rags and socks and play forever.[1] Max and his mother returned to his original home of Turin, Italy, twice for lengthy periods, during which he took his love of baseball back with him. In his first visit, at age fourteen, Ott took along his baseball mitt and ball. Soon he organized the local children into two teams and staged what appears to have been the first game of baseball in Italy, in 1919. During his two-year stay, he and his friends played regularly.

When Ott returned once more to Italy after World War II, U.S. soldiers had succeeded in teaching and developing softball—rather than baseball—throughout the region surrounding Rome, and north into

Milan. Ott worked hard to get Italians playing baseball again, finally succeeding in 1948. A year later eighteen teams had been organized. The apex of Italian baseball—the national team—was instituted in 1952, and Italy played its first international contest against Spain. The Italians lost badly to a Spanish team stacked with Venezuelans, but they learned an invaluable lesson for European baseball: bring in auxiliaries from baseball-rich countries. In 1954, using foreign players, the Italian national team won its first European Championship, and for the next dozen years the Italians and the Dutch battled for European supremacy. That dominance is evident both in the national team and in what is called "club baseball."

The National Team

Dan Bonanno is an American who, after playing college ball, was recruited to play for the Italian national team in 1982. He points out that the national team holds a privileged position: "In Italy they're pretty well developed. Consequently, their Olympic Committee and the Italian Baseball Federation back the national team. There's a lot of money going to the national team. They always go to the Olympics."[2] MLBI's European director, Clive Russell, says that all of Europe is similarly focused: "Essentially, the development of baseball in Europe at the federation level is all around the Olympics, and around the potential for your team to qualify for the Olympics. . . . So if your country wins medals and participates strongly, that gives you a buzz in your country, not to mention substantial funding for you through your federation."[3]

Buoyed by foreign players, the Italians sought to integrate those foreigners into local life. The *oriundo,* or foreign Italian resident—typically an American player with Italian roots—was able to obtain an Italian passport and legally play for the national team, and to earn a living by playing and coaching throughout Italy in between international competitions. From 1975 to 1980 Italy won European Championships, and baseball was becoming entrenched throughout the country. Playing fields proliferated, full-time groundskeepers were hired, teams were formed, and children at all levels learned the sport. With this degree of recognition, corporate sponsorships began to emerge. Parmalat, Chesterfield, and Mediolanum all signed on. The highwater mark was reached in 1983, when a strong

Italian team swept the Dutch at the European Championships to represent Europe at the 1984 Olympics, where the game was appearing as a demonstration sport.

At the Los Angeles Olympics, Italy faced the Dominican Republic in its first game and played this Latin American powerhouse tightly, losing 10–7. Then came two lopsided losses: 16–1 against the United States and 10–1 against Taiwan. Following these two rather predictable defeats, Italian observers began to question both the national proficiency at the sport and the value of oriundi. "The Italian national team got killed in that Olympics and a lot of the Italian guys had to stay home, unhappily," recalls Bonanno. "Some guy from the States, John Guchianni, gets a new name, Giovanni Guchianni. And the guy can't speak a lick of Italian. The Italians didn't like that too much. [Aldo] Notari [the head of the Italian Federation and International Baseball Federation] didn't like it either, and he had it in for MLB, so they changed the rules."[4]

Perhaps, the critics thought, Italy would be better served by developing local talent. Notari strove to rid the Italian Federation of baseball of oriundi. Some were grandfathered in, but only a handful of non-Italians—including two on the national team—were henceforth permitted to play. The popularity baseball had managed to attain declined as a result. Notari pushed the Cuban connection in place of the relationship with MLB. "MLB was out of the picture for years because of the agreement Italians had with Cuba," the former major leaguer Jim Davenport, now coaching the Italian national team, recalled, "and MLB didn't want to have a thing to do with it."[5] Notari stood in opposition to MLB and its efforts to Americanize the game. In place of having professional American coaches, Notari opted for Cubans, whose baseball accomplishments are well known, and who are easy to approach in this capacity. Notari was attempting to promote opportunities for Italians, and retain control over the game. The results were mixed: club baseball suffered, while the national team remained stable.

Baseball clubs in Italy are independent of the national team. As Bonanno explains, "The club thing is run privately. It has nothing to do with the Federation. This [the clubhouse where the interview was conducted] is Rimini. If Rimini wins the championship, the people and their organization are really happy. The federation is like, 'All right, but we want these guys playing on the national team.'"[6] According to Mauro Mazotti, manager of the Fortituto club, the two entities are more closely linked in Olympic years because a club's players can be coaxed into playing for the Italian national squad with the promise of expanded media coverage. "We find people are more interested in hiring Italian-American players, particularly during an Olympic year. This is because the Olympics are a showcase for players—even more than with those independent leagues."[7]

Club Baseball

Defining club baseball in Italy as "paid amateurs," Dan Bonanno points to the self-reliance of clubs:

> It's a club system. . . . The Italian Baseball Federation is the governing body for the league, but the team gets no money from the federation. There are ten Series A teams. They pay dues to the federation, and the federation supplies them umpires, scorers, scheduling. There is no legally binding tie between the team and the league. If Bologna wants out, it can leave. The national team gets funding from several big sources [the Olympic Committee, lotteries, federations], but local teams don't get a dime. They have to find all their own sponsors [and] fund their team, mostly through wealthy owners.[8]

Mazotti adds that the club structure is a function of the absence of sports from the Italian school system: "If you don't have sports in school, then you have to form clubs to play. Here, we have to pay to play [athletes bear the cost of playing their way onto a club]. We [Fortituto] have a board of ten to twelve people, wealthy people who have baseball as their hobby."[9] For "hobbyists," the profit motive of running and marketing a team is minimal at best.

If club baseball is underfunded and shunned by the lotteries and the national baseball federation, clubs nevertheless have the freedom to do what they want with regard to foreigners. Most baseball people in Italy—and they are few, relative to the behemoths of Italian sport, soccer and basketball—agree that the 1980s could have been a launching pad for getting Italians into professional North American baseball. "In the eighties, when we were playing better ball, there were about twenty guys who could play pro ball, sign contracts," contends Dan Bonanno, a veteran of that decade. Dan Newman has an Italian grandfather, and following a two-year stint in the Houston Astros organization, he began his career in the Italian league. Recalling the 1980s optimism and the subsequent fall, he recalled, "They thought it was going to be a sport that would take off! It was a 'new sport,' and they had more American coaches in the 1980s, more foreign players, more sponsors. Then they eliminated the foreigners and the fans went away. Developing the players at the grassroots level was better in the eighties, too. After they eliminated the Americans, a lot of young players lost interest because they wanted to play with Americans, be coached by Americans, speak English."[10]

Bonanno concurs: "At that point there were a couple of teams that could compete; their pitching was a lot better. I would say that they were 'A' ball [the lowest of three levels in the U.S. minor leagues]. There were some strong talented players here then, AAA guys, guys who had had a cup of coffee [a brief major league career]; ex–major leaguers like Lenny Randall, Joe Ferguson for the Dodgers came over here, and Rick Waits, who pitched eleven years in the majors, came over."[11]

The caliber of baseball—both on the national team and on clubs— declined so badly between 1988 and 1998 that the national federation reversed itself and agreed to let Italian-Americans back in. Bonanno recounts his own recruitment: "I was at Grand Canyon University in Phoenix, and we won the NAIA National Championship. The team from Parma had their people over there doing research to see what Italian-Americans could possibly fit that category. So I was able to show that my grandfather was an Italian citizen, and I got a passport to come over to play."[12]

What Is Wrong with Italian Baseball?

LACK OF PROFESSIONALISM Why can't the Italians develop more players who could be signed to contracts by major league teams? Club baseball is simply too disorganized, and there is nothing in Italian baseball to propel it forward. Club baseball lacks the requisite degree of professionalism needed to drive competition. "The owners have to stop treating it like a hobby," asserts Dan Bonanno, who has had to deal with the system for more than two decades. "We've seen in the eighties how

baseball tried to take off when sponsors were involved. Then people running the club were promoting it more, and it was on radio and TV. Then
it reverted to that level of ownership of a local club team, like, 'Hey. It's
February; what are we going to do this year?' And you got people pulling
money out of their pockets."[13] Mazotti chimes in: "The main thing we're
missing over here are serious executives. Over here, they don't run the
club for profit. Your executives don't even work full-time. They're all
part-timers."[14] Even an occasional owner shares this critique of Italian
baseball: "As far as marketing goes, we just don't know how to do it, and
we're paying for this Italian mentality. You get a sponsor giving money,
and that's what you base your budget on. Thirty years ago basketball was
big and baseball was on the upswing. But baseball didn't take it to the
next level, because they didn't know how to market."[15]

INDEPENDENT LEAGUES   Today there is a new threat for Italian
baseball: the independent leagues that have begun to spring up in North
America. They offer another venue for talented players hoping to play
professionally. "Once we were pretty competitive as far as getting players
to come here," Mazotti recalls. "After you finished your career in the
minor leagues or major leagues, where did you go? To Mexico? A lot of
guys didn't like that. Europe, and Italy was a nice option. You could
make a nice salary here, an apartment and a car [with insurance]. But
now with the independent leagues people say, 'Why do I have to go to
Europe to earn more or less what I could be earning at home? And
I could be playing more, and having more scouts look at me.'"[16]

THE POLITICS OF THE SPORT IN ITALY   Because clubs are bought
for reasons of vanity and ego satisfaction, an understanding prevails
among owners to close ranks against anyone who would reform or
rationalize the sport. It probably does little good for MLBI to attempt to
get Italians to modernize their game, because the motives for owning
teams are so irrational. Owners like to socialize as a group, consider
themselves members of a tight little cartel. As Falzone puts it, "There
seems a desire among owners to keep the game small because it stays
under the control of just a few . . . the federation. If you develop the
game and it gets bigger, the people at the core of the organization are
going to lose control. And that's the politics of Italian baseball."[17]

LACK OF HUNGER   One irony working against baseball in Italy, and in Europe generally, is the relative lack of hunger in the populace. Establishing a new sport in an impoverished country, where there are few competing institutions and where the sport can be used by significant numbers of young men for upward mobility, makes it easier to grow the game. Bill Holmberg manages San Marino, a middle-level team in the tiny republic surrounded by Italy. He has been involved in coaching and teaching the game for decades, in the United States, Africa, and Europe. In response to my question about the future of players in Italy compared with those in South Africa, he acknowledged that the latter had much more to learn, but ventured to guess that South Africans would eventually overtake Italians because they need it more: "People [in South Africa] are hungry, and when you have hunger, you've got people who are willing to work hard for a chance, which our kids [Italians he's coaching] don't want to do."[18] For Holmberg, it's that simple. Upward mobility is a powerful force in directing human energy.

By that standard, Italians will never knock on the door of major league baseball. Dan Bonanno is also familiar with the South African baseball programs, and likewise subscribes to Holmberg's view: "Italians live pretty well. They eat well. Here, with the 'Momma syndrome,' people have it good at home. They travel, playing ball, and like a lot of men in Italy, they stay home till they're in their thirties. In Italy it's family, dinner at home, and you get their freedom too. They're content! But, if you look at Africa, those guys are hungry. You know, a kid who comes to a tryout: no shirt on, no glove, and who throws 88 mph. They got incentive."[19]

That complacency, that "comfortably numb" level of play was shaken a bit when an unknown, Jason Simontacchi, signed with the Minnesota Twins right out of the Italian leagues. After being released by both the Royals and the Pirates, Simontacchi, whose grandfather was an Italian citizen, had secured an Italian passport and played for Rimini in 2000. There he found a change-up and put together a memorable season: twelve wins, one loss, and a 1.71 earned run average. The capper came when he went on to represent Italy in the Sydney Olympics of 2000. He beat South Africa, then narrowly lost to the United States when he committed an eighth-inning throwing error. Atlanta Braves Manager Bobby Cox wondered out loud, after watching him pitch, "I don't know how

Italy lost the Olympics."[20] Long-dead dreams of baseball futures were resurrected everywhere in the Italian leagues. Mark Cherbone was playing for Fortitudo when Simontacchi was pitching so effectively in 2002 for the St. Louis Cardinals, who had picked him up as a free agent. Cherbone, too, began playing as if there might be a call from his agent regarding a scout who'd seen him play. "I love being here," he said. "I got to play on the Olympic team. We beat the Australians, and I pitched four scoreless innings. We had the U.S. tied into the ninth, and were beating the Cubans 5–1 going into the fifth. So we can play some of the world's best and stay with them."[21]

WAITING FOR GODOT Is there anything Italian about Italian baseball? I asked the Bologna players that question one night after a game. Italians and Americans agreed that Italian fans don't know much about the game, but that what they lack in savvy they make up for in decibels. Italian fans of a team feel more passionately about a game that they only partially understand than any Red Sox diehard ever could. "Five hundred Italian fans make more noise than five thousand Americans'" said one player. "They're unreal!" "Yeah, but they still don't really know shit about the game," objected another. "I really don't know why they even come." His friend thought for a brief second, and offered: "I think it's the lights. They're attracted by the lights."

That question stayed with me as, later in the week, I boarded a train to Godot. The doubleheader I was going to see would begin at 10:30 A.M. It was Saturday, and the train out of Bologna was packed with beachgoers. Godot was a stop on the way, a small agricultural community. I got there at 12:30, just as the first game was ending, and wondered what we would all be doing before the second game. Only a few relatives and friends watched.

As the ninth inning played out, four or five older women emerged from a square, unadorned, cinderblock structure adjacent to the field. They came lugging six or seven long folding picnic tables, which they set end to end. When play ended and the players gathered around us, a feast had magically appeared, and everyone converged on the food. The tables had been set with linens, paper plates, and plastic utensils; large bowls held different pastas, chicken dishes, salads; and wine and, later, good coffee and desserts were set out. For the next four hours there was little talk of baseball but lots of eating and drinking in this field in the middle of a sunny farm setting.

Food is so central to Italian life that the Italian League players weave food into every nook and cranny of the game. Waiting for the players to gather for one contest, David Bidini observed, "Mirko Rocchetti, an infielder with the Peones, arrived at the park carrying a tray of cornetti, brioche, and biscotti. . . . Ricky Viccaro showed up a half-hour into the game, swinging a red thermos of espresso, which he cracked in the fifth inning. . . . Someone else placed boxes of sweets on racks above the bench, and they were polished off in no time."[22] Why shouldn't Italian baseball reflect Italian life, and here, in the middle of . . . nothing, really, I saw that it should and did. Good food, good friends, wine, and laughter. Life was good, and baseball would remain a hobby.

Germany

Pictures exist of Americans playing baseball after World War I, but Germans were officially introduced to baseball in the summer of 1936, via the pomp and majesty of the Olympic Games. At the Berlin Olympics, baseball was played as a demonstration sport by two collegiate teams in front of 100,000 spectators. The sport did not take hold at that time, in part, I suspect, because the German National Socialists deemed the game irrelevant to their larger goals. Baseball had no roots in the thousand-year-old traditions boasted by the leaders of the Third Reich. In fact, though, Germany holds one little-known distinction related to the origins of baseball. In 1796 Johann Christoph Friedrich Guts Muths published the earliest printed rules for the game of baseball . . . in central Germany.[23] This fact was to be overwhelmed by the folk-notion that baseball is rooted in the English schoolboy's game of rounders, and by the institutional origin myth of Abner Doubleday and Cooperstown.

After World War II the game was reintroduced via the large U.S. military presence in Germany. American forces stationed there organized teams among themselves and played in a loosely structured league. As a result, German children and youth learned the game. Klaus Helmig was one of them: "Well, I saw the American soldiers playing here. There were a lot of people with the troops, and they had an army league here in Germany even in 1950. I was just a boy, you know. I was so impressed with the white ball, you know, the pearl. We just tried to chase foul balls."[24]

The occupation forces sought to "de-Nazify" Germany by introducing a variety of democratic institutions, primarily through an agency called the German Youth Activities, designed to advance the American way of life. George Pascal, a leading sports marketer in Germany, points out that "baseball was a big part of that. It was a chance to play a sport that wasn't soccer, and Americans gave out candy along with the equipment."[25] By 1948 there were 140 German teams organized throughout the country, and by 1951 they had already organized a German championship tournament. Klaus Helmig and his brother Hanjorg moved to Mannheim and started their own team in 1952. "We had street teams in the area where we had that stadium where the American military played," Klaus Helmig recalls. "They had occupied the German stadium and made a baseball park out of it, and we watched the Americans play after school."[26] After the games, it was common for the Americans to teach the game's fundamentals to these young Germans.

By 1954 enough countries were playing the sport that a European Championship had been started. Strong pressure from soccer, however, was keeping a check on the rise of baseball. Klaus Helmig points out that older Germans who did not identify with baseball pressed the case of soccer: "They didn't care about young Germans playing an American sport, which they didn't understand anyway. They [Americans] were still former enemies, and baseball was considered a crazy game." For younger Germans, though, baseball continued to possess an allure: "We watched often. I remember here in Mannheim, the army outfit that played was a transportation outfit, which was all black. The army was still segregated here after the last world war. They were called the Tornadoes, and they were fantastic."[27]

The Helmig boys practiced every day, and as they grew up they played alongside and even against some of the military teams. "We played several years, and when we got older we had a pretty good team," according to Klaus. "Then one day when we were coming home we saw a car parked in our driveway, and it had 'Baltimore Orioles' on it. A scout was looking for us, and talking to our mother. My father had died the year before, and my mother agreed to have us sign with the Orioles, you know. Me and my brother signed with the Orioles." That was in 1956. Klaus and Hanjorg were the first Germans ever signed to professional baseball contracts. The publicity people for the Orioles saw the potential for press exposure, and so the two young men were introduced to America with far more fanfare than most low-level signings received. "They showed us all around," Klaus recalls. "We went to the Naval Academy, and New York at the Waldorf Astoria at the Annual Baseball Writers Association Dinner. They even got tuxedos for us and we were special guests because we were the first Germans ever signed. We were guests of the White House. The president was not there, but we were."[28]

After being watched for several weeks at the Orioles' Scottsdale, Arizona, spring facility, the two were sent to different teams in Class D, then the lowest level of the minors. Klaus played in Paris, Texas, in the Sooner State League, while his brother was sent to Thompson, Georgia. The German experiment didn't last long. Neither of the Helmigs was destined for glory on the field, but the two German rookies played a curiously interesting role in the history of baseball, of global movements of players, and of race relations.

Breaking the Color Barrier

One can only imagine how disgusted Adolf Hitler would have been had he been alive to see these two sons of the Third Reich engaging in a public act of race mixing. Yet in the summer of 1956 Klaus and Hanjorg Helmig continued their American odyssey by playing in the Negro Leagues. Two white boys—two German white boys, two German white boys a scant decade after the Third Reich failed—were playing and living the Negro Leagues life! If Klaus thought this was culturally extraordinary he did not let on:

> And so we were released in the middle of the summer, both of us at the same time; and we went back to Baltimore. We were working in the National Brewing Company, which belonged to Mr. Jerold Hoffberger. He was the owner of the Orioles then. We played semipro ball there, and then we got scouted by this Negro League club, the Baltimore Elite Stars, in 1956. There was one gentleman, Levi was his name, a businessman and sports pro-

moter. And he thought maybe he could bring us into the black leagues. He made the contact with them, and we practiced and played with them for maybe a couple of months. We were the only white guys on the team.[29]

The idea of two Germans playing in the Negro Leagues was intriguing, so I asked Klaus what it had been like for whites, for Germans, to play and live around blacks two years after *Brown v. Board of Education* became landmark civil rights legislation. The Helmigs had helped break a reverse color barrier by becoming two of the first whites—if not the very first—to play in the Negro Leagues. Helmig felt that because they were Germans, it was easier for them than it would have been for American white boys:

> We never heard anything bad said about our color. Just occasionally, "Come on white boys, hit the ball!" They wanted to give us a chance, you know. The Orioles didn't hold onto us, so these black teams invited us to play. They were very nice to us, very friendly. As a matter of fact, we stayed with a black family in downtown Baltimore.
>
> We went on the road: North Carolina, Virginia, Delaware, and we played with them. I remember that we were invited to a barbeque, and the people wanted to know where we were from. We said, "We are from Germany." And they wanted to be very friendly with us. They invited us to eat. They were there with their wives, and girlfriends, and families. . . . Sometimes we arrived at the games early after driving all through the night. We would sit on blankets, you know, relaxing and taking a rest.
>
> There were some really good ballplayers there. I remember one time we played the New York Black Yankees. My brother pitched. I played outfield and we lost 1–0. The guy stole home on my brother![30]

Returning to Europe, the Helmig brothers went directly to play in the 1956 European Championships in Rome. In 1957 Germany fielded a team that hoped to represent Europe in the National Baseball Congress's World Series in Wichita, Kansas. Instead, the Dutch won the tournament—a result that still leaves Klaus Helmig with bitter feelings:

> The Dutch were always strong. They learned their baseball from the sailors in Amsterdam. We wanted to take a German team to the States that year, but there was the game against the Dutch. The umpire was from Belgium, and he was drinking beer. He had his brother standing behind the backstop. He made some of the calls for his umpire brother, terrible calls. Then it was about the sixth inning, and we couldn't stand it anymore, you know. We charged him, and had some kind of melee, you know. A few of our guys got thrown out, and we lost the game. We came from the States, and we couldn't believe somebody could do that.[31]

Baseball's attempt to gain a foothold in Germany suffered a major defeat when the bulk of the U.S. troops left the country in the mid-1950s. The programs were disbanded or badly neglected, and the next generation of children was not exposed to the game. According to George Pascal, "As American forces left, we lost interest in the programs. There was no continuity, and the kids of the 1950s grew up and never taught their kids how to play baseball. By the 1970s, baseball died."[32]

MitchFranke.com

After the Helmigs, no German signed with a major league team until nineteen-year-old Mitch Franke in 2001. Milwaukee Brewers scout Chris Miller thought enough of Franke to give him a tryout. At six-foot-one, 187 pounds, the switch-hitting Franke was raw, but the Brewers saw potential.

The media warmed to Franke, and he was the subject of articles and of television spots aired back home in Germany. Franke's celebrity status quickly went to his head, and he set up an Internet site to chronicle his fortunes—an excusable gesture, given his youth and his generation's reliance on the Net. On Franke's site, www.MitchFranke.de (an English-language version can be found at www.MitchFranke.com), he proclaims, "I'm proud to be the first German baseball player on a U.S. Minor League team." Klaus Helmig must wince at that one. By promoting himself so publicly, Franke set himself up to be publicly disappointed. Failing to develop any of the potential the Brewers had seen in him, he was released on March 26, 2003. The Web site seems not to have been updated since.

Two other Germans signed around the same time: catcher Simon Gühring, with the Brewers, and pitcher Tim Henkenjohann, with the Twins. By the end of 2003, they too had been released. These young men were all signed because they played on club teams and on the German national team, but it remains unclear which is the more direct path to a pro contract.

As is true across Europe, the national team is more aggressively promoted than are the club teams. But George Pascal, the managing director of IPS, a marketing sport production firm in Germany, sees a sharper focus there on grassroots development of players: "In Germany there's an emphasis on growing the sport and making it more popular. Other countries are putting all their efforts on the national team, like Russia for example. . . . So basically Germany has a healthy system."[33] This has been the joint venture of the German Federation, private interests, and Major League Baseball International. MLBI has had its Pitch, Hit, and Run Program entrenched in England and Germany since 2000, and it introduced the program in Italy in 2003. Pitch, Hit, and Run is the earliest intervention program in baseball, designed to reach children ages seven to eleven, via a school-based curriculum. Pascal, who has overseen this process in Germany, claims to have placed it in eight hundred schools, and he says he receives two to three proposals each week from schools that want to add the program. The Pitch, Hit, and Run program feeds the Play Ball program, a school-league format in which children play baseball competitively. In Germany these leagues have been located mostly in areas that have strong club presences, like Bonn and Reigensburg. The idea is to build links from Pitch, Hit, and Run all the way to the national team.

Each club pays fees to the national federation to enter into league competition at a level appropriate to its achievement. The Bundesliga is the elite level of club baseball. The problems plaguing these clubs are the same everywhere: lack of professionalism translates most immediately into inability to market and run the team profitably. This is an even greater problem in Germany than in Italy because the game is far less advanced, even though more Germans play the game. Most publications claim some twenty-eight thousand baseball players in the country, but the vast majority of them are actually softball players.

Club baseball has shown a disappointing inability to close the gap between Germany and the powerhouse Dutch and Italian leagues. Nor has the German national team been able yet to force its way into the elite company of Netherlands and Italy. Yet there is cause for optimism, at least in the eyes of Jim Small of MLBI: "We've definitely made progress, particularly in Germany. There are several kids in professional ball."[34] All those players have since been released, however.

The notion that baseball is a niche sport that must break out to join the mainstream also represents a marketing problem. Germany is a difficult environment for baseball in part because only 10 percent of the population can be defined as sport fans, according to a study carried out for MLBI by John D. Powers in 2002. Even within that small segment, only 6 percent—fewer than one German in a hundred, overall—are hard-core fans, and 15 percent are moderate; the vast majority are classified as passive fans. Marketing to such a small population poses its own problems. Germany has baseball-related strengths, however, that marketing can build upon: 21 percent of German sports fans encounter major league baseball in some form at least once a week, and those fans tend to be younger than the followers of Bundesliga soccer. Furthermore, the grassroots programs have succeeded in making children aware of the game. American pop culture also has a certain cachet in Germany, a condition that baseball should be able to exploit. Hip-hop artists, for instance, are routinely shown wearing MLB-licensed caps or jerseys, and those images are seen around the world. That sort of brand recognition potential shouldn't be disregarded.

Building a television constituency is also critical, according to everyone from Klaus Helmig to marketers like George Pascal. Major league games need to be shown, of course, but must be supplemented by "up-close and personal" programming. *Baseball Max,* an international TV magazine that is translated into German and shown on Saturday mornings, is an example of a program designed to use baseball's icons to foster youth identification with the sport. *Baseball Max* includes special content tailored to countries that have players in the major leagues. A German player who reaches the major leagues would become the spearhead of a television campaign to increase baseball fandom in the country.

Would this kind of effort constitute cultural imperialism? Is baseball irredeemably American-identified? Pascal doesn't think so: "The idea is not to have Germany identify baseball as American. It's Baseball Germany! [Like] Baseball Japan, [Germans must] have their own brand of the game. The idea is not to have everyone play American baseball or have the Americanisms of baseball."[35] Interestingly, at the Bonn European Championships in 2001 there was a German attempt to co-opt the MLB icon. While the crowds were filing in to watch one of the games, someone placed bumper stickers all around the stadium. The background was an approximation of the MLB logo, over which appeared the text "Der kult der Zang" (The cult of Zang). None of MLB's people cared who or what Zang was, but MLBI's Clive Russell was outraged by this unauthorized use of MLB's logo. "I want these removed immediately," he barked at the German official overseeing the European Championship. "This is an illegal use of MLB's logo, and if they are not immediately taken down, we will pull our backing of these games." Der kult der Zang disappeared instantly, and MLB brand integrity was safe . . . in Germany. Whether or not MLB's response was heavy-handed, the incident was similar to the flap over Japanese posters advertising the 2004 All-Stars exhibitions. Clearly there is a no-tolerance policy toward meddling with the brand.

As with Italy, I tried to gain some sense of whether there was such a thing as German-identified baseball while attending the European Championship. The entire affair, however, replicated an American event. The teams appeared to be international, sporting the country's name on its shirts, but some of the teams were heavily or mostly American or Canadian (England). The spectacle and event could just as easily have been in Milwaukee. Even the music was programmed by MLBI, so that as the German national team took the field or as individual batters approached the batter's box, one might hear Queen's "We will, we will rock you," or, oddly enough, strains of the Hebrew "Havah Nagilah." The stadium announcer was a stocky, female, German-speaking version of Billy Crystal, but the format she followed might have been scripted in the United States. What was clear was that Germans had yet to create anything to culturally lay claim to the game.

United Kingdom

Despite MLBI's conscientious attempts to develop the game in the United Kingdom, baseball is flagging there. Jim Small is guarded: "It hasn't developed as fast as we had hoped." MLBI has invested a substantial part of its budget into both Germany and the United Kingdom in a concerted effort at game development and marketing. The results have been underwhelming. Why has the game had such a difficult time taking root in England? What is the future of baseball there?

Historians of British baseball are fond of pointing out not only that baseball came from the English game rounders but that the English have actually been playing baseball for more than a century (since 1889)— almost as long as Dominicans. The difference between the sport's trajectories in those two countries is striking, but British baseball historians without fail like to point to anything that can legitimate the game in Great Britain.

Josh Chetwynd is a blend of journalist and player. Born in England and raised in the United States, Chetwynd played baseball at Northwestern University and then in the Frontier League (1995). When presented with the opportunity to play on the British national team in 1996, he leapt at it. Since then he has worked around, studied, and played the British brand of baseball. Chetwynd was working in MLBI's London office in 2002 when I first encountered him. He quickly proceeded to let me know how long-standing—by European standards—the game is in the United Kingdom.[36]

A. G. Spalding, the U.S. baseball legend and entrepreneur-turned-proselytizer, included England on the 1888–1889 world tour he organized for his Chicago White Stockings and an opposing all-star team. Fifteen years earlier, the Boston Red Stockings and the Philadelphia Athletics had played in England but made nowhere near the splash of Spalding's exhibition. The games played in London in the spring of 1889 included among the respectable crowds the Prince of Wales. Although the spectacle impressed the prince, he—not surprisingly—declared "cricket as superior." Indeed, although Spalding's tour drew large crowds, most British fans echoed the prince, finding the game unintelligible and low scoring (a euphemism for tedious). A few months later a collection of collegiate players from the States toured England. Chetwynd notes that the college players were responsible for getting the British to play the game alongside them. The resulting interest gave birth to a league, subsidized by one of England's leading industrialists, Sir Francis Ley.

The world wars put the brakes on growth for the transplanted sport. Slowly, baseball made a comeback following the First World War, culminating in the decade of the 1930s, often referred to as the game's "golden age." Because of the efforts of Sir John Moores, a league of eighteen amateur teams was operating in 1935. Moores was one of Great Britain's most successful gambling operators. His Littlewoods Football Pools Company served as a base for a more diversified operation which opened stores all over England, enabling him to subsidize the creation of a professional baseball league in 1936. Some of the teams in that league even reported earning profits; Scarborough, for example, had average receipts of £70 a game. American and Canadian players were prominent on the teams, fostering some local resentment.

That decade was notable also for the 1938 series in which a team from England defeated the U.S. Olympic squad. Not surprisingly, the British consider this their greatest baseball victory. In an effort to gain international experience before the 1940 Tokyo Games, the U.S. team had come to England for a tuneup, a five-game series against a collection of players from the Yorkshire-Lancashire League. The British team was really primarily Canadian, but no one seemed too concerned. To the surprise of everyone, including the British, they beat the Americans in four of the five contests. The victories were convincing, too. British pitchers twice shut out the Americans, and the British team showed the ability to come from behind as well. Chetwynd, like other British baseball historians, calls it Great Britain's "greatest Baseball victory."[37]

The post–World War II era saw a relatively listless brand of baseball being played in the United Kingdom. Lacking the benefactors of the earlier era, British baseball continues to plod along, hampered by organizational dysfunctions and the rising popularity of soccer. The current line on the subject, according to MLBI's head, Paul Archey, is that baseball has not "developed as fast as we'd hoped it would": the nation has a diminished ability to generate new players capable of moving up the ladder to the ranks of the clubs and ultimately to the national team. To say that the play of the national team has never quite jelled is an understatement. The European Championships have been held twenty-eight times, beginning in 1954. With only two exceptions (Spain in 1955 and Belgium in 1967), the Netherlands and Italy have won every tournament. Great Britain came in second in 1967 but has typically been among the bottom dwellers in the A-Pool. MLBI's head of European operations, Clive Russell, explains, "In 2003, because they don't have enough funding from the government, the British national team came to the European Championships without having played a single game together! The chaos surrounding them and the poor organization meant that their uniforms almost didn't show up on time. They didn't know if their hotels would be paid for on time. It was a mess!"[38] There is no shortage of reasons for these failures, but the bottom line is that the sport of baseball has failed to take serious root in the United Kingdom. This is not for lack of effort by MLBI, however.

MLBI

Major League Baseball International established itself in 1990 in the United Kingdom, where it ran its flagship programs. As in all such endeavors, direction was needed, along with ample resources. Clive Russell was brought in to provide those needs in 1997, as well as to head MLBI in Europe and Africa. Beginning in 2001 MLBI decided to concentrate on Germany and the United Kingdom, in a serious attempt to upgrade baseball so that those nations might eventually compete with the powerhouses of the Netherlands and Italy. Recalls Russell, "I realized that we were too thin on the ground to be everything to everybody; and so we had to focus our activities and efforts for a couple of reasons: to get better value for money in terms of our investment, and to track what that return is. We really wanted to focus on a couple of countries where we thought we could establish a firm basis of game development and business."[39]

Despite having a vision, strategy, and capital, MLBI needed to understand that "growing the game" in the United Kingdom and Europe is as much social engineering as it is marketing and starting up children's programs. The game must be rooted in a community, it must exploit social rivalries, and it must evolve meaningful rituals. And how do you go about generating enthusiasm for the game? Do you involve as many young players as possible, with the goal of ultimately building a strong national team, which can garner Olympic funding? Or do you cull the elite players in hopes of having some sign professional contracts and make it to the major leagues. MLBI's Paul Archey refers to these two paths as "push" and "pull," respectively. Success, revenue, and attention all work to lure the best talent to the game. Russell concurs, "If the Germans had a $5 million budget, then they could start enticing the kind of athletes they need to. That's the big issue in Europe: enticing the right kind of athlete."[40]

The "push" of successful grassroots programs could theoretically promote widespread involvement with a generation of young players. There should be an unbroken chain of leagues that link children to the clubs and the national team. The numbers show that the Pitch, Hit, and Run Program is in fifteen hundred schools in South Africa, more than eight hundred in Germany, and six hundred in the United Kingdom. Success has been claimed in each country, at least on the formal level. As Jim Small says, "We've seen [in the case of the school-based programs] the tripling of the numbers playing since we started in the U.K. in 1996. In 1997 there were 21 coaches, and now there are 443. Back then there were 6 coaches on the national team, today there are 30."[41]

Success, however, means more than the numbers of coaches, or the number of schools that have adopted Pitch, Hit, and Run. Bob Fromer, a transplanted New Yorker who has lived in the United Kingdom for decades, heads up grassroots efforts for Pitch, Hit, and Run and the Play Ball programs. While pointing out the programs' successes, he has grown increasingly frustrated at the lack of funding. "Politically," he complains, "'the line' is that [PH&R] is a success because it's drawing far more kids in than it would any other way. Is it drawing as many kids in as it should? No. The reason is that we have a culture such as this, which is completely dominated by soccer, and with a government that has no sympathy toward minority sports."[42]

Great Britain's Play Ball program, which builds on Pitch, Hit, and Run, is not sufficiently funded and relies excessively upon volunteers. In a moment of critical candor, Russell concedes, "We were in [the United Kingdom and Germany] four years too early. In those years the vast majority of our efforts were wasted. For instance, we started running Pitch, Hit, and Run expanding by 250 schools a year without the proper infrastructure, and relying almost exclusively on volunteers. In areas where we see the strongest programs, they're the smallest."[43]

The linkage between PH&R, and Play Ball, as well as the linkage between the layers of British baseball, is also weakly developed. MLBI's Envoy Program is another link. It takes American and Canadian coaches to work with the more talented players in countries trying to develop baseball programs. Pat Doyle, who directed the Envoy Program in 2002, noted the frustration with underfunding felt by that development people the world over: "To be able to say, 'Okay, we had an Envoy in Bonn for five weeks.' What happened there? 'We saw X number of kids.' Well, how many of them continue to play ball? There's plenty we could do with the right funding."[44]

Growing the game has to have an ideological component—something that makes kids dream and fantasize about the game. Michael Jordan did more to spread the gospel of the National Basketball Association worldwide than any combination of its programs and marketing. In the twenty-first century that is the role of television and marketing. Here, again, U.K. baseball is in a bind: you can't get good exposure if you're not already exposed. Although, as Russell points out, the era of twenty-four-hour sports networks brings an unprecedented opportunity to any sport in Europe, "minority sports" still must overcome their disadvantages.

The J.D. Powers marketing study commissioned by MLBI in 2001 indicated that U.K. baseball/softball has its work cut out for it. A mere 9 percent of British sports fans ranked major league baseball as their favorite sports organization, and a mere 7 percent have ever participated in either baseball or softball. If getting a country's best athletes to play a sport is the most effective way to establish that sport in the nation's consciousness and give it institutional respectability, then U.K. baseball is a tough sell. The best athletes go into sports that are already established—soccer, primarily. By contrast, the sole British-born and -bred athlete to sign a professional baseball contract—Gavin Marshall, a twenty-six-year-old right-handed pitcher who plays in the independent Frontier League—is barely a blip on the British sporting radar screen.

By summer 2004 MLBI had begun rethinking its investment in the United Kingdom. Jim Small, echoing MLBI current policy, was talking about redistributing MLBI's resources: "We've kind of reallocated some things. We've cut the Pitch, Hit, and Run spending quite a bit, and reinvested that money into television programming. We're looking at a baseball profile. We started an anthology half-hour TV show that is geared toward a non-baseball-playing market. It has a ten- to twelve-minute mini-condensed game, a couple of features on players, and a how-to-play segment."[45] Clive Russell knows that the window of opportunity for European baseball is open neither wide nor long. He grows a tad restive when he feels that European baseball is being judged inappropriately:

> The reason our "push" strategy failed is that they never really invested enough to get it done, and we spread our resources too thin. I look at it a lot more optimistically than Jim [Small] or Paul [Archey] do. . . . They look at "How many kids have we had that have moved on to do this or that? How many players have been signed?" They don't see the difficulty of developing these things. It's not cheap to do. More and more, these arguments fall on deaf ears for various reasons, mostly because of the amount of money coming out of Japan. If you're talking "push," then we're cut. They say, "Look. We've spent however many millions of dollars and we're not seeing enough."[46]

Europe's Baseball Future

The realization that baseball in Europe is not progressing toward tier two status any time soon has forced MLBI to shift its strategy. The notion of the game thriving via a grassroots movement has given way to a plan of developing, wherever possible, impact players, or what Jim Small calls "high performance athletes." Small is echoing the policy shift generated from the baseball operations side of MLB. Sandy Alderson, formerly of the Commissioner's Office, is perhaps the chief architect of the push for what he calls "senior development": identifying the top players in a country and developing them at an academy. In this rarified atmosphere, Alderson feels, some of the players can develop into major leaguers.

Australia is his model: "The Australian academy has been in operation since 2002, and in the three years of its operation we've doubled the number of players signed out of Australia." There are now one hundred Australians under professional baseball contracts. Alderson's reasoning is simple and clear: "It is central to our international strategy. We seek to develop players who can come to the United States and prosper and create interest in their home countries." Turning his attention to Europe, Alderson notes that Europe hasn't produced players. He intends to transplant the Australian model to Europe: "What we hope to do this year [2005] is have our first European academy. . . . If you took the best six or seven players from each country and brought them together in an academy for seven or eight weeks, you'd really begin to see tremendous progress and gain some acceptance on the part of these countries."[47]

Having a Yao Ming experience would go a long way toward getting the media attention that baseball needs in Europe as well. "It sure would pull the game up at the grass roots level," Small says, "because then there will be a context for baseball in Europe which there isn't right now. We're not in the newspapers enough. We're not part of the sports scene."[48]

A more immediate danger for European baseball can be found in International Olympic Committee's decision in July 2005 to eliminate baseball from its program. The IOC has urged MLB to commit to allowing its players to participate. Commissioner Selig has dismissed the idea, claiming that it would constitute a major disruption to the baseball season to have players take off two to three weeks in the midst of pennant races. The consequences of Selig's decision are significant for tier three countries, however, because the funding that makes baseball viable in most European countries is dependent upon IOC distribution of money to the various national committees. "Essentially the development of baseball in Europe at the Federation level is all around the Olympics," Russell says. "Other than football [soccer]—which has its own event [the World Cup]—every other sport that's an Olympic sport is attuned to its national Olympic participation. If your country medals and competes strongly, that gives you a leg up in your country, because then you get Olympic funding for your particular Federation. It's absolutely enormous!"[49] The Dutch team, for instance, got between $3 million and

$5 million for its baseball program in 2001. MLBI's Jim Small believes that for some countries IOC money is the difference between a future and no future: "I think there's enough critical mass in France, Germany, or the Czech Republic, but elsewhere I don't know."[50]

Fielding national teams requires a substantial infusion of money. The costs of training for and participating in international competition can be prohibitive; without IOC subsidies some countries would be in danger of losing baseball altogether. If the United Kingdom, which has more than a century of baseball under its belt, has an uncertain future in the game, what of countries that have only recently been introduced to the sport? Global baseball should be judged not only by Latin America and Asia but also by baseball backwaters like Europe and Africa. That's where the test is.

Take Ukraine, for instance. Ukraine formed its first national baseball team in 1994. For MLBI Ukraine is one of the long-term projects within a bigger long-term project, Europe. Basil Tarasko is a coach at Baruch College in New York, but since 1991 he has spent his free time traveling to coach the Ukrainian national team. At the 2001 European Championships in Bonn, the Italian national team stayed at my hotel, a well-appointed place in the old city center. The Ukrainian team had more modest accommodations: "We're staying in a youth hostel. It's forty deutschmarks a night and we got five people to a room," Tarasko noted matter-of-factly.[51]

The Ukrainians have developed fairly well considering their recent introduction to the game, but the conditions under which they play baseball hold them back. In 2001 Ukraine hosted the Big League European Championship for players aged sixteen to eighteen. Six countries, including Belgium, Germany, Moldovia, and Lithuania, were scheduled to compete but only Poland showed up. Money to send teams was scarce. The Ukrainians beat the Poles in three straight games, earning a trip to Easley, South Carolina, for the World Big League Championships. All that was needed now was the $75 fee per player for visas. That, however, proved to be a major stumbling block, Tarasko pointed out: "It only costs $75, you may say, but $75 for the parents of our players is a considerable sum."[52] The team's manager wound up borrowing the money for the visas at the last minute, and the team headed for South Carolina. There they faced a powerful team from Venezuela, losing 10–0. In that game the local police chief noticed that the Ukrainians were playing in tennis shoes because they couldn't afford cleats. Wanting the European visitors to have the same resources as the other teams, the Easley Police Department sent out the call to local businesses for equipment, which arrived in time for Ukraine's second game. Against Saipan the Ukrainians won 6–5. Then they lost a heartbreaker to Canada, 8–7. They won one game and lost three overall, but they played admirably against teams from countries with strong baseball roots. Their struggles and determination epitomize the challenges facing MLBI in parts of the world that offer potential for growth. Basil Tarasko recounts his debacles as if they were cultural romps laced with humor. He recalls the Ukrainian team's first international tournament, for instance:

> In 1993 I traveled with the first Ukrainian National team from Kiev to Trieste, Italy. That was fifty-one hours: no toilet, no nothing. Only those little sausages, and two-liter bottles of water. We get to the hotel three days late, by the way, so they throw us out of the tournament. Our schedule said we play Russia. We get to the field and nobody's there, so I found someone and I said, "Look at the schedule. We're supposed to be playing Russia." He said, "Oh, no, no. You had to show up three days ago to enter the tournament." We had paid for the hotel, and so we stayed and managed to play a scrimmage against Lithuania. . . . [Ours was] the only national team that got money the last day before the trip. We get to the border and they give us the money. It's a poor country.[53]

At present, the more affluent areas of Europe and the baseball world don't compete under these Spartan conditions and ragtag mindsets. But that could be the direction in which much of European baseball is headed if the IOC should eliminate baseball as an Olympic sport. Olympic money has kept baseball afloat in all of Europe's backwater baseball havens.

The relative economic privation of the Ukraine also makes it a place where people flock to those paths that lead to opportunity. As in the Dominican Republic, where baseball offers both the dream, and the reality, of escape from a life of hardship, baseball in the Ukraine and Russia could be developed as a pathway of upward mobility. If that should happen, if a Ukrainian or two makes it to the big leagues, there is good reason to think that the rush will be on. This remains speculation, however, in the face of European baseball's biggest obstacle: expulsion from the Olympics. "You'd see baseball just drop off the radar screen in weaker countries," predicts Small.[54]

7

SOUTH AFRICA: BASEBALL AND THE
NEW POLITICS

Edwin Bennett, a Colored South African and one of the driving forces behind baseball in the country, was an activist in the antiapartheid movement. He fashioned an interesting family ritual when his children were growing up under apartheid. Each night, as his family gathered around the television before bedtime, they would wait for the South African national anthem to be played. His three children would line up about ten feet from the television set, and as the anthem was ending, Bennett would shout, "Go!" The children would rush to see who could turn the anthem off first. In that symbolic act we see the extent to which apartheid, and resistance to it, had infiltrated every pore of South African life, every little encounter, every seemingly innocent gesture. Bennett reflects, "Just the satisfaction of turning it off must have made them feel good; although I doubt if their little minds could have understood that in this minute act, they were busy with the struggle."[1]

Barry Armitage is a White South African who, in 2000, at the age of twenty, was signed as a pitcher by the Kansas City Royals. He was one of the first South African players ever to sign professionally. By 2003 seven South Africans were under contract with various major league teams. A year later, Armitage was one of only two who remained. He is almost too young to remember apartheid, he says: "I was thirteen when apartheid ended and the new South Africa began. Today we have—at the local level—White clubs, Colored clubs, and a few Black clubs, but when we play the big games for the national team we have only one club. In

South Africa 40 percent of your team has to be 'of race' [Black and Colored], and baseball is more than that. We get sponsorship because its one of the few sports were you get such a mix naturally. We get money from the government because baseball is not a race sport."[2]

Armitage, the stepson of an international softball player, is from Durban and grew up playing baseball exclusively from the age of five, but the game was barely known, and the young player's world was insular and remote. Even though Armitage is a pioneer of sorts, there is little awareness of him in his home country. "Funny," he admits, "but I've had more interviews with the press here [in the United States]. I've never had one in my own country, nothing mentioned about my making it, or playing well, or anything."[3] The South African game is still in its infancy, all but unknown, and Armitage and Bennett are separated by a generation, politics, and race, but they are linked as baseball pioneers.

No matter how recent baseball in South Africa might be, no examination of it can be divorced from the history of apartheid. In the following discussion of South African baseball, I look at the linkages between antiapartheid movements, baseball, and schools. One person, in particular, serves as a living link between these three phenomena: Edwin Bennett, an ex-librarian, tireless antiapartheid activist, and baseball trailblazer. He has served as the development officer for SABU, the South African Baseball Union, since the end of apartheid in 1992.

Apartheid, Sport, and History

Apartheid in South Africa was only the most blatant institutional system of oppression; it was certainly not the earliest.[4] When the Dutch East India Company first settled into the area of the Cape of Good Hope in 1652, it created the template for the apartheid rule eventually established in 1948 by the National Party. The Dutch East India Company instituted a race-based system of economic and legal status that made land ownership and office holding the exclusive privilege of company personnel and European citizens.[5] Unskilled or semiskilled Afrikaners needed legislation in every area to keep slightly ahead of Black laborers, and that discrimination only served to exacerbate the racial fear and hatred in South African society. Religion, education, political life, and even recreation came to be influenced by this cultural atmosphere. By the 1880s Blacks were barred from sport in South Africa.

South Africans invest as much or more collective energy on sport as do any people in the world, prompting Dennis Brutus, a prominent anti-apartheid activist, to claim, "Disasters elsewhere and international affairs are mere trifles compared to a rugby victory—and even anticipation of a victory." Even though the "disadvantaged" peoples (a term of art for non-Whites in contemporary South Africa) lacked the resources and facilities that Whites enjoyed, both groups included avid sportsmen, underscoring the role of sport as a powerful tool for social change. Sport was, as Brutus continued, "the soft underbelly of the white psyche."[6]

Dennis Brutus began the South African Sports Association (SASA) in 1958 after battling with the International Olympic Committee over recognition of black weightlifters. SASA was a conglomeration of black federations but included sympathetic members of all groups—the first nonracial sports organization—and it was heavily supported by the African National Congress (ANC). Its goal was to administer Black sports and organize protests against discriminatory practices in South African sport. As the groups making up SASA became more militant, they were banned and harassed by the government. Brutus was banned as a Communist the following year, making it illegal for him to belong to any organization or to teach, write, or otherwise function politically.[7]

In 1963 SASA metamorphosed into the South African Non-Racial Olympic Committee (SANROC), whose goal became the destruction of apartheid in sport and institution of a system in keeping with Olympic principles. The primary mechanisms proposed for this effort were the expulsion of the Whites-only South African National Olympic Committee (SANOC) from the Olympic movement and organization of an international boycott against apartheid sport. While en route to West Germany to meet with IOC officials, Brutus was intercepted by Portuguese officials in Mozambique and handed over to South African police. They returned him to Johannesburg, where he would face trial and certain prison. Convinced that he would be assassinated, Brutus tried to escape and was shot. As he lay bleeding in the street, the driver of a Whites-only ambulance, seeing that the victim was colored, continued on his way. An hour later a Black ambulance arrived. Brutus survived in exile in London.

The domestic void in nonracial sports resistance was filled by the formation of South African Council on Sports (SACOS) in the early 1970s. One
member of SACOS was a librarian–turned–sports activist named Edwin
Bennett. He was to become assistant secretary of the Transvaal Council
on Sport.

The Republic of South Africa dealt with dissidents brutally—exiling
them, imprisoning them, and even killing them. International sporting
bodies were slow to respond to these political policies, unwilling to over-
step their bounds by intruding into the republic's internal affairs. South
Africa was also well placed in the international sports arena. Its history of
formal Olympic involvement dated to 1908, and it was a founding member of the International Rugby Board and the International Cricket
Conference. Calls for the sports boycott of South Africa led by Brutus
and others to the international community, and to IOC head Avery
Brundage, were at first scarcely heeded. Yet despite Brundage's foot-
dragging, the IOC threatened the South African National Olympic
Committee with suspension if it did not accede to the Olympic charter
on racial discrimination.[8] The IOC rejected South Africa for the Tokyo
Games in 1964 and for the Mexico City Olympics in 1968.

Rebel Tours

Organized in response to South Africa's increasing sports isolation
through the 1980s, Rebel Tours involved invitations offered and accepted
by a now increasingly illegitimate agency: South African sport. One of the
first such events brought a group of British cricketers to South Africa in
1982. These events were promoted at great cost to the South African government. Just the first two legs of the 1990–1991 English Rebel Tour cost
fourteen million rand. The players were very well paid mercenaries, accord
ing to Booth, most receiving between £83,000 and £110,000, and cricket
captain Mike Gatting receiving £200,000.[9]

In traditionally White sports, such as rugby, the South African government was able to circumvent the ever-tightening noose of isolation
through its historically established ties. Even here, however, there was
growing international disapproval of apartheid. In 1981 New Zealand
Prime Minister Rob Muldoon was steadfastly behind the Springboks'

rugby tour of that year, no matter what critics of South Africa had to say. This tour resulted in numerous clashes between police and those both protesting and supporting the Rebel Tour.

While both the National Sports Congress (NSC) and SACOS were determined to protest and disrupt these tours, only the NSC had the people in place at the local levels to carry this out. Edwin Bennett played a role in this resistance, a role similar to that played by many other activists:

> We took on the Rebel Cricket Tour of Mike Gatting to South Africa. I was given a particular area to organize. We made our goals clear: there would be no match. And the then Town Club of Johannesburg met with us. They "asked" us to assemble in certain areas and move up [protest] periodically; and only a few at a time. That was not going to happen. That was no protest. They beat us up good and solid that day. But what they didn't know was that we were mobilizing in the other towns as well, and for the first time we would be seeing the ANC flag being openly carried.
>
> When Gatting came to Johannesburg's airport, they had a garrison of police searching cars, and because I looked White I played a trick on them. I was dressed up as a businessman and drove to the police checkpoint. There I said, "I'm late for my plane. You men better keep those Black people out of the airport!" They let me through, and in the meantime I've got all of the posters in my car. I carried them into the terminal and the other activists followed me into the toilet, and we distributed the material. We mobilized quite a few people and got quite a bit of international coverage.[10]

Booth seconds the notion that the protests were significant, pointing out that at Kimberley more than three thousand protesters met the English cricketers: "The tour ended after three weeks of adverse publicity."[11]

Antiapartheid Use of Schools

The idea of educating Blacks for their "rightful" place was a cornerstone of the National Party's racial policy. "Racial relations cannot improve," cautioned Minister of Native Affairs Hendrick Verwoerd in

1953, "if the result of Native education is the creation of frustrated people who . . . have expectations in life which circumstances in South Africa do not allow to be fulfilled."[12]

While these legislative acts rankled many, organized resistance really escalated in the mid-1970s. In 1976 the deputy minister of education, Andres Treurnicht, attempted to force all schools to teach math and social studies in Afrikaans, the language of the white nationalists. Soweto exploded, and in June of that year fifteen thousand students organized a protest, triggering a chain of similar events throughout Black communities. Recalling his involvement with SACOS during the 1980s, Edwin Bennett gives an example of the resistance: "We mobilized a lot of schools. For instance, if a big corporation—like Simba Chips—wanted to give a huge sum to Grand Prix racing, and only wanted to give us a few boxes of chips as a donation, we would immediately go on a boycott of their goods. We would also go to their competitors to let them know why we would be buying their goods."[13]

Bennett's ability to gain access and to organize in school settings served as a perfect link between MLBI's attempt to develop South African baseball and the schools' search for postapartheid projects for the "New South Africa."

Baseball in South Africa

If, as baseball insiders like to say, one "fishes where the fish are" (in this case, the Dominican Republic), then the Royals, in going to South Africa, left their sanity open to question. Although South Africans saw the game played by American miners around the turn of the twentieth century, baseball is essentially nonexistent as a mass phenomenon. This is tier three, with a few pockets of players and fans in the Cape Town area and in Johannesburg. Efforts by various major league teams and the Commissioner's Office to develop the sport have only begun. Obstacles along the way include lack of even a rudimentary understanding of the game, the need to compete against entrenched sports, and the challenge of creating and sustaining interests. On the other hand—and this should not be minimized—baseball represents something new and uncontaminated by the country's historic turmoil.

Oral histories concur that baseball has its South African roots in the 1930s. Pett Yus, former president of apartheid's White baseball organization, the South African Baseball Federation, saw the game's origins in his native Cape Town: "The way it started was that a lot of American ships used to dock here. As a result we had a lot of Americans living in Cape Town. We had a crowd called Mormons, religious people from Utah in the U.S., and baseball started with these Mormons, when they started playing in *Winderbosch* Commons. These were pickup games, but they grew."[14]

When South Africans began playing baseball, they, of course, did so along racial lines. The South African Baseball Association (SABA) was the Black federation. Most of the baseball traced to Blacks was centered in Cape Town and dates back only to the 1950s, although it probably precedes formal apartheid.

Most of the history of South African sports has tended to focus on such high-profile sports as rugby, cricket, and soccer, and on the Olympics. These were the most racially separated sports, and to this day they carry the marks of apartheid. The Springboks are South Africa's national rugby team, one of the most successful in the world. This team and the sport have always had a strong White identification. In the wake of unification a rancorous debate ensued over whether or not to continue to call the national team the Springboks, because the name was so identified with White supremacy. In 1991 Sam Ramsamy, the president of the National Olympic Committee of South Africa (NOCSA), was infuriated by the suggestion that this symbol of oppression of Blacks should remain the symbol that identifies South Africa to the entire world. But others, including the new South Africa's first president, Nelson Mandela, argued that the springbok should be retained as a symbol but that its meaning must be reinterpreted.[15] Only after South Africa beat Australia did popular sentiment swing toward the Springboks. The Sowetan headline the next day blared "Amabokaboko"—The Boks! The Boks!—and an unanticipated victory over the world champions seemed to turn public opinion when even Nelson Mandela could not.

The less consequential sports, it seems, were never objects of so much emotion or scrutiny, even in the era of apartheid. In the case of baseball, at least, it appears that there was even occasional circumvention of official policy. Pett Yus, who played in the White baseball leagues of the 1950s, recalls clandestine baseball games against Black teams:

> As you know, we had White baseball and Black baseball, and we were miles apart. We were to have nothing to do with each other. But I actually got into trouble because we used to arrange games. We had to keep quiet about it, of course, and we'd go off and play them in their area. And of course by the time the police heard about it, it was too late. I used to phone the chap who was president of the Western Province and ask him, "Listen, Kwaphi, how about a game at your field?" We went to play there quietly. We'd arrange our ride, play the games, have a few good beers afterward, and become friendly. People showed up to watch, but only if they were in the know. You couldn't spread it around. Not allowed. It was madness.
>
> They caught us and actually arrested us. We got off lightly, [but] they warned us that the next time we'd be in serious trouble with the police. But we were all friendly in baseball.[16]

With the end of apartheid came the merger of the two baseball federations. Majority rule may have been the law of the land, but apartheid did not simply disappear in either practice or belief. I saw this in my trip to Cape Town, where I was taken to one of the better baseball facilities, in a White area, Bellville. The lighting was adequate, and the field was well maintained—modest by American standards, but good by local standards. A few days later I went to visit the Chukker Sports Complex in the Black area of Cape Town. Here the facility was shoddier, threadbare, maintained only with great effort and efficient use of limited resources. There was a strong sense of pride, however, as people declared that Chukker was one of the best teams in the country, producing two players who had signed professional contracts with American teams, as well as players from the South African national team, Sweden, and Nigeria. Under majority rule White and Black federations were required to pool their resources and distribute it evenly. This had not happened. Whites used their money to create better facilities; Blacks and Coloreds, because they didn't have the same resources, continued to lag behind even in the new South Africa.

It was in the first days of majority rule, in 1992, that the South African Baseball Union approached Edwin Bennett, whose connections to the Black community made him desirable. Bennett became the development officer, a position he continues to hold.

It was not easy to grow the game. Funding went to elite sports, but in 1993 the National Sports Congress struck a deal with the Australian government to provide instructors, and baseball was one of the sports the Australians taught. Bennett and those with him still had to begin at the most basic level:

> With their help we got things moving. They spent all of ninety-three days in the Eastern Cape and Soweto. We managed to make our own tee-stands, soft-touch balls, little wooden bats. It took off particularly well in the Eastern Cape because they had a rich tradition of clubs with rugby and cricket. We also knocked on a lot of corporate doors and eventually the government started helping as well.
>
> With little grants we were able to make multilathe wooden bats. I made them out of maranti wood. My brothers would varnish them.[17]

It had always been important to Bennett that children be the primary beneficiaries of his efforts. So his hiring as development officer for SABU enabled Bennett to use his connections to the educational system to prepare for Major League Baseball's arrival.

MLBI Enters South Africa

When Major League Baseball International devised its flagship program, Pitch, Hit, and Run, it did so precisely for countries like South Africa. Australia may have been where the program was first implemented, but South Africa was an ideal forum. Young children experiencing a new curriculum in a changed social atmosphere were eager to try all of the government's programs. The Pitch, Hit, and Run program was not the first such program in South Africa. In 1986 the Cricket Union, using modified bats and soft balls, launched a similar program, teaching cricket to children in the Black townships.[18] The Cricket Union boasted that in just four years it had introduced fifty thousand Black children to this miniature version of cricket and trained twenty-five hundred coaches.

Neither Jim Small nor Clive Russell knew the extent of Bennett's contacts in the government, so neither could anticipate how pivotal he would be to MLBI's plans. Bennett, on the other hand, knew the capabilities of his networks: "We give them [MLBI] what they don't get from other countries. We give them children!" Bennett is confident in the speed and depth of his grassroots approach to growing the game.

> It's because of the networks, political networks, that we can make things happen so quickly. When I walk into any province, and I want to speak with so-and-so, I speak with them. No waiting. We are involved in the rural towns, and that's where it is growing for us, not in the cities. We take the game where there is nothing, and we create interest. We are regarded as a top-ten sport in this country. At the school level, United School Sports Association of South Africa [USSASA], we have been awarded the top sport honor. This fits in beautifully with the Pitch, Hit, and Run Program.[19]

Not all schools were so excited by the prospect of learning baseball, however. The older, elite White schools were—not surprisingly—at times resistant to SABU presentations. Bennett recalls, "At two schools I was personally chased out. Some of my regional coordinators of Pitch, Hit, and Run were also asked to leave schools. We made proper presentations in saying we wanted to introduce baseball to the school. Some administrators were polite: 'We don't like baseball. We prefer cricket.' Others said, 'Look, I don't want to hear anything about this sport of yours. Just get out!' "[20]

In a sense, there was still some race coding that affected the view of baseball. The Kansas City Royals scout and SABU coach Mike Randall, who is White, confirms this association: "Our educational system, especially in the advantaged White areas, used to be cricket only [during apartheid and before]. If anybody went in there and tried to talk about baseball, the headmasters chased you away. They saw you as a threat. Now everyone has a constitutional right to do whatever they want, so we can go into these schools. What Edwin's done is lay the groundwork for providing another sporting opportunity for young people."[21] In Black schools, volunteers are willing to teach anything, while paid instructors in White elite schools teach only the sports they know: rugby and cricket. This racial divide extends to Black teachers, who want to introduce as many sports as possible, particularly those that they were denied as youngsters. It doesn't matter at all if these baseball instructors are predominately women (since 80 percent of teachers in the country are women) or that they barely know the game themselves; at the inception one needs to blanket the area.

Opinions differ on how best to develop the sport. While Bennett prefers to see stage one as a numbers game, Bill Holmberg, an American coach with extensive experience in Italy feels differently. He spent four months in 2001 assessing the MLBI programs in South Africa. While he was impressed at how expansive the Pitch, Hit, and Run Program was, that was also his criticism. Holmberg would prefer to consolidate small initial steps based on intensive instruction, followed by slow building of skill sets. "Look, Edwin is a very talented guy," Holmberg says. "I wouldn't tell him how to organize a political rally, but don't tell me how to organize player development. One of the problems with Edwin is that he had all his kids out, exposed to the game, but I never saw any of them playing on the club teams. They had exposure, all that equipment. The next stop would be to funnel them into organized clubs." Holmberg prefers an approach that concentrates attention on one or a few areas where one can bring the best coaching to maximize the level of play: "Centrally locate in one area. Work it hard, and then branch out. I went to some places where we went out and we were sitting out there and we didn't even have a field. Thirty-five, forty kids, some good athletes, with crappy facilities. We tried hitting ground balls with them. You'd throw the ball up, hit a nice ground ball, and the ball would move like it's in a pinball machine. You can't teach an infielder in those settings."[22] Holmberg's frustrations are easy enough to understand. His talent lies in elite player development, while SABU is concerned with all skill levels. Given the fiscal limitations on Pitch, Hit, and Run—and given the competition for scarce national funding—quantifiable success is at a premium. So Bennett can legitimately claim that Pitch, Hit, and Run has gone into fifteen hundred schools to more than 400,000 children. MLBI and the South African governmental agencies are pleased with numbers like that.

There are, however, other ways of assessing the impact of MLBI's grassroots programs, among them anecdotal evidence suggesting that teaching baseball is only one part of a larger form of instruction, involving life-changing experiences. Bennett recalls the lengths to which some of the people in his program go to play this sport:

> Some Black kids come to an under-eighteen tournament, and they drove right through the night. They were brought in an open vehicle, and it rained all night. They were drenched. They looked gaunt, like they were Sudanese. We had some uniforms for them that were given to us by a very old man. They were old, but these kids needed them. They had no running shoes. They played barefoot, and one of the first things that the umpires warned us was, "It's dangerous to play barefoot." I said to them, "It's either these kids play barefoot, or we don't have a game." In Black townships we play wherever and however we can.[23]

Game developers understand that this is as much about culture and class as it is about baseball, so they seize every opportunity to maximize the experiences that children will have outside of the game. It's almost as if they want to have these children go through mild forms of culture shock.

Coaching Dilemma

The biggest and most immediate hurdle for SABU is to effectively build a set of links that lead from the most elementary instructional baseball of the Pitch, Hit, and Run program to the level of the club and even the national team. This goes to the heart of Bill Holmberg's frustration with South African baseball, the absence of coaching.

Over the past decade South Africans have had Australians and Cubans come in to lend a hand in coaching. MLBI has its Envoy Program, which brings coaches into countries for a month to instruct the best talent, but little is done to develop indigenous coaching. Billy Mengengelele of the Durban area is a real rarity, an African coach, who works tirelessly with young ball players, but he underscores the problem: too big a country, too few coaches.

Mike Randall, a Cape Towner who has coached at a range of levels in South Africa, has recently been brought on by SABU to address this failing.

"MLB has built its player base here through the Pitch, Hit, and Run program," Randall says. "They're looking to accelerate this process. My first goal is to develop the coaching standards, and in doing that I'll be spending time with them on the field while they're training and drilling the kids."[24] The strategy for building baseball in South Africa involves building linkages. It seems as if the South Africans are already aware of the problems and working at them in their own way and at their own pace. While everyone I spoke with was cordial, I sensed that there were differences in approach between MLBI and SABU. MLBI wants to make the links through their programs and personnel. Bill Holmberg went to South Africa as a special consultant and, together with Dan Bonanno, devised a training manual and a program for getting the game to the next level. The illustrated manual contained more than sixty pages on teaching fundamental skills to young players and organizing school leagues.

Bennett and Randall at SABU acknowledged the value of MLBI's contribution but insisted upon putting it into their terms. Randall is going ahead with his plan of instituting school leagues, and progress is being made—albeit slowly—on training coaches. The main problem is that he has to do this on his own, and in that capacity he is being pulled in different directions. As a scout for the Kansas City Royals he's constantly looking for talent. But some might question the efficacy of going into rural areas where no one has ever been signed: all seven of the South Africans to sign with major league teams thus far have come from urban areas. SABU has concentrated a lot of effort in the country, not only at the rudimentary levels of game development but also in courting athletes from other sports. Both Bennett and Randall are attempting to cull established sports talent preserves. Bennett is quick to point out that the Eastern Cape is the "heartland of rugby," where he can make an effort at finding young athletes willing to give baseball a chance; Randall, meanwhile, attends elite cricket matches in search of players. "Our player base is so small that I look at ways of finding other athletes," Randall says. "This includes White and Colored. I would attend cricket matches at random. I'd approach the school master and tell him I'd like to watch the game. He'd ask, 'What are you looking for?' I'd tell him I'm looking for guys who can throw the ball."[25]

Soccer, rugby, and cricket all can provide models for how to develop players as well. Randall would someday like to establish a baseball academy in

Cape Town as productive as any of those in the Dominican Republic. When looking for a model, he doesn't look to Salcedo, the Royals' Dominican academy, but rather one established by the Dutch soccer club Ajax:

> They've got a satellite club here. They've got a full-on soccer academy here where they scout players beginning at ten or eleven years old. They actually go around and pick up kids after school, and they take them to the academy for specialized soccer training. When they're finished, they are weighed, and professional dieticians give them a meal. They've got a guy who is responsible for instruction in their schooling and to help them with homework. When they're finished, they've got transportation back to their homes.
>
> They're so advanced. You know how we have this racial thing in our country. They set it up so that a White physiotherapist or biokineticist works with a Black kid. But because the Black kid most often doesn't open up to a White guy, they've hired Black assistants and professionals to make it easier.[26]

What parent wouldn't want his or her child in such an after-school program? Randall knows that it's a long, long way to that type of facility, but because he's South African, he knows that it exists, and he knows that it's the kind of academy that would succeed in baseball. MLBI can't match it; no major league team would bother because there is so little to be gotten out of the country. But the Royals are on square one, and they are being recognized as the point men for MLB.

Royals in South Africa

The Royals are the most recognized baseball franchise in South Africa. The Yankees mean nothing there. Of the seven professional baseball contracts signed by South Africans, three of them were with Kansas City, and given the Royals' institutional placement in the nation, more signings are likely. This is the outcome of the philosophy of the Royals under General Manager Allard Baird. Kansas City's presence in South Africa reflects the need of a small-market team to scout the margins, but the success of that presence is the outcome of Baird's progressive leanings. Something Edwin Bennett mentioned brought this into sharp relief for me: "Out of the blue I get thirty-two dozen balls from Allard Baird that were used [by the Royals] at spring training. Those balls are like gold to us! And he says, 'Just make sure that they get into the right people's hands.'"[27]

Two elements are worthy of note here. "Out of the blue . . .": SABU wasn't expecting a thing. Almost half a world away, in the midst of spring training chaos, Baird had South Africa on his mind. "Just make sure that they get into the right people's hands": Baird not only understood the logistical and political dimensions of South African baseball but identified with the most disadvantaged part of it, the kids often overlooked in the rural areas. He knew that Bennett would be likely to use those balls for his USSASA program, and Baird wanted to support that effort. The Royals cemented their presence in South Africa with this kind of handling of a tier three environment.

Baird came to South Africa almost accidentally. One could say that had he been a less curious person—or just a little sleepier one morning in 1999—he'd have missed the opportunity altogether. Baird describes the serendipitous origin of his South African experiment, while he was still an assistant general manager for the Royals:

> There was a presentation to the general managers and assistant G.M.s, and you know how sometimes during those times when it's not really baseball-related, you sort of zone out.
>
> Well, all of a sudden they started talking about statistics, and how it's the fastest-growing sport in the country. And [snaps fingers] it's South Africa! Before that meeting I'd heard that baseball was being introduced there, but then the numbers, the statistics, the aggressiveness from a baseball marketing standpoint were really impressive. That was the start of it.[28]

The ability to see opportunity where others don't—where he hadn't previously—is the common denominator in descriptions of Baird. The manager of business operations for the Royals, Carol Kyte, sees him as "an out-of-the-box kind of guy who's always trying to go to places where others don't."[29]

It is one of Baird's best traits: he can see into a baseball situation, no matter how rough, the way someone with a fine eye can see the potential in a neglected house. Getting past that which is immediately apparent is a talent, so while a connoisseur of houses looks at architectural features that are hidden from the ordinary eye, Baird looks at young prospects with an eye to promising physical attributes, subtle abilities, and people who might make it happen: "I think right now you don't see very good players, but you do see a good system. South African Baseball Union has really set up a program over there that's in many ways better than what we have in the U.S. as far as structure and discipline."[30]

Baird embarked on his first trip with the idea of assessing South African baseball. If he signed someone, that would be a bonus, but he wanted to get a sense of "whether these guys could play or whether [good baseball] is forty years away. Do we get involved now? Later? Or at all?" SABU arranged everything for the Royals' entourage, so that they would see baseball from the moment they landed. "It was a sixteen-hour trip," Baird recalls. "We came off of the airplane, and they had a tryout camp set up for us."[31]

What Baird saw on that first trip was a diamond in the rough. The potential existed, and under the criteria of the Royals' small-market strategy—"high risk, high reward"—South Africa was a good bet. Some in the Royals organization were reticent about the potential. Luis Silverio, director of player development in the Dominican Republic, who accompanied Baird on the first trip to South Africa, didn't sugarcoat the baseball picture there:

> They're a long way behind. In years its tough to say, maybe twenty-five to thirty years behind. . . . They're way behind body-wise. Young kids don't know how to play baseball—that alone is ten years' worth of work, at least. That's where the coaching comes in, and they need a lot of coaching. I mean, you have ladies coaching kids how to play ball. They don't know how to teach baseball. There's no way you can compare a fifteen-year-old Dominican kid with a fifteen-year-old South African. It's gonna take a long, long time.[32]

Cape Town, Durban, and Johannesburg, at least, were places where baseball was being played at a basic level of competence. In the rural areas there was tremendous excitement over the game but almost no skill. Allard spun that circumstance into something quite positive:

You get to East London [a Black African rural area with little baseball], and we were going to run a tryout camp where a lot of Black African kids were. We had sixty-seven kids there, and probably a third had shoes. A lot of girls had their skirts on, but we worked them out anyway. Probably four kids had gloves. But I talked to sixty-seven kids, and their eyes never left me! You go to the States and talk to a group of kids, and they're busy looking around. A half an hour into the tryout I told Luis, "Let's try to teach!" And so we spent time throwing a baseball, we lectured afterward, but what it all came down to was "How do I get a glove? How do we get balls?"[33]

The Kansas City Royals are at the center of a remarkable convergence. They are the most recognized team in South Africa. "I think we're doing a great job there," concludes Baird. "There's a sportscaster there who comes on a sports show wearing a K.C. hat, and there are Royals stickers all over the set."[34] This is what branding is supposed to be, according to marketing people, but it is also the way it should be done by socially responsible people. Whether the Royals' efforts ever result in South Africa's becoming a hotbed for baseball talent, they have created a template that should be widely emulated.

The Royals have worked to entrench themselves into South African baseball in such a way as to become the most important conduit for the spread of the American pastime—more than other clubs and more even than Major League Baseball International. They did it by paying close attention—in part, because they had no choice, but also because they valued indigenous agencies like the South African Baseball Union. They did it by hiring local scouts rather than bringing more Americans over. Finally, they did it by understanding that they were guests, and that they had something rewarding to offer South Africa.

What MLBI, the Royals, and SABU are doing in South Africa goes far beyond baseball. While it is sport that they are concerned with, the consequences of their activities reach into the realm of social change. For Edwin Bennett and his colleagues, these grassroots programs constitute their attempt to redress the failure of previous governments to provide their children—Black children—with opportunities to play. Bennett stated this clearly in his initial meetings with SABU back in 1992: "I told them I had two conditions: 'You will play in the townships, and all children will participate in your games.'"[35]

MLBI acknowledges this sociological aspect only in passing. At the core of MLBI's interests is game development, and in comparing Holmberg's or Dan Bonanno's view with Bennett's, we see the differences most clearly. MLBI is happy to be perceived as part of the new South Africa, but sees the perception only as a fortunate coincidence. Because of the lengthy gestation of tier three programs, they are not featured as prominently as MLBI's more immediately rewarding programs. Nevertheless, the industry is concerned with growing the game at all levels, so its grassroots programs will only get more important over time. Sandy Alderson, until 2005 MLB's senior vice president, has discussed such things as the "Yao Ming factor": the potential for reverberations from having a single athlete from a tier three country who can make an impact both in the league and in his country. That is the outcome MLBI hopes for from its presence in places like South Africa.

The Royals operate somewhat out of character for a baseball franchise. On the one hand, as a small-market franchise, they carefully scout the margins of the baseball world, but their commitment to South Africa exceeds anything we might normally expect. They clearly are not being driven by any immediate payoffs from a player perspective.

The country has a long way to go in baseball terms. The game is still not being played above the school level by Blacks. Coloreds, primarily in Cape Town, play, and Whites in pockets of cities play, but links between school-aged children and the club structure have yet to be made on any large scale. When a South African becomes a major league star, however, that anonymity may disappear. Whoever that first South African star will be, he will have to thank Barry Armitage, who paved the way for him.

Barry pitches in the Royals' farm system, most recently for the Class AA Wichita affiliate. He has pitched unspectacularly but successfully in relief—well enough to have made the Midwest League All-Star team while pitching for Class A Burlington. Barry has gone farther than any South African playing baseball, and that he does so in anonymity is telling. "Baseball is quite small in South Africa," he acknowledges. "I mean, all my friends play it, and they follow my career, but really, nobody knows who I am. . . . There's never been a story about me in the press in my own country. Baseball just doesn't really get into the public eye."[36] This is what the policy makers in MLB are busily trying to change; the question is how best to do so. Do you "push" it via better links between grass roots programs? Or do you identify the elite players and cultivate them in a rarified atmosphere to get them into the majors as quickly as possible?

And yet, in another sense, it really doesn't matter, because baseball has beaten the taint of racism that haunts the country. It is now considered one of the desirable sports for the new South Africa, and if cultivated carefully, baseball can become a respectable part of the sports pantheon.

8

WHEN WILL THERE BE A REAL WORLD SERIES?

One oft-voiced objection to the World Series is, simply, that it excludes most of the world. Outside of the United States and one city in Canada, people quickly point up the combination of arrogance and defensiveness in suggesting that the rest of the world does not really matter when it comes to baseball. Therein lies the game's fundamental contradiction: will Major League Baseball become global or remain American?

At least as early as 1991, reports began surfacing of MLB having turned the corner on globalization. Baseball executives began alluding to "international competition in a non-confrontational, global, geo-political sense."[1] The acknowledged prophet of internationalization, Peter O'Malley, that year declared, "Financially, international baseball won't bring [licensing or broadcast] revenues next year or even the year after that. It's a long[-term] play."[2] With Major League Baseball International (MLBI) still in its infancy, not much else was passing for international baseball.[3] The industry had done next to nothing and trailed its competition pretty badly. The National Football League had already boldly moved into Europe, setting up a league and drawing large numbers of fans.[4] The National Basketball Association had been involved in international programs for some time as well.

By the late 1990s MLB still had not done much as an organization to globalize the sport. That had been left up to franchises with vision. The San Diego Padres, for instance, arranged to play 1997 regular-season games in Monterrey, Mexico, and in Honolulu—part of the United

States, but one with cultural ties to Asia. When John Moores bought the team, he pushed marketing into nearby Mexico, offering fan ticket incentives, an apparel store in Tijuana, and televised games. He also marketed to Honolulu, then a novel gesture in the industry. "Baseball's marketing is absolutely woeful," Moores declared. "It would be a natural, obviously, to play some games in Japan and have a World Cup. But baseball has done almost nothing." The Commissioner's Office could only offer up vague generalities: "I believe we're in the very early stages of internationalization. . . . We have a myriad of plans."[5]

Today, Commissioner Bud Selig and the MLB brass are firmly on the global bandwagon, having spent the better part of the past six years making up for lost time. When the New York Mets and Chicago Cubs opened the 2000 season in Tokyo, for instance, Selig declared—with just a hint of smugness—"What we're doing here is what anyone would do in the 21st century. It's a global economy. It's not the world of the 1950s or 1960s."[6] Yet in a separate interview with the Yomiuri baseball reporter Jim Allen, Selig's provincialism was more evident. Allen told me: "When the Mets and Cubs came here to open the season, . . . I asked Selig, 'What is Major League Baseball doing to promote the game around the world in countries where baseball is not already well developed?' He said, 'We're bringing Major League Baseball to Japan; I think that's a big step.' I said, 'No, no, no, Japan already has professional baseball.' And he said, 'Oh, yes.' And I asked, 'What about countries that don't have professional baseball?' And he said, 'Well, we can't push it.'"[7]

Clearly, this is somewhat at odds with the more expansive comments that Selig's office had prepared for the press assembled in Tokyo. Allen does, however, give Selig credit: "For a Commissioner to get two teams to play in Japan—considering how limited Major League owners are—is, to me, a massive accomplishment."[8] The juxtaposition of the commissioner's progressive and parochial personae mirrors tensions that exist within the structure of Major League Baseball itself. There is definitely a commitment on the part of MLB to develop a greater global presence for the game. Doing so, while relinquishing a measure of control, makes MLB uneasy, however. Is it MLB expansionism or global partnership? The latter would curb the power and influence of MLB in the short-run but aid the growth of the game (and of MLB) in the future. The

Commissioner's Office is simultaneously seeking to develop the sport in areas in which it is weak, to maximize revenue streams around the world, and to bring the baseball world together . . . all under the banner of MLB. These goals are not only difficult but in some measure incompatible with the game's present-day policies.

Before we determine whether or not MLB is globalizing, we need to figure out just what being "global" really is. Is Major League Baseball's playing of games abroad global? Does having significant numbers of foreign players constitute globalization? Can "global" be taken to be a harbinger of true partnerships between equals?

The G-Word

While the views of leading analysts and scholars of globalization differ considerably, they converge around certain attributes and processes. First, globalization refers to capitalism as a world system on a level never before encountered. There are no longer any competing economic systems and ideologies. With the fall of the Soviet Union, capitalism's major obstacle to worldwide domination was removed. In a corollary to this principle, industrial nations are expanding around an open market–based system, pitting multinational corporations against states, and blocs of states against each other.

Interconnectivity—a qualitatively heightened interdependence of commerce (corporate and small), governments, and individuals around the world—is another key element of globalization. All systems are interdependent: contacts among societies and cultures have been increasing—sometimes dramatically—for thousands of years. The Greek historian Polybius noted this in the second century in linking the Mediterranean world with that of Asia.[9] Unlike earlier expanding links, however, which were based on an incomplete awareness of "the world," the current interconnectivity is truly global.

A corollary of this global interconnectedness is what David Harvey refers to as the "time-space compression": a series of technological breakthroughs in communication and transportation—microchips, fiber optics, satellites, and the Internet—that make it possible to move capital and information across the world instantaneously at the push of a button.[10]

The opening chapter of Thomas Friedman's *The Lexus and the Olive Tree* leads with a photograph that depicts a personal side of this technologically inspired space-time contraction.[11] The picture is of an Orthodox Jew praying at Jerusalem's Wailing Wall. Bearded and in traditional garb of black hat and coat, he is deep in prayer. In his hand, however, he is holding a cell phone, which he has placed against the Wall so that his relative in France can also receive the special blessing associated with the site. In economic terms, Harvey points out, "It is now possible for a large multinational corporation like Texas Instruments to operate plants with simultaneous decision-making with respect to financial, market, input costs, quality control, and labour process conditions in more than fifty different locations across the globe."[12]

Capital and information can be moved more quickly and cheaply than ever, and the speed and cheapness of communication continue to increase. All of the voice traffic that crisscrosses the Atlantic Ocean at any time can be carried by a pair of fibers no thicker than a human hair.[13] Comparing all this with previous technological revolutions, the anthropologist Manuel Castells concludes, "Information technology is to this revolution what new sources of energy were to the successive industrial revolutions."[14] This has consequences for individuals as well: "These technologies are making it possible not only for traditional nation-states and corporations to reach farther, faster, cheaper and deeper around the world than ever before, but also for individuals to do so," writes Thomas Friedman.[15]

Globalization Is New

The concept of globalization tantalizes with its newness and future-feel. But is globalization, as many are claiming, really a *new* order? Not everyone thinks so. For skeptics, globalization is traditional capitalism on steroids: recognizable but grown much more muscular. They argue that the types of breakthroughs so touted by globalists had already been established: in the breakthrough of the telephone, for instance, and in the expansiveness of trade, a basic order of interconnectivity that has been a staple since mercantilism. Paul Hirst and Grahame Thompson, among others, have argued that contemporary trading blocs and global interdependence are both actually weaker than they were at the turn of the twentieth century.[16] But most scholars are convinced that while some precedent existed for globalization, the current manifestation differs in its extensiveness, intensity, and the velocity of its movement.[17]

It may seem unnecessary to remind people that globalization is synonymous with capitalism, but the way the term is being used suggests that globalization is capable of morphing into anything, even its opposite. Under globalization, capital moves quickly into and out of institutions and countries in search of optimum conditions. Friedman refers to the "electronic herd"—groups of investors roaming the earth in search of profit-conducive environments. The herd likewise moves out of long-established havens. In the developed world this phenomenon is manifested in the success of corporations to press for open markets through pacts such as NAFTA, and in the dramatically increased outsourcing of jobs and production, especially to countries like India and Pakistan.[18] Some American companies have even begun to build outsourcing into their original business plans.[19] Those who still think of U.S. corporations as concerned with protecting the American workforce should meet one Ravi Chiruvolu, a general partner with Charter Venture Capital. His firm, located in Palo Alto, California, bankrolls fledgling technology companies. Charter Venture Capital does not even consider investing in the United States. Says Chiruvolu, "My view is you should not start a company from scratch in the United States ever again."[20] He represents the new mindset that refuses to be constrained by national affiliations.

The anthropologist Anna Tsing points to one of globalization's most seductive elements: "Globalization is a crystal ball that promises to tell us of an almost-but-not-quite-there globality."[21] "Hyperglobalists" like Friedman claim that globalization can alter the geopolitical nature of the world. For Friedman there is a "democratic" future in globalization that can be good for all concerned, especially the have-nots. Accordingly, "First World vs. Third World" schisms can fade as the economic playing field is leveled. For industrial nations globalization means reduced trade barriers, more affordable consumer goods, and an enhanced lifestyle. This is also part of the promise hyperglobalists espouse. For the poor, a chance is held out for economic salvation: employment and a better life. But does this utopian picture actually jibe with the more sobering currents of hard-nosed capitalism?

Not to critics like the Nobel Prize–winning economist Joseph Stiglitz, who has written extensively about the "broken promise" of globalization. Revolutions in communication and transportation and the breakdown of trade barriers should be benefiting most of the world. They aren't because, according to Stiglitz, "we have no world government, accountable to the people of every country, to oversee the globalization process in a fashion comparable to the way national governments guided the nationalization process. Instead, we have a system that might be called *global governance without global government,* one in which a few institutions— the World Bank, the IMF, the WTO—and a few players . . . dominate the scene."[22] Tina Rosenberg echoes this assessment of globalization: "No nation has ever developed over the long term under the rules being imposed today on third-world countries by the institutions controlling globalization."[23] Convinced that developing nations other than China and India are not enjoying the benefits of globalization, Rosenberg offers a list of reforms. Given the Janus-faced nature of globalization, there is no shortage of critiques offering reforms to ensure that the promise is fulfilled.[24] For instance, the Mexican government should have insisted upon technology transfer when it first struck its deal in 1995 with the giant automaker Volkswagen. The Mexican VW factory is the nation's largest factory, employing about twenty-six thousand, the result of a $1 billion investment. "The value Mexico adds to the Beetles it exports is mainly labor," Tina Rosenberg points out. "Without technology transfer, maquila work is marked for extinction. . . . Mexico is increasingly competing with China and Bangladesh—where labor goes for as little as 9 cents an hour. . . . Businesses, in fact, are already leaving to go to China."[25] Hence the state has not only a role in globalization but an essential role. If reforms like compulsory technology transfer, suggested by Rosenberg, were implemented, they might help to deliver the promise.

Globalization's Two Continua

It might be helpful to think of globalization as existing along two continua. The first is political and economic. One end of the continuum is what I call "testicular globalization," which takes its cues from twentieth-century Cold War economics. This form of globalization seizes upon current technology and enhanced trade opportunities but functions with a twentieth-century geopolitical mindset: armed with its policies (for example, protectionism) testicular globalization works to retain the economic dominance of the industrialized West at the expense of the rest. At the other end is a more democratic version. I call it "tough-love globalization": it includes not only the cardinal features of contemporary globalization (for example, time and space contraction) but also a degree of decentralization of power. While tough-love globalization is inclusive of corporations and nations—encouraging the have-nots to enter into the matrix if they can—it stops short of institutionally seeking to distribute power and wealth. Tough love is about merit, and though it opens the door to opportunity, it brooks no failure. This is not to be confused with a utopian vision, concerned primarily with distributing the benefits of globalization. Tough-love globalization merely allows entry to those that can take advantage of it, turning its back on all others; in this way it differs from the other pole.

A second continuum of globalization is based upon cultural criteria, primarily the tension between global and local forces. Here we have at one end globalization linked with "Americanization." From this pole the spread of American commodities around the world is synonymous with American influence and power. McDonald's, Coca-Cola, Hollywood films, Nike, Starbucks, and so on fan out to every corner of the globe, and every country not only is privy to our culture but falls under its sway. As consumers of American culture, people around the world inevitably wind up losing their own. Many see American sport as playing a significant role in this process.

The "Americanization" thesis favors a one-dimensional use of commodities: the appearance of commodities and objects at other ends of the earth—"tribesmen" wearing Dallas Cowboy caps—is illustrative of globalization. But what anthropologists call cultural diffusion has happened for millennia, as has trade spanning great distances. These are not examples of globalization. A commodity purchased is not, in and of itself, proof of the homogenization of culture or of American domination. Consumers can and do purchase goods from abroad while attaching very different—at times antagonistic—meanings to them. Hence at the other end of the cultural continuum we have the triumph of the local or indigenous—whatever we use to describe that entity—in the face of globalized forces. "Cultural resistance" is the term often given this response.[26] Some refer to it as "Creolization," but whatever the terminology, it implies a refusal to simply capitulate, not only to the artifact and the idea but to the agency as well.

An illustration of culture and globalization appeared in an article written by Mitchell Stephens more than a decade ago: "[Mitzi] Goheen, an anthropology professor at Amherst, recalls a graduate student from Kenya who was relieved, upon arriving in the United States, to discover that he could get Kentucky Fried Chicken here, too."[27] In this cultural inversion, the student finds solace in being able to eat "his food," Kenyan food . . . KFC. When a product has successfully entered a foreign market, it does so in part because it seems local, not foreign. When a Kenyan can appropriate the colonialist's own artifact as his own, then the cultural meaning of the artifact has changed. KFC as Kenyan and KFC as illustrative of Americanization: a rich tension, one that blurs the distinction between local and foreign.[28]

Global Sport Studies

The field of sport studies has also been busy carving out a niche within the globalization discussion.[29] Most of the effort has been an attempt to figure out the perspective that best suits the subject matter (for example, neo-Marxist, postmodern, figurational); case studies are represented primarily as articles and chapters. A partial exception may be found in the work of John Sugden and Alan Tomlinson, who have compiled a body of work around the Fédération Internationale de Football Association (FIFA), the world soccer governing organization.[30] Their critical analysis of the politics and economics of FIFA offer insights into one of the two most globalized sport entities (the International Olympic Committee being the other). The most important figure in the literature on sport globalization is Joseph Maguire, who since the late 1980s has produced a powerful corpus of work on globalization and sport.[31] Since the late 1980s, Maguire has examined basketball, soccer, American football, ice hockey, and cricket from a perspective that essentially revolves around culture and change. While "figurational sociology" has yet to find its true intellectual roots (it shares space with history and with anthropology), Maguire has given us a collection of cases that explore the tensions between pressures exerted by such powerful global sporting interests as American football or British cricket and local (national) responses. Borrowing Norbert Elias's terms, "diminishing contrasts" versus "increasing varieties," Maguire updates them within the context of globalization debates.[32]

Branding the Game, the Industry, the Nation

The economic and cultural dimensions of globalization intersect around the notion of international marketing. For Major League Baseball (or any corporate agency) to expand abroad requires an understanding that what it strives to do is nothing short of instigating culture change in the context of consumption and practice. No American sport has been more successful in international marketing than has the National Basketball Association. NBA marketers understand that international development is more than an adjunct, it is their future life's blood. "We are a mature business in the U.S. and the growth is outside the U.S.," admits Heidi Ueberroth, vice president for global media properties and marketing for the NBA.[33] The NBA has succeeded in Europe, where MLB is struggling. The NBA has rooted there, has managed to develop numbers of impact NBA players, and has generated long-range plans of opening franchises in Europe. These efforts included tried and true methods: getting young players involved and setting up leagues for them to play in, and building strong national teams and club structures. In contrast, MLBI's grassroots campaigns, like Play Ball, remain alien efforts to insert a cultural product—a corporate brand—into systems that don't recognize it. MLBI's European efforts have languished by comparison to what the NBA has done there. Even worse, much of MLBI's work continues to appear as if baseball were a foreign body. (It is, of course, but so is the NBA, although it doesn't come off as such. Indeed, there is the rub.)

These days marketing strategy is about promoting "the brand." Most marketing mavens are concerned with making the connection between consumer and goods along psychological or cognitive lines, argues Douglas Holt, a professor of marketing at Oxford University. For Holt and a growing number of cutting-edge marketers, "branding" is really a cultural project. Holt, a trained anthropologist, lays out what is an essentially anthropological argument.[34]

When a brand attains icon status, Holt argues, it does so because it has fused with its culture's myths, reflecting its collective fears and desires. Hence, for instance, the Volkswagen Beetle, a German-based vehicle that in the 1960s and 1970s became an iconic brand in the United States, a cultural brand, did so in large part because it managed to convey a sense of bohemian rejection of mainstream American taste in cars. Beetles became "American" by embodying our cultural notions of egalitarianism; "the Bug" became an expression of a refusal to follow fashion, and by extension to engage in social climbing. Detroit was manufacturing and pushing the notion that cars were to be traded in frequently in order to remain trendy and fashionable. The Beetle ads satirized those social-climbing pretensions by exalting the car's unchanging utilitarian qualities. It worked. For Holt, the VW ad campaign was able to reflect cultural issues to create an iconic brand. Intercultural branding compounds the test, because now one must find the central myths of other cultures and make them resonate locally.

Cultural branding differs little, if at all, from attempts by nations to craft perceptions of themselves in foreign settings, and any discussion of Major League Baseball moving abroad must take into account local attitudes toward the United States. "Nation branding" is what foreign policy makers, corporate moguls, and branding gurus call such attempts to burnish foreign perceptions of a nation. It is closely related to propaganda; hence former Secretary of State Colin Powell hired Madison Avenue marketers to "rebrand American foreign policy" in the Middle East.[35] Advertisements, magazines, and television programming were enlisted to alter perceptions of the United States in this troubled region, to no avail. The British marketing expert Simon Anholt points out that the brand has to reflect foreign and domestic policy to be accepted abroad.[36] The brand cannot, in other words, be purely fiction; it must stand for something real. MLB must be something that can metamorphose into an international brand. This is no small task for something as linked to America as is baseball.

Baseball and Cross-cultural Branding

In light of the connection between the enterprise, the brand, and political and cultural perception abroad, what would it take to have baseball take root in Germany and in the United Kingdom, where soccer is so dominant, or to develop the game in South Africa, with its unique sport and racial history? What would it take to have MLB expand its base in Japan, China, or Korea, three distinct Asian nations with different degrees of baseball sophistication? These are the questions MLB has been asking. Promoters have built a range of programs and business strategies around traditional marketing principles to answer these questions, but they may have been selling themselves short. Mavens such as Tim Brosnan, Paul Archey, and Jim Small feel strongly that you can market yourself into any situation and out of any problem, but even they have given short shrift to cultural branding. Incorporation of sociocultural factors into an overall strategy or business plan, especially where international efforts are involved, might boost MLB's programs and goals. The following strategies make use of social and cultural features. In isolation, such strategies would probably fail to foster the growth of foreign sport. Bundled with conventional marketing notions, however, they could promote meaningful growth.

Keeping the Marketing Ear to the Ground

In Japan in the summer of 2004, "old school" baseball Shoguns and their hold on the game were challenged by a phalanx of young Internet owners. As a result, the cultural geography of the game changed. Takafumi Horie of the Internet portal Livedoor, Masayoshi Son of the Internet service provider Softbank Corp., and Hiroshi Mikitani of the online retailer Rakuten all made bids to buy ailing professional teams in Nippon Professional Baseball. The way that fans sided with Horie made it appear as if the old feudal traditions were falling out of favor in the intergenerational showdown. The old guard knows virtually nothing of the Internet and is distrustful of those that do. When Horie attempted to buy the Kintetsu Buffaloes, he was simultaneously rebuffed by the old owners and mobbed by enthusiastic young fans as he walked into the gift store at the stadium. He mixed with the fans, wearing T-shirt and jeans and talking like a modern marketing guru. A Yomiuri Giants executive berated Livedoor's youthful founder, pointing out that the reason everyone stood against him getting into NPB was that he never wore a tie![37]

MLBI has done well with the staid, powerful business interests in Japan but is also comfortable with the new breed. "These guys are more switched on. They're going to create a more vibrant league," acknowledged MLBI's Jim Small.[38] In looking at the social cleavages of the game, however, MLBI might consider how to more strongly associate itself with the changing face of Japanese baseball in an exciting and mutually advantageous way. At present, MLBI is content to work with any and all dimensions of Japanese baseball, but if it took a more proactive role, it could change a key perception that Japanese have of Major League Baseball: as outsiders, gaijin. MLB has been slow to understand just how intractable the Japanese are in terms of perceiving its ambassadors as Americans, as foreign influences, which is to say corrupting. The poster announcing the postseason MLB-NPB exhibition series—the one that Jim Small insisted be changed because MLB was presented as a bat painted red, white, and blue—was a telling example of the ingrained resistance MLB must overcome.

Allowing Japanese fans to vote for the major league All-Star teams and see season-opening games in Tokyo are nice gestures, but MLB could be promoting much more effectively. Parties that have been closest to the action—Sandy Alderson, Paul Archey, and Jim Small—all feel that ties between the two baseball countries are stronger than ever. At bottom, however, MLB is competing for a larger share of the Japanese market, and that is a market reality that cannot be changed. Small, for instance, applauds Japanese modernization as good for MLBI: "These new owners are likely to do all kinds of marketing things to get people to go to the ballpark. It's great, because if NPB is better, that's better for us. If baseball is strong here, that's good, because we can compete with them and show that our brand of baseball is more desirable."[39] The tension between encouraging and competing with the other organization involves a heightened sensitivity around a range of issues. Institutional ties between NPB and MLB obscure some cultural issues on the part of the Japanese, but also on the part of the Americans. There needs to be a marketing campaign that convinces Japanese fans that MLB is part of their cooperative, not colonial future. Shifting the marketing axis to make culture a driving force could promote this perception among the Japanese.

Marketing Social Consciousness

Baseball in South Africa couldn't be more different than in Japan. Outside of Johannesburg and Cape Town the sport is poorly understood, while it is Japan's number one sport. While in Japan there is seemingly unlimited revenue to be generated, in South Africa simply teaching the game stretches MLBI and the South African Baseball Union (SABU) to the limits.

On a fundamental level, grassroots development of the game is at odds with what MLBI was created to do, which is to generate revenue for the owners. Jim Small recognizes this when he talks of tier three development as "growing the game." The business will come later, he claims. There is a real question whether MLB and its owners share the vision of growing the game enough to spend the kind of time and resources it takes to develop the game in tier three settings. But if Archey and MLBI have their way, then cultural knowledge of the local world will be brought to bear, which would doubtless aid this effort.

"Cause marketing" is the convergence of an economic interest (be it product or corporate sponsorship) with social responsibility. Small first alerted me to baseball's unique position in postapartheid South Africa: "By talking to [the SABU development officer Edwin Bennett] and seeing his background, it became obvious to me that it's something beyond baseball. That baseball—and I hesitate to say this because I don't want to give baseball more credit than it deserves—is helping in its own small way to rebuild a nation." While appreciating the sensibility of doing the right thing, however, Small minimizes the desirability of moral marketing: "To market anything there needs to be a significant business interest. In sponsorships, for instance, cause marketing in baseball doesn't completely match up. If we're going to go into a South African company and be successful from a business perspective, we have to be able to show them that we can move product."[40]

I would argue differently, namely that in South Africa there exists one of those rare synergistic moments where being responsible is good for all parties. On the social responsibility side of the ledger, South African Baseball Union's Bennett approaches baseball as a social activist. For him, getting schoolchildren to play baseball is indistinguishable from building a new South Africa. Baseball gives them hope: "Three of our kids from Pitch, Hit, and Run went to the World Children's Baseball Fair [in Regina, Calgary]. One of their teachers from the rural areas said to them, 'The farther north you go, the colder it becomes,' and these children got off the plane wearing parkas on a very hot day. It was their first flight, their first trip in a car on the way to the first flight."[41]

In signing on as baseball sponsors, South African firms could be made to feel that they are part of this societal future. Major corporations throughout the world are increasingly adopting some version of what has become known as corporate responsibility. Officials are assigned to initiatives in which the corporation can play a responsible role in local affairs, in no small part because its officers understand that committing to the community can further long-term economic interests. In South Africa baseball is being promoted in a multiracial format, guaranteeing that all children and young people are gaining equal access to it. Governmental agencies now regard baseball as a "priority sport," eligible for funding such as National Lottery monies. Through this allocation, backstops and lights have been installed in existing fields all over the country, including in Black townships. With baseball being recognized as part of the country's new origin myth, corporations have an additional incentive for signing on.

Inventing Tradition

The historian Eric Hobsbawm coined the term "invented tradition" to connote a practice, behavior, or ritual that is of recent origins but has the feel of something quite old.[42] An invented tradition functions to foster a sense of community among disparate clusters of people. The British coronation, of nineteenth-century origins, is one such ritual. In baseball, invented tradition has the potential to be harnessed to a range of rituals, behaviors, and passions—some trivial, others serious—to create a sense of a shared world. Structuring a league, in this instance, works off of the same impulses as conflict resolution or community development.

Manipulating social tension for marketing purposes is hardly new. The fans of the Boston Red Sox and New York Yankees have been buying into their mutual disdain for decades. This is particularly the case among Red Sox fans, who until 2004 were consumed by a hatred of the Yankees' success, in contrast with the Red Sox's chronic failure, an attitude that many outside of New England regarded as collectively neurotic. A whole range of products has been created to reflect this toxicity. "Yankees Suck" T-shirts, and Yankee Hater hats and shirts are among the more tasteful products to be found throughout Red Sox Nation. The torrent of passion that fuels the rivalry underwrote television ratings and attendance and raised the players' fervor. Similar rivalries can be found in football, for instance, in small Texas towns, or in soccer, (Manchester United vs. Arsenal in England, for example). To my knowledge, however, few have marketed mutual hatred more successfully than those consumed by the Red Sox–Yankees rivalry. The functional significance of this "invented tradition" is not simply that it might help displace resentment but that it creates a fellowship within communities, and a kind of oxymoronic bond between communities. It also takes on a timeless quality, as if the rivalry has always existed. The mutual hostility is part of a ritualized dance that exhilarates fans and forges their collective identities.

If one were to take this as a template for structuring a league, there is no limit to what might be fashioned. Social tensions might be successfully channeled to diffuse negative energy and build cohesion. MLBI's European programs might take a page from this. In any given city the Play Ball program could be organized to include schools with strong local rivalries based upon neighborhood or other social tensions. The building of leagues forged around class tensions has been shown to have a powerful draw upon fans, as is the case in Brazilian soccer.[43] Yet another example of corralling social tension comes from the Israeli Premier League, which is made up of eleven Jewish teams plus Bnei Sakhnin, a team comprising mostly Arabs, with a few Jews, and based in the Palestinian Upper Galilee. With bipartisan crowds in attendance, the air at their games is thick with vile anti-Arab invectives. Arab players are called suicide bombers, while their Jewish players are regarded by Jewish fans as traitors. Bnei Sakhnin is a microcosm of the Arab-Israeli conflict, as well as a hopeful harbinger of its peaceful resolution, but the team's existence has infused the league with a passion that is verbalized and liable to spill over outside of the pitch.[44] Bnei Sakhnin won the Israeli Cup in 2003 and earned the right to face the English power Newcastle United in the first round of the UEFA Cup. Fresh from this victory the Arab team captain, Abbas Suan, and another Arab Israeli, Walid Badir, became part of the Israeli national team vying for World Cup contention. Each man played a decisive role in enabling Israel to tie Ireland and, later, France. Suan's picture adorned state lottery ads throughout Israel, and many referred to him by the biblical phrase for "savior of Israel." Of course, in such a land others continue to revile him, but what is clear is that he and his successful team have the capability of bridging the waters that divide Palestinians and Israelis.[45] Invented traditions exploiting dramatic events and heated rivalries have the capacity to build interest, which in turn can fuel existing myths or create new ones. In short, social tension can build a fan base.

Invented tradition may also come from the most benign sources as well. Small rituals that become ingrained have the ability to resonate and build collective identity and a barely perceived affinity for something or someone. One of South Africa's two minor league players, Barry Armitage, has established a low-key tradition in Durban:

> What we try to do in Durban is that every Friday night we have a Little League game from 5 to 8 P.M. Then at 8 o'clock we have a men's game, in which I pitch. The thinking is to get the youngsters and their parents to stick around to watch what they should be pulling for. I'll get introduced as Barry Armitage who plays for the Kansas City Royals farm team, and the kids would get excited and ask, "When can we see you on TV?" and "When are you going to be in the major leagues?"[46]

This Friday-night, secular, proto-ritual gives youngsters a chance to conjure dreams about South Africans playing in the Unites States. Furthermore, that it is a family gathering with entertainment, food, and hero worship helps to ground the game in a particular place. Armitage and his community could forge the ritualized building block of a small but significant baseball outpost. Were a sponsor to come in and underwrite this event, the connection might deepen. Badly needed media attention might come its way, further growing the game.

In Lowell, Massachusetts, at Lowell Spinners games another little ritual with marketing potential has arisen. At the Spinners' wonderful new six thousand–seat ballpark the team owner instituted a practice that captivated youngsters. As they entered the park, they enrolled in a raffle. Just before the home team took to the field, the announcer would summon nine youngsters whose names have been drawn, and each would come down to the field and accompany a player to his position. Once all nine players were on the field, each with his young fan in tow, they engaged in a brief ritual—tossing a ball back and forth, kicking the pitching rubber—and the children left the field transformed. These youngsters will never forget the experience of getting this close to their heroes and taking part in such a public spectacle. Moreover, all the young people in the stands have internalized this experience as well, and they can't wait for the next game to see whether they'll be called upon. This two-minute rite has profound consequences for bonding the youths with the team, the park, and the game, and offers a useful template for firms and corporations looking to identify their brands in consumers' minds. The promotions and fan-friendly events that are ubiquitous in minor league baseball form the foundation of invented tradition.

Inventing tradition, marketing social causes, and blending baseball with cultural myths are all strategies by which MLBI can creatively enjoy success and deepen the game's roots in foreign soil. The two global continua intersect around international marketing: there culture and economy fuse, and while marketing poses challenges for outsiders seeking to gain economic entry, it also offers opportunities for creativity. How does Major League Baseball stack up as a force for globalization?

Major League Baseball as Globalization

The most important development in the effort to globalize the game has been the centralization of power by the Commissioner's Office. The ability of teams to function independently—especially outside of North America—has been curbed considerably since 2000. This was done in the interests of shoring up some of the most serious problems that baseball faced in the 1990s. Labor strife in 1994 brought fan disillusionment in its wake, contributing to lagging television ratings and a growing economic disparity under which only well-heeled franchises seemed capable of reaching postseason play. A sense of foreboding prevailed, even among owners. In the first days of 2000 the owners voted unanimously to extend unprecedented authority to the commissioner to ameliorate structural disparities in the sport and generally oversee the health of the game. Bud Selig, formerly the owner of the small-market Milwaukee Brewers, used this opportunity to aggressively promote revenue sharing, which in his mind was the single most effective cure for the economic woes of MLB. To shape this program he set out on a bold effort to centralize a range of economic ventures that had been in the hands of teams.

Three years earlier, in 1997, following a weekend series between the San Diego Padres and the St. Louis Cardinals in Hawaii, the Padres, who had orchestrated the event, got to pocket a healthy return on their investment; the series had drawn well, and the team sold $150,000 worth of merchandise. Cardinals Manager Tony LaRussa was prompted to comment on the Padres' sudden windfall: "Baseball should be more global and spread out. But I get a feeling that the Padres are spreading out. I thought this was baseball, and we're all supposed to be sharing in it, but if we're just spreading the Padres' reach, what the hell. The world is getting smaller all the time. I don't know if it makes any sense to spread it for one club."[47] The sentiment of sharing the wealth was one that Commissioner Selig sympathized with.

One of the first moves by Selig following the expansion of the Commissioner's Office powers was the assumption of all team Internet rights and operations. Recognizing that Internet operations could potentially generate significant revenues, Selig pushed to have his office control these portals. Radio, television, and video broadcasts also came under new scrutiny and control as well. In fact, anything and everything that generated income was fair game for revenue distribution. Selig's office moved in a variety of directions. For instance, through agreements with four banks, MLB set up a lending pool for its teams of more than $1 billion, the largest such pool in the history of sports.[48] The game went on the offensive in politics as well, outspending all other sports in lobbying Congress on a range of issues from trade with Cuba to public funding for stadiums.[49]

Up until 2000 Major League Baseball International had been a somewhat marginal division of the Commissioner's Office, but when Tim Brosnan—then heading MLBI—finally convinced a majority of owners that the game was increasingly going to be foreign-directed and that resulting revenue was limited only by imagination, the office became energized. Older programs, such as the year-end Japanese-U.S. All-Star Game, received new life, and fresh programs and ideas were floated. New initiatives were generated on the baseball operations side of the Commissioner's Office as well. I've selected four global efforts to examine: the proposed worldwide draft of players; the World Baseball Classic; Team USA in the Olympics; and the MLB-NPB All-Star series. These represent the increasingly global interconnectedness of the sport; yet each is also rife with sectarian sensibilities that can undercut global efforts.

World Draft

During contentious 2002 labor negotiations, the Major League Baseball Players Association and team owners were at odds on a wide range of issues, but one that both sides agreed upon was instituting a worldwide draft. This draft would extend the Major League Baseball First-Year Player Draft, covering amateur players in the United States, Canada, and Puerto Rico, to include amateurs anywhere in the world. Each June all thirty major league teams participate in a selection rite of the best high school graduates, college upperclassmen, and unenrolled twenty-one-year-olds. The clubs take turns in reverse order of the previous season's finish—the last-place teams pick first. The draft goes on for fifty rounds. Once selected, a player can sign only with the drafting team—or the team to which his rights are subsequently traded or sold—until seven days before the next draft takes place.

The current incarnation of the worldwide draft was floated in 2001; it wasn't the first, however. A proposal for a such a draft was approved as early as 1993 by MLB scouting directors, but it got nowhere. Actually, a precursor to the world draft had been carried out in the Dominican Republic in 1985, and it too ended with a whimper.[50] Ralph Avila, then Los Angeles Dodgers vice president for Latin American operations, participated in that effort. His actions were probably the most telling thing about that draft: Avila simply refused to draft anyone! Round after round he simply stated, "The Los Angeles Dodgers pass."[51] When queried by his distraught bosses, he stated matter-of-factly that he chose no one because the players listed as having entered the draft were of no interest to him. In short order, Avila and his scouts found and signed three players who they felt would have a chance, but who had not appeared on the list of draftable players: Ramon Martínez, Juan Guzmán, and Juan Bell. The Dodgers had by then established a thorough scouting operation which crisscrossed the island in search of talent, while most teams contented themselves with holding tryouts in the few larger cities. Avila knew where the talent was islandwide and made the effort to go after them.

In the wake of the 2002 collective bargaining agreement, the Commissioner's Office argued for a worldwide draft in the interest of promoting competitive balance. Baseball's view was that foreign free-agent signings favor clubs with money. MLB Executive Vice President Sandy Alderson, who held the position until summer 2005, had been the most vocal proponent for the draft: "It would give clubs more equal access to players on the international level. When 40 percent of your players are foreign born, there's a need to equalize access."[52] This principle is particularly applicable to the Dominican Republic. Until the mid-1990s, it was uncommon for players from that country to receive bonuses of more than $5,000. Indeed, one of the main reasons that the Dominican talent explosion took place was that it was a cost-effective environment in which to find high-end talent. Since 1999, however, six-figure and even seven-figure signings have become increasingly common. The Dodgers gave Joel Guzmán $2.25 million in July 2001, prompting Anaheim Angels General Manager Bill Stoneman to comment on big-market teams: "Face it, if the New York Yankees spot a guy in one of the Latin American countries, or anywhere, and they want him, they will outspend all others to get him. And with their revenue, they can. A worldwide draft is just a good idea. Talent will be more evenly distributed."[53] Hence two considerations are posited to justify MLB's desire to regulate the international flow of labor: the critical mass of foreign players and the need to level the playing field between large- and small-market teams.

Proponents of the worldwide draft can be found in all camps. Some small-market general managers, such as Dean Taylor, formerly of the Milwaukee Brewers, contend that in theory it should work: "It'll prevent the Dodgers from going in and signing a guy for $2 million in the Dominican, and outbid[ding] the smaller-market team. If they want that player, they're going to have to use their first-, second-, or third-round draft pick; and in doing so that going to leave another player somewhere else open."[54] If major league organizations are forced to make a finite number of choices, a logical way of leveling the field could be constructed.

The problem with reforming the present system is that it also benefits small-market clubs. Despite increased bonuses, free-agent signings in Latin America remain significantly less expensive than domestic ones. A club with budget constraints but able to effectively scout can find excellent players that it can still afford to sign. One small-market executive who asked not to be named disagrees with Alderson's proposal, pointing out the economic disadvantage of a world draft:

> I'm not trying to throw darts, but there's more here than meets the eye. The logic [of the world draft] is that I may get a chance to draft a big-name guy, and the worldwide draft might minimize the bonus. But the way things are now, instead of spending $1 million on a player who might end up being a dud, I can go out and sign fifty Dominican or Venezuelan kids for $20,000 each and have a pretty good chance that some of them will develop into good players. With a world draft in place, I can't do that anymore. Now I may have to take a kid I like in the sixth or eight round and pay him $100,000 or whatever the sixth-round money is. Why screw up the chance to sign all these guys for reasonable money?[55]

Additional problems threaten the smooth running of an international draft. For instance, even while claiming that it would be a "true world-wide draft," Alderson admitted that the system would have exceptions. Some say that the exceptions would rule the system. Countries with professional leagues, like Japan, Mexico, and Korea, would be exempt from the draft, thus effectively removing three of the bigger player-developing nations. One of the most talked-about consequences of the worldwide draft will be what it does to amateur baseball in the Dominican Republic and Venezuela. Some teams are concerned that their academies will be shut down, replaced by one central facility, and that their signing bonuses—finally the same as Americans'—will result in fewer Dominicans being signed. There will also be difficulty in calculating signing bonuses when the kinds of players vary so widely between countries. That is one reason why Major League Baseball Players Association lawyer Michael

Weiner has argued for centralized academies run by MLB: "We're still concerned that there should be a way for a 16-year-old Latin American player to be favorably compared to American high school players. Centralizing the academies is a way to do that, to create some commonly developed background."[56] Ben Cherington, vice president of player personnel for the Red Sox, doubts that this will take place: "You're still going to have to train and develop kids in those countries. It's not going to change those kids' readiness to come to the States and play, so there's still going to be a need for a training facility. I'm not convinced that they'll be lessened in importance."[57]

There is also a certain amount of resistance to the draft from within baseball-rich foreign countries. Some in the Dominican Republic see the draft as an attempt to interfere with the way Dominicans run the game. Former Dominican Senator Victor García Sued threatened to organize opposition to the proposed world draft: "I'm going to our government, and I'm going to the governments of several other countries to fight against Selig. . . . An international draft would hurt the Latin American players." Garcia, it should be mentioned, runs his own academy.[58] Garcia's opposition centers on the disadvantage that Dominicans face because most come from poor backgrounds and suffer from substandard nutrition. He claims that boys in the United States and the Far East are two to three years ahead of Dominican players in physical development.

Jesús Alou, who heads the Red Sox's Dominican academy, sees the international draft as altering the way he goes about scouting and signing:

> I believe that the [worldwide] draft is going to change a few of the things we do now. For example, I'm a fisherman. Right now, if we were fishing in the Dominican Republic, we'd go out and fish with hooks. The scouts in the United States put no hook on their line. In other words, the scout over there goes out all year, but they can't land a guy, and say to him, "Hey, sign over here." This is due to the draft. Over here, we hook into a guy and if we think he's good, he's on board. Signed right away. The [worldwide] draft will change all that. That's why I say, they go out to fish without a hook. Here we get a gaff; we put it out there, and bring them in."[59]

Scouts prefer to operate within a system in which they can play an important role in securing talent, and the Dominican Republic has—for better or worse—been that kind of system.

In 2002 all that divided the Players Association, the Commissioner's Office, and the clubs were the number of rounds to be held in this world-wide draft. By the end of the 2004 season, however, the issue of the worldwide draft was all but dead. "We're farther from it today than we were two years ago," admitted Alderson.[60] "Why are we talking about a system that everyone pretty much agrees doesn't work, and imposing it on an area where just about everyone likes the system the way it is now?" was the way one baseball executive put it.[61] Once the worldwide draft escaped the confines of North America, it became subject to national interests and local practices, none of which could be easily governed or controlled by MLB. The worldwide draft is an instance of a meritorious globalized idea that succumbed to localized pressure. Structurally speaking, MLB does not have the institutional wherewithal to force the issue.

Team USA at the Olympics

In looking back at the IOC's decision to allow professionals to compete in basketball in Barcelona in 1992, one can see the organizers were—to a significant degree—motivated by market share. By including pros—indeed, some of the best of the pros—they would be securing the Games' position as the preeminent global sports event for some time to come. Was it mere coincidence that baseball was formally adopted by the Olympics at about that time?[62]

Team USA finally got to play baseball for real in 1992. The acknowledged kingpins of amateur baseball, the Cuban national team, won gold that year in Barcelona and again in Atlanta in 1996. U.S. baseball fans all argued that if the American team could escape its amateur straitjacket, it would win, and the U.S. team managed to prevail even without major leaguers in the 2000 Games in Sydney, Australia. The Americans, it was thought, were finally on their way to reclaiming their position atop the baseball world. The Commissioner's Office was somewhat miffed that the national team had to play in the Pan American Games to qualify for the 2004 Olympics, but having put together a strong squad of minor leaguers and some former major leaguers, Team USA reluctantly set about the business of continuing its mastery. Funny thing happened on the way to Athens: Team USA lost to Mexico 2–1 and failed to qualify for the Olympics. Howls of disbelief emanated from various corners of the baseball establishment, none louder than Tom Lasorda's: "I can't believe it. It's a shock and a disgrace that the Americans won't be represented in the Olympics." Countered a more cosmopolitan Sandy Alderson, "I don't think it's a setback for US baseball. I think it's a validation of the internationalization of the game." But the old boys all over the United States sided with Lasorda, who continued, "Baseball is America's game. It doesn't belong to the Japanese or the Cubans or the Koreans or the Italians. This is sad, very sad."[63] Far sadder is Lasorda. Having spent as much time traveling in the name of the game as he had, he was unaccountably blind to the realities of global baseball.

Any hopes that Olympic baseball would follow in the tracks of the "Dream Team" that basketball had assembled in 1992—when the likes of Michael Jordan, Charles Barkley, and Larry Bird were first allowed to compete in that sport as professionals—immediately ran into serious obstacles. The Olympic officials who speculated in this area were rebuffed at once; no one at MLB ever considered such an approach. Given the summer Olympics' schedule, the Games would badly disrupt the baseball season and pose a threat to clubs in the thick of pennant races. Sandy Alderson commented on that as early as 2000: "We didn't even take the possibility of major league players taking part in the Olympics into consideration. At this point, we're not ready to hold up the regular season and postseason."[64]

The IOC didn't respond immediately, but it took note. Seemingly out of the blue in late August 2002, the IOC's executive board discussed an internal report that recommended the elimination of baseball, softball, and the modern pentathlon. Unwilling to make the move just then, the executive board put off a decision until its meeting later in November, but the proposal sent shock waves through the international baseball community.[65] The last time a sport had been dropped from the Olympics was in 1936, when polo was axed. Was baseball, which had been put on hold for nine decades, going to be dismissed after only four Olympics? The report cited several reasons for recommending its removal; foremost was that baseball's top players were not participating.

Aldo Notari, the president of the International Baseball Federation, fretted that being dropped from the Olympics would be a "disaster for the development of baseball in the world."[66] It would indeed! Many countries in which the game is still in its formative stages depend upon Olympic Committee money to subsidize a national team and international competition. All of Europe and Africa and sections of other continents might be fatally affected by such a ruling.

A flurry of meetings to determine a strategy for countering this proposal took place throughout September 2002. At the heart of the matter was MLB's unwillingness to engage the IOC. "One nice letter from MLB and the union, saying in Beijing the best players will be participating, and problem solved," said Notari.[67] MLBI circulated information on the IOC board members, evaluating each in terms of his voting on the issue. If board members held some hope that MLB would comply with the request that major league players appear on the rosters, they couldn't have been more wrong. MLB's Bob DuPuy reiterated, "We would like very much to have the best players in the Olympics, but our schedule, our season and the expectations of our fans make that difficult at the present time.[68] Some Olympic officials cavalierly suggested shutting down the annual All-Star Game.

Sandy Alderson, who has been at the center of this impasse, was convinced that he could find a middle ground. Cognizant of how important the Olympics are to the economic development of peripheral countries, Alderson pieced together a proposal that might placate the IOC:

> One possibility is that we hold a three-day tournament, single elimination, which would make it easier to let certain players participate. If we were to vary that with a two- or three-day hiatus in the major league season, we could begin to make it work. Another thing we could do is when NBC televises the gold medal game, the rest of MLB would be blacked out. You could create a situation where anybody who is a baseball fan throughout the world would, on a Wednesday night in August, watch the gold medal game. That's a very strong statement. A short tournament would also cut down the number of players you need, and that addresses another IOC concern.[69]

While Alderson tried to find a workable solution, some privately bristled at the "arrogance" of the IOC. These critics feel that the IOC is fiscally motivated, seeking ways of reducing the television competition that comes from a major league season during the summer.

Alderson never got a chance to work his ideas into a presentable counterproposal. On July 7, 2005, in a secret vote, the IOC voted to eliminate both baseball and softball from the Olympic venue beginning in 2012. The absence of major leaguers on the teams, as well as lower standards for drug testing than in other sports, seemed decisive, but many associated with international baseball saw an anti-American element to the vote. Bob Watson, MLB's general manager of professional operations, certainly felt this to be the case: "This was not just a slap in the face at the United States, but a slap at the sport of baseball."[70] Major League Baseball will not be directly affected by such a move, indicated Donald Fehr, head of the Major League Baseball Players Association: "Baseball will go on just fine."[71] Commissioner Selig attempted to minimize the IOC move: "I don't know if frankly I consider it a blow. I'm sorry they made the decision, but we're moving on in a very dramatic way to internationalize the sport."[72] Selig was clearly spinning, because he is aware of what such a decision really means at the peripheries of the sport. National teams around the world will take serious economic hits because of this decision. Cuba, for instance, will feel the loss directly: "Not having the Olympics will be a big hit [on] Cuba and for the fans in Cuba," lamented White Sox pitcher José Contreras, himself a Cuban defector. "That's like the World Series for people [there]."[73] The loss of Olympic funding will devastate many of the tier three baseball-playing countries around the world.

Going into the winter of 2005–2006, there was talk of MLB getting back in the IOC's good graces. Attending a meeting of the International Baseball Federation in Switzerland in October 2005, DuPuy, MLB's president, came away with newfound optimism. Citing the growth of the sport around the world, and the growth in the number of baseball federations from 60 in 1990 to 122, Dupuy felt that MLB would persuade IOC members to request another vote in the winter Olympics in Turin, Italy.[74] The appeal failed, and while MLB had prepared itself for such an eventuality, there is little doubt that the sport will be hurt in those countries where it is weakest. One thing is certain: in the minds of many in the international community baseball is linked with the United States, and by extension with American foreign policy and pop cultural influences.

The IOC move has, without question, encouraged the creation by MLB of an international competition—witness Selig's promise that MLB was "moving on in a very dramatic way to internationalize the sport." The elimination of baseball from the Olympics put the notion of a World Baseball Classic on a fast track. But in running its own international event, MLB might expand its internationalization program while at the same time risking its global identity.

The MLB-NPB All-Star Series

The forerunner of the all-star series between Major League Baseball and Nippon Professional Baseball dates to 1908, when the Reach All Americans went to Japan for a nineteen-game tour.[75] Individual major league teams made trips there off and on over the following decades. Beginning in 1986, however, the event has involved an all-star collection of major leaguers who visit Japan every other year. Through the late 1960s the tours were won handily by the American teams, but from then on there was a qualitative improvement in the Japanese game. The series now features hard-fought contests.

Part goodwill tour, part nationalist contest, and part marketing ploy, the series is treated seriously by major leaguers. The event is nationally televised and played at venues all over Japan. The 2004 series, for example (which MLB won, five games to three), was held in Tokyo, Osaka, Sapporo, and Nagoya, covering south, central, and northern reaches of the country. These days, the MLB All-Star team generally features one of the majors' Japanese players. Ichiro's presence on the 2002 MLB team created enormous interest among Japanese, but in 2004, the Mets pitcher Kazuhisa Ishii didn't pique the interest of the Japanese fan as had Ichiro and Hideki Matsui. According to Jim Small, "Attendance was down from the past series, because we didn't have Ichiro or Matsui, but we averaged thirty-eight thousand over eight games, with a pretty hefty ticket price. That shows there's a pretty big appetite here."[76]

Does this event further the globalization of the sport? Insofar as it has become an emblem of the increasingly two-way flow of the game, the all-star series has global significance: Japanese players appear on the MLB rosters, and non-Japanese players on the NPB side. These transnational affiliations can undercut the perception of the game as a strictly national-ist affair. The production of the event has also become more important as well. MLBI treats its dealings with Japan as its most important global interaction, as evidenced by the placement there of Small, the vice presi-dent of international market development, at the head of MLBI's first foreign office. The July 2004 press conference announcing the all-star series was packed. Jim Small considers this kind of event a "'brand bomb,' an intense focus on our brand for almost two weeks. So we have prime-time games on Japanese television."[77]

The 2004 major league All-Star team featured some of the game's biggest stars—Roger Clemens and Manny Ramírez, for example—who dutifully played their ambassadorial roles. Clemens visited the U.S. embassy and opened a new Adidas store. Ramírez was present at a sake ceremony. Everywhere they went crowds clamored for them. Braves catcher Johnny Estrada was struck by the Japanese and their courteous ways. "You never get booed here," he noted. "When you don't have time to sign something, they just bow. Of course, we don't know what they're saying. So they could be bowing and saying something bad about us."[78]

The media companies that sponsor this event find that these tours gen-erate widespread enthusiasm, but the return of Japanese major leaguers to their native soil adds a twist. Japan's favored sons are coming home, all right, but they are coming home wearing the uniform of the other side, the gaijin. Nationalist impulses are quite strongly felt by Japanese, and having their players identified with the other side poses a problem for some; at the same time, the presence of Japanese players on American rosters is a powerful indication of globalizing forces. "There are really hardcore baseball fans here," says MLBI's Small. "What Ichiro and Matsui did was expand awareness to people who were NPB fans, but not MLB fans. Baseball was born in America, but now belongs to the world."[79]

World Baseball Classic

In the fall of 2001 Bud Selig declared his intentions to bring MLB to global stature by holding a World Cup–like event. "The mechanics are difficult," he admitted, "but I will say this to you:

There will be a World Cup. And I really hope it's while I'm still Commissioner."[80] "Difficult mechanics" and Selig's uncertainty that he would be there to watch it come to fruition hardly gave the impression that such an even was imminent. A baseball World Cup already exists under the aegis of the International Baseball Federation. In it, Team USA competes with its best amateurs, augmented by minor leaguers and occasional players with major league experience. For a true FIFA-style baseball World Cup to exist, however, only the best would do. The concept has been floated from time to time. MLBI's Tim Brosnan and Paul Archey began envisioning such an event as early as 1993. "We started to put this idea together amongst ourselves that baseball wasn't going to become a global game just by force-feeding people the game over the airwaves," Brosnan recalls. "We were going to need to spoon-feed people the game in person. . . . We started with this germ of an idea that playing games in a lot of *different ways* was going to be critical to the success of the business. . . . What if we did something like the Olympics, but it wasn't the Olympics?"[81] Paul Beeston, executive vice president of baseball operations in 2001, felt that if the thorny issue of timing the event could be worked out—no one would tolerate a two-week break in the heart of the major league season—a "real" World Cup might be realized by 2003. But Beeston's target date of 2003 came and went, and little progress was made, even taking into account that MLB had devoted most of its energies the previous year negotiating a new collective bargaining agreement. Still, MLB Executive Vice President for Business Tim Brosnan promised, "The interest in a World Cup is real. . . . It's come from an 'if' proposal to a 'when' proposal."[82] Most proponents believed that 2005 would be the ideal time, right between the 2004 Olympics and the soccer World Cup in 2006.

The selection process remained problematic. How many and which teams would compete? Some choices were obvious: the United States, Japan, South Korea, Taiwan, the Dominican Republic, Venezuela, Puerto Rico, and Mexico—the certain eight. By November of 2004 MLBI, which was heading this effort, had decided upon a sixteen-team format—extending additional invitations to Panama, Canada, Australia, Cuba, Italy, the Netherlands, South Africa, and China. Little else was settled.

When 2004 rolled in, there was still the same talk—and only talk. In February MLB President and Chief Operating Officer Bob DuPuy again intoned, "The Commissioner and ownership are very enthusiastic about having such an event."[83] By May, MLB had cleared one hurdle—the drug testing issue—but then things got sticky. Word came in July, at the All-Star Game, that the Japanese and South Koreans were unhappy with the way the World Cup was being organized, and by the exclusivity of the decision-making process. Particulars bothered them as well. The event was tentatively set for March 4–21. The Japanese, who begin their season in March, felt as if their time constraints were not being taken into account. At bottom, when originally approached about the "World Baseball Classic," they perceived it in terms of a FIFA-like World Cup, organized by a board that represented the countries competing. When they realized that it was, in fact, an MLBI-run invitational tournament, the Koreans and Japanese grew irate. "At this point the MLB and [the Players Association] have decided to host an event that they will *invite us to*. We want more input than that," tersely insisted Michael Park, manager of baseball operations at the Korean Baseball Organization.[84] The commissioners of the Korean Baseball Organization and Nippon Professional Baseball considered boycotting the World Cup. Recognizing that no credible tournament could take place without these Asian countries, MLB realized that a 2005 World Cup debut was impossible. MLB organizers spun an explanation to the North American media, claiming that the Japanese needed more time: "The year delay from a stated goal of staging it prior to next season [2005] was done primarily to accommodate the Japanese, who can't field a team in 2005 because of contraction and restructuring of their own major leagues."[85]

If NPB had planned to gain leverage by creating an Asian block with Korea, Taiwan, and China, thereby stalling the World Baseball Classic, the Japanese executives overestimated their influence and underestimated the organization of MLBI. Nevertheless, the MLB Commissioner's Office worked feverishly to get the World Baseball Classic back on track, meeting frequently with Japanese officials. On July 11, 2005, the event was, at long last, publicly paraded. It would commence on March 2, 2006, and end on March 20. The sixteen teams would be divided into four pools: (1) China, Taiwan, Japan, and Korea; (2) Canada, Mexico,

South Africa, and the United States; (3) Puerto Rico, Cuba, Panama, and the Netherlands; (4) the Dominican Republic, Venezuela, Australia, and Italy. The competition would proceed in round-robin fashion at each level until the single-elimination semifinals and finals. First-round games would be played in Tokyo, San Juan, Florida, and Arizona. All the others would be in major league parks.

Rumblings from Japan continued, however, even through 2005, as the Japanese media regularly printed objections on the part of the Japanese players' association and NPB. Again, objections were raised over the issue of the March games (immediately preceding the Japanese season), as well as revenue distribution.[86] MLB patiently broke down the economics of the event in order to convince NPB officials of an equal distribution. According to the International Baseball Federation's Aldo Notari and MLB Players Association head Gene Orza, once the costs of putting on the tournament are recouped, the net profits would be split into two pools.[87] The national federations representing each country would divide 53 percent of the remaining revenue along the following lines:

Major League Baseball	17.5%
Major League Baseball Players Association	17.5%
All other professional leagues	13%
International Baseball Federation	5%

The remaining 47 percent of the net profits are to be divided as prize money. The eight teams that fail to advance beyond the first round would each receive 1 percent. The four teams that lose in the second round would each get 3 percent. The two teams falling in the semifinals would each get 5 percent. The second-place team would get 7 percent, and the winner 10 percent.

At first glance, the shares of MLB and the MLB Players Association, a combined 35 percent of the net profits, jump out as bloated, compared with the shares of the rest of the nations playing in the tournament. This rankled the Japanese. MLB's Jim Small went on record to address this:

> To say this is a money grab for the MLB is absolutely erroneous. . . . All the money made around the world goes into one pot and all of the expenses are taken out of that pot. Whatever is left, the

profit is split up. . . . The MLB and MLBPA are entitled to the
largest percentage of the net profit. It you take the percentage we
are getting and divided it by 30 [all MLB teams], it is the exact
same net number as the NPB percentage divided by 12 (all NPB
teams). What that means is that the New York Yankees make the
exact same amount per share as the Rakuten Golden Eagles, and
the Yankees have all of the risk.[88]

Even in the face of this reasoned and economically defensible distribution, NPB and players continue to bristle. MLB's Bob DuPuy, who,
among others, meets with the Japanese representatives to explain the
economic breakdown in rational terms, says, "We've made a lot of
progress on venues—and, frankly, we've made a lot of progress on the
Japanese."[89] Still, others report that the Japanese continue to harbor
resentment. "This whole thing smacks of imperialism on the part of
MLB. Why didn't they build a consensus on this before announcing their
plans?" commented one high-ranking Japanese official.[90] Here we have
the essence of the disagreement: MLB has charged onto the world stage
with this event in tow. The World Baseball Classic is another Major
League Baseball production, politically and economically crafted by and
for MLB, with an international cast. The Japanese, on the other hand,
feel as if they have been bullied to accept, rather than approached in a
spirit of cooperation to build a consensus. By the reckoning of the
Japanese, MLB's approach lacked the requisite ritualistic and diplomatic
choreography. Jack Sakazaki, a Tokyo-based sports consultant, argues,
"It's cultural differences that trigger these problems. . . . MLB's attitude
is, 'We're taking the risk, we'll make the deal.' It is arrogant, and it ticks
the Japanese off."[91] Differences in the way the two cultures negotiate
also play a role; the sometimes hard-nosed business style of the
Americans rubs the Japanese consensus builders the wrong way. At least
one report speculated that these differences factored into the Japanese
assessment of MLB negotiators.[92]

While Japan and Korea were pressing their point, it was also quickly
apparent that MLB had no intention of losing control over this important tournament. MLBI's Jim Small has been dealing with NPB on this
issue throughout negotiations, and at times his frustration has shown:

"They feel like we're shoving it down their throats. They're excited enough, but they don't understand why *we're* running it. They look at it like the FIFA World Cup, and it's not that way. This is a tournament that MLB is operating, and these guys are invited, and the Dominican Republic is invited, and so on."[93] The FIFA decentralized model is built around continental federations, and that fuels interest and international commitment worldwide. I am drawn back to the early vision of MLB's Brosnan of what this event would be: "We talked about leagues, we talked about Olympics. . . . And then we talked about, 'Why can't there be *something that was ours, that we could own, our own stage?*"[94] The World Baseball Classic was clearly being planned as an American event to be supported by the rest of the world. If internationalism was part of the picture, it was to be internationalism in service of an MLB event. When MLB officials grow exasperated with the Japanese or Koreans, claiming that the WBC is "not about business or politics," they are only partly correct.[95] It is, in this instance, about the cultural perceptions of how business and politics are handled and acted out.

MLBI is right in feeling that this was its creation, and MLBI's staff labored to put all of the pieces together. Further, MLB is shouldering the considerable up-front costs of the event's production. Paul Archey and others have worked hard to negotiate the logistics and revenue potential embedded in the event. Yet there has been a failure to present this to others as a work in progress, and one that will—perhaps next time—be more globally inclusive. In the end, the WBC—for whatever reasons—is global in form, but national in essence. Uneasy with this, no doubt, MLBI offered the Japanese two seats on the WBC steering committee in 2009. Something was missed, however, in the initial approach, so that by the time these efforts were made, they appeared forced and tardy.

If MLB needed a mirror held up to it to see its nationalist persona, it received one less than three months before the WBC was set to begin. On December 13, 2005, the U.S. Treasury Department informed Major League Baseball that Cuba, which had finally agreed to play in the inaugural event, would not be permitted to enter the tournament. The U.S. trade embargo against Cuba—a policy almost a half-century old—would be violated if the Cubans received the money that each participating team gets. Prodded by the Cuban-American community, the Bush administration brought national policy into the mix. Without Cuba, some of the event's much needed luster would be missing, not to mention the loss of a great competitor. Other participants responded rapidly. Puerto Rico threatened to withdraw as a site for the games if the Cubans were not permitted to play. Venezuela volunteered to be a site. Cuban Americans demanded to have their own team at the WBC. Baseball was being trumped by partisan political interests.

As Paul Archey and other MLB officials were busily trying to get the government to rescind its decision, they should have had an epiphany: MLB was, for the moment, standing in opposition to the parochial nationalist impulses—the very ones it often acts upon. In resisting the dictates of its own government, MLB had a mirror held to its face—a valuable transnational lesson.

In the end, the U.S. government rescinded its ban on Cuba; the Japanese showed up; players donned colorful uniforms, presenting the world with national eye candy; and the tournament was played with remarkable gusto. Upsets occurred, as Mexico bounced the favored Americans, and the Dominican Republic and Venezuela were likewise vanquished. Cuba and Japan played for the title to widespread excitement and surprise. Television ratings were impressive and attendance healthy; but if the doyens of this event think that the success justified the means, they are wrong. The nationalism that was—in this instance—tamed, lending luster to the event, can likewise undo it if, in the future, MLB does not structure the WBC more equitably.

MLB's Technological Juggernaut

What most people perceive as Major League Baseball's most globalized index is the cosmopolitan makeup of its work force: 29 percent of its players that are foreign born. While transnational labor is a meaningful variable, large labor migrations—nineteenth-century Irish emigration to the United States, for example, and Turkish labor migration to Germany in the twentieth century—have characterized most of the Industrial Age. What is truly most globalized about MLB is its ability to bring the game to any corner of the planet. Major League Baseball International has been busily negotiating contracts for television rights with countries around the world. In 2004 MLBI signed a record contract with Japan, and the Dominican broadcaster Canal de Notícias signed a four-year deal valued in the low seven figures.[97] Even Europe has been opened up to televising baseball; Germany, Italy, and the Netherlands receive regular broadcasts.

Major League Baseball Advanced Media (MLBAM) is the Internet division of MLB, headed by Bob Bowman and supervised on a day-to-day basis by Dinn Mann, its editor in chief. MLBAM is at the leading edge of the sports world. It is "the world's largest producer of live online content," claims Mann. In 2003 it presented more than forty thousand hours of programming. By year's end there had been 650 million visits to MLB.com.[98]

As impressive as are the numbers that MLB.com has put up, the speed with which it did so is more impressive still. In June 2000 all major league clubs agreed to cede the running of their Internet sites to the Commissioner's Office. Before that, the quality of sites was uneven at best. Some teams had good sites. Some even used the Internet aggressively. The San Diego Padres and Arizona Diamondbacks reached into Mexico and other nontraditional pockets. In setting up MLB.com, the Commissioner's Office assumed control of information regarding teams and jettisoned or reassigned a host of independent writers and others who had become employed by individual teams.

Setting up MLBAM was a bold but risky move. With a combined $90 million investment from team owners, MLB.com ate up $75 million in its first three years of operation. By the end of 2002, however, it became profitable, and in 2005 MLBAM grossed $220 million. The company has a triangulated revenue strategy in place: e-commerce, sponsorships, and multimedia subscriptions. MLBAM has been successful in attracting sponsors—Internet providers mostly, like Microsoft, AOL, and Comcast—that use the site as a lure for potential subscribers. All three revenue sources have been surprisingly successful—especially the subscriptions. Conventional wisdom has it that people are reluctant to pay for anything online.[99] Still, even here, MLBAM has succeeded. In 2003 there were 550,000 subscribers to a vast array of content; by 2005 there were 1,300,000. For $100 a season, a subscriber can have access to live audio of any game played, and live video of 250 games per year. "MLB is unique because it's unscripted and there's a constant flow of content," Dinn Mann boasts. "There's no other sport with 2,700 games a year and up to 15 games a day."[100] Additionally, the user gets a dizzying array of offerings: highlight packages, postgame analysis and video, archived games, video highlight downloads, and wireless service. The free site MLB.com has current stats, scores, box scores, real-time events, news, tickets, merchandise, history, memorabilia, and more. So successful has this enterprise been that in the fall of 2004 it was rumored that MLBAM would soon go onto the stock market with an initial public offering.[101]

The "Connectedness" of MLB

The global labor flow of baseball has been one of the main drivers of its interdependence. Foreign players in the major leagues galvanize widespread interest in the game among their countrymen. MLB's Sandy Alderson perceives this as the heart and soul of baseball globalization. Referring to the baseball academy that MLB has successfully developed in Australia, Alderson claims a clear global vision, one based on what he calls "senior development," the development of players who can make it to the major leagues: "The baseball academy we have in Australia is central to our international strategy; which is to develop players who can come to the United States and prosper. With that they create interest in their home countries."[102]

Overall, the interconnectedness of Major League Baseball is still in its formative stages. MLB has global reach, but it is spotty: strong in some places, weak in others, nonexistent in many. When baseball globalization has reached a mature stage, MLB will have grown so that it will be responsive to changes in any area of the globe, as the banking industry is sensitive to economic hiccups around the world.

Crafting a World Series

MLB and its international arm have aggressively fostered the game and the brand around the world. We have seen that Paul Archey and Jim Small use the language of globalization, along with Commissioner Selig and Sandy Alderson. There is no doubt that MLB is committed to spreading the game internationally, just as there is no question that it has made significant progress since the early 1990s. It is also clear to me, at least, that there are many talented people in the Commissioner's Office, people who understand this process in a range of ways. That being said, the question as to what kind of globalization program MLB is pursuing remains to be answered.

MLBI's definition of globalization is simultaneously narrow and broad. Being responsible for generating revenue from broadcast rights, licensing, corporate sponsorship, and events makes MLBI the foreign business division of the sport. MLBI is also charged, however, with developing the game where it exists only minimally, and this poses a challenge. If MLBI operates within its conventional parameters, it can succeed economically over the short run. But only by working to build in unconventional fashion can MLBI move to the forefront of global sport formation and make the industry a global success in the coming century.

MLBI and the cutting edge division MLBAM have shown that they are committed to expanding the business of Major League Baseball. They have been impressive in this regard, but there is a shortsightedness to it all. For Major League Baseball to become a global force it will take more than sophisticated technology and advanced marketing; it will take a global view in which MLB grows by reducing its dependence on strict economic and political control. *MLB will actually have to decenter somewhat.*

I have noted that the most important development in the globalization of the sport had been the commissioner's centralizing control of the sport; why would I now say that baseball needs to decenter? The authority to act for the industry gives MLB the ability to act globally, decisively, and quickly, but it must take care not to become the eight hundred–pound gorilla in its dealings with others. Confederates will promote a healthier, longer-lived organization than will serfs.

At the level of the franchise there is a much greater range of opinion regarding globalization. Some owners and general managers remain mildly annoyed at the prospect of a global game, but most—in the abstract, at least—support the trend. Some clubs are quite aggressively internationalist. The Royals, as we have seen, are going global: thinking at the same time about their own needs and about the long-term prospects of expanding the game. The New York Mets have developed an organizational structure that is truly transnational. General Manager Omar Minaya, a Dominican-born U.S. citizen, has worked to ensure that the Mets have Latino administrators at all levels. This has the effect of blurring national boundaries and turning the Mets into the industry's first transnational entity.[103]

All enterprises seeking to globalize do so for some combination of factors: to maximize profits, for example, or to expand their vision, or promote world domination, or to successfully compete. With the possible exception of the founding philosophy of the United Nations, there are no completely benign reasons for globalizing. MLB's efforts have self-interest at their core. There is, nevertheless, a more benign direction for globalization to take—"tough love globalizing"—which doesn't seek to colonize. The formation of major league–level franchises in other parts of the world is the single most important step that MLB can take to globalize. Logistics aside, bringing a team from Tokyo or Caracas into Major League Baseball is one form this could take.

A more far-reaching and perhaps more structurally sensible way to accomplish globalization might be to realign Major League Baseball so as to enable foreign franchises into the league. A Pacific Rim division, which could accommodate Asian teams along with existing West Coast major league teams, would be a viable structure within MLB. As futuristic as it sounds, Tokyo, Seoul, Taiwan, and Sidney might be in the same division as Seattle, San Francisco, one Los Angeles team, and San Diego. A Pan-American Division might include Florida, Tampa Bay, Texas, Houston, and Arizona, along with Havana, Monterrey, and Caracas. The remaining major league clubs would be split into an Eastern and a Western Division. To foster this restructuring, the level of baseball played in Korea and Taiwan would have to be elevated. Without this commitment to forge real partnerships with other regions of the world—itself a process of decentralizing—MLB will only continue to internationalize in the manner that I termed "testicular globalization." That way lies stagnation.

A global flow of baseball capital should also be pursued. Foreign ownership of franchises should never again inspire nationalist indignities like those visited upon Hiroshi Yamauchi when he purchased the Seattle Mariners. If Hyundai wants to buy the Havana team, or Ted Turner sell his Atlanta Braves and insist on purchasing the Tokyo franchise, both should be encouraged. If Toyota can upgrade the Monterrey club, so be it. The purpose of globalization is to break down the nationalism that is built into Major League Baseball or the Nippon Professional Baseball leagues. The global flow of capital and franchises should mirror that of the globalized sports labor that has led the way. Fears that local professional leagues will be weakened or turned into feeder leagues for MLB ring of protectionist nationalism, and will be rendered obsolete if the structure and economics of the game open up completely. Can the Japanese object to Tokyo becoming a major league club if their companies own major league clubs in the United States, and if the best Japanese players are found on major league rosters in Seoul, Chicago, and Caracas? Can owners continue indefinitely to be ethnocentric if their teams are multicultural, their players given every opportunity to advance to major league level, and if the ownership of franchises runs the gamut from Canadians to Americans to Venezuelans? MLB's Sandy Alderson theorizes, "I think it's possible to extend the game elsewhere in North America or the Western Hemisphere or beyond. Keep in mind that teams from Hawaii are able to compete at the collegiate level as well as previously in the professional level of baseball. So what kind of step is it from Hawaii to Japan, for example? I don't think it's that difficult to project the game over the next decade or two to have developed a global structure."[104]

By "global structure," does Alderson conceive of a decentered Major League Baseball down the road? At this writing, baseball is far from decentering, in part because the game has so far to grow; because of this, Alderson thinks that decentralization is "decades away." His view is based on a pragmatic appraisal of where the game is now, and how fast it is growing:

> When I think of globalization conceptually, using FIFA as an example of decentralization, I think of the following. In FIFA the game is played well in a lot of places, and the economics in those places can support the opportunities that come their way. That kind of dual strength lends itself to decentralization. Baseball isn't there yet. There are only a few places in the world where the level of the game matches up with the level of the economy. Until you see more places develop, MLB will continue to have the power it presently has (to pay the salaries it does, to develop players wherever they are).[105]

Alderson explains why globalization is not likely *now*, but MLB has to determine whether it will encourage globalization in the future. Few general managers and owners actively espouse moving in this direction with any haste.

There is no baseball Moses on the horizon to lead the game into the twenty-first century, but a scattering of forward-thinkers can be found. Former Boston Red Sox General Manager Dan Duquette, for instance, has claimed, "I've always thought that Cuba or Venezuela would be a great place to establish a major league franchise."[106] San Diego Padres chairman John Moores concurs: "You'd like to see two Latin American franchises, maybe in Havana and Mexico City, in the next 20 years."[107] I am certain that baseball administrators who hail from foreign countries do not need to be convinced of the advisability of globalizing the franchise base. New York Mets G.M. Omar Minaya and San Francisco Giants Manager Felipe Alou, both Dominicans by birth, advocate locating franchises abroad. Some significant global interpenetration is already evident in the global labor flow in professional leagues around the world. We see it in MLB's advanced information technologies division, which has made the game globally available in exciting new ways, and in the willingness to send teams around the world both in and out of season. What we need now is to have MLB transfer its know-how in unassuming ways, crafting partnerships in the course of forging new structures that may one day emerge transformed. In short, MLB has to decide between embracing testicular or tough-love globalization. Should it decide on the latter, we can then talk about a real World Series.

NOTES

Introduction

1. Jim Small, interview by the author, January 12, 2000.
2. Ibid.
3. Ibid.
4. Ken Belson, "Getting Champions' Caps to the Game Before the Final Whistle," *New York Times*, May 28, 2003.
5. Bob Hohler, "Guerrero Wins by Country Mile," *Boston Globe*, November 17, 2004.
6. Charlie Nobles, "Baseball Players from Over There Get a Shot Over Here," *New York Times*, May 18, 2005.
7. Tim Weiner, "Baseballs Being Made in a Sweatshop," www.sportsbusiness news.com (The Daily Dose), January 26, 2004 (originally published as "Low-Wage Costa Ricans Make Baseballs for Millionaires," *New York Times*, January 25, 2004).
8. Thomas L. Friedman, *The World Is Flat: A Brief History of the Twenty-first Century* (New York: Farrar, Straus and Giroux, 2005), 114.
9. Ibid., 32.
10. Michael Lewis, *Moneyball: The Art of Winning an Unfair Game* (New York: Norton, 2003).
11. Jim Small, interview by the author, January 26, 2004.

Chapter 1. The Crisis at the Core

1. Joe Strauss, "Baseball Making Comeback, Has the Game Begun to Heal?" www.sportsbusinessnews.com (The Daily Dose), November 5, 2003 (originally published as "Baseball Puts on Its Rally Cap," *St. Louis Post-Dispatch*, November 2, 2003).
2. "Commissioner Selig's Accomplishments," MLB press release, August 19, 2004.

3. Justice B. Hill, "Selig Wants to Make Game Global," www.indians.com, August 23, 2004.

4. Quoted in "Selig's Accomplishments."

5. Quoted in Howard Zinn, *The Twentieth Century: A People's History* (New York: Harper Collins, 1984), 2.

6. Edward Gibbon, *The Decline and Fall of the Roman Empire* (New York: Modern Library, 1966), 860.

7. Marvin Harris, *The Rise of Anthropological Theory: A History of Theories of Culture* (New York: Crowell, 1968).

8. Russell Adams, "Local TV Ratings Looking Up for Most Clubs," *Sports-Business Journal*, July 12–18, 2004, 6.

9. Barry M. Bloom, "MLB Sets Attendance Mark," www.MLB.com, October 3, 2004.

10. For major league totals I assumed the twenty-five man roster that has, with occasional deviations, been standard for most of the season. Minor league totals are based upon the premise that each team has one affiliate at each of three levels, plus a rookie league team in the United States and one in the Dominican Summer League.

11. "Harris Interactive Poll: Baseball vs. Other Sports," *Baseball America,* March 29–April 11, 2004, 22.

12. *Street and Smith's SportsBusiness Journal: By the Numbers Annual Research Guide,* 2004, 41. The Harris Poll is cited in Bill Plaschke, "This Sport Just Can't Get to First Base," *Los Angeles Times,* May 1, 2005.

13. Jules Tygiel, *Baseball's Great Experiment: Jackie Robinson and His Legacy* (Oxford: Oxford University Press, 1983), 186.

14. Mike Royko, *Chicago Daily News,* October 26, 1972, quoted in Tygiel, *Baseball's Great Experiment,* 186.

15. Quoted in Brent Staples, "Where Are the Black Fans?" *New York Times Sunday Magazine,* May 17, 1987, 23.

16. Aaron Kuriloff, "Baseball Is Striking Out in the City," *New Orleans Times-Picayune,* March 19, 2000, citing a survey by Mediamark Research.

17. *By the Numbers,* 2003, 23.

18. A sampling of pricing around MLB shows that the Los Angeles Dodgers have a package for a family of four at $48 (as of 2004) that includes tickets, parking, and concessions. Other teams have similar deals (sometimes substituting souvenirs for parking): the Cardinals for $60, the Yankees for $80, and the Mariners for $50. Families living in communities whose teams offer such "family packs" might be able to take a child or two to a couple of games a season. But the spontaneous decision—"Hey, whatcha doin'? Wanna take in a game?"—seems to have been priced out of existence.

19. Terry Lefton, "The Aging Baseball Market," *Brandweek* 34, no. 3 (1993): 11.

20. Allen St. John, "Baseball's Billion-dollar Question: Who's on Deck?" *American Demographics* 20, no. 10 (1998): 60–62.

21. Rick Horrow, "The Business of MLB at the All-Star Break," www.SportsLine.com, July 12, 2004.

22. Eric Fisher, "Baseball Asks, 'Where are the Kids?'" *Washington Times,* May 22, 2004.

23. Eric Spanberg, "Attracting Kids to Major Sports No Child's Play," *Sports-Business Journal,* June 16–22, 2003, 22.

24. *By the Numbers,* 2003, 85.

25. Quoted in Fisher, "Baseball Asks."

26. Quoted in Todd Wilkinson, "USA: A Whole New Ballgame," *Christian Science Monitor,* March 27, 2000, 1.

27. Center for the Study of Sport in Society, Race Report Card, 2005.

28. Frank White, interview by the author, February 8, 2002.

29. Peter Gammons, Baseball Notes, *Boston Globe,* July 28, 1991.

30. Harry Edwards, "The Crisis of Black Athletes on the Eve of the 21st Century," *Society* 37, no. 3 (2000): 9–13.

31. Center for the Study of Sport in Society, Race Report Card, 2005.

32. Quoted in Kuriloff, "Baseball Is Striking Out."

33. Ibid.

34. Quoted ibid.

35. Mike Klis, "Fewer Blacks Step Up to Plate in Pro Baseball," *Denver Post,* May 11, 2003.

36. Quoted in Rick Hummel, "Baseball No Longer Is Attracting Many Young Black Players," *St. Louis Post-Dispatch,* April 13, 2003. At least one person familiar with the situation contends that if baseball were granted more college scholarships, the game would be able to attract more African-American talent.

37. Quoted in Ben Bolch, "MLB Steps Up in Compton," *Los Angeles Times,* August 6, 2003.

38. Marcy Frank, "Youth Participation in Sports Hits the Couch," *SportsBusiness Journal,* November 27–December 3, 2000, 6.

39. Matthew Futterman, "Little League Baseball Facing Serious Challenges," www.sportsbusinessnews.com (The Daily Dose), August 7, 2003 (originally published in the *Newark Star-Ledger*).

40. Dave McKibben, "Where Have All the Little Leaguers Gone?" www.sports businessnews.com (The Daily Dose), August 14, 2004 (originally published in the *Los Angeles Times*).

41. Quoted in Rick Westhead, "Survey Says, MLB Needs to Be More Competitive," *Bloomberg News,* December 20, 2001, 22.

42. The luxury tax is a fine of sorts for teams that exceed a certain payroll limit. Its purpose is to encourage parity by restraining excessive spending on free agents by big-market teams. For 2006 two teams will have exceeded the $136.5 million threshold on payroll: the New York Yankees ($213.1 million) and the Boston Red Sox ($141.9 million). For the Yankees this is their third violation, and their luxury tax is pegged at 40 percent of the overage (roughly $34 million); for the Red Sox it is their second violation (30 percent tax, or $4 million).

43. Andrew Zimbalist, *May the Best Team Win: Baseball Economics and Public Policy* (Washington, D.C.: Brookings Institution, 2003).

44. Tim Brown, "Bare Markets," *Los Angeles Times,* April 1, 2005, D12.

45. Eric Fisher, "The 'Troubling Times' MLB Appears to Be Facing," www.sportsbusinessnews.com (The Daily Dose), December 1, 2003 (originally published in the *Washington Times*).

46. Allard Baird, interview by the author, March 23, 2004.

47. Zimbalist, *May the Best Team Win,* 103–104.

48. Kevin Baxter, "At Baseball's Annual Winter Meetings, It's the Haves vs. the Have-nots," www.sportsbusinessnews.com (The Daily Dose), December 9, 2004 (originally published in the *Miami Herald*).

Chapter 2. The Kansas City Royals

1. John Holway, ed., *Voices from the Great Black Baseball Leagues* (New York: Da Capo, 1992), 92.

2. Art Stewart, interview by the author, March 20, 2004.

3. Ibid.

4. Frank White, interview by the author, February 8, 2002.

5. Stewart interview.

6. White interview.

7. Ibid.

8. Stewart interview.

9. Ibid.

10. Jerry Crasnick, *Baseball America,* September 15–28, 2003, 4.

11. Mike Bauman, www.MLB.com, March 24, 2004.

12. Allard Baird, interview by the author, March 26, 2004.

13. Allard Baird, interview by the author, August 3, 2002.

14. Ibid.

15. Allard Baird, interview by the author, May 3, 2002.

16. Quoted in Thom Loverro, "A Suggestion That MLB Look at Pay for Play," *Washington Times,* May 19, 2003.

17. Allard Baird, interview by the author, March 28, 2004.

18. Michael Lewis, *Moneyball: The Art of Winning an Unfair Game* (New York: Norton, 2003), 16.

19. Allard Baird, interview by the author, May 12, 2002.

20. Ibid.

21. Ibid.

22. Allard Baird, interview by the author, March 29, 2004.

23. Quoted in Gordon Edes, "Manager's Musings Worth Considering," *Boston Globe,* April 14, 2002.

24. Allard Baird, interview by the author, May 2, 2002. In baseball lingo a "five-tool" player is one who can hit, hit for power, run, field, and throw.

25. White interview.

26. Luis Silverio, interview by the author, August 23, 2002.

27. Ibid.

28. Allard Baird, interview by the author, February 18, 2002.

29. Allard Baird, interview by the author, May 2, 2003.

30. Through 2005 there were still two South Africans in the Royals system: Barry Armitage and Eric McClellan.

31. Allard Baird, interview by the author, August 5, 2000.

32. Clive Russell, interview by the author, July 2, 2002.

33. dr1.com, Daily News, July 30, 2002.

34. Luis Silverio, interview by the author, February 8, 2002.

35. Ibid.

36. Ibid.

37. Ibid.

38 Ibid.

39. Quoted in Edes, "Manager's Musings."

40. Quoted ibid.

41. Baird interview, March 29, 2004.

42. Ibid.

43. Quoted in Tracy Ringolsby, "Hope Returns to Kansas City," *Baseball America*, February 16–24, 2004, 9.

44. Allard Baird, interview by the author, December 14, 2005.

45. Ibid.

46. Ibid.

Chapter 3. The Los Angeles Dodgers

1. Quoted in Jesse Katz, "Artless Dodgers: They Were Once L.A.'s Team, Proof of the City's Ascendance. Now We Hardly Know Their Names," *Los Angeles Magazine*, April 2002, 54.

2. Quoted ibid.

3. Bill Shaikin, "The Yankees: Bottom Line and Baseball Parity," *Los Angeles Times*, April 1, 2004.

4. Commissioner's Office Blue Ribbon Report 2001, in "Is Money Everything?" Jim Banks, www.MLB.com, December 6, 2001.

5. Quoted in Bob Hohler, "Epstein Says There Is Limit on Spending," *Boston Globe*, December 13, 2003.

6. Fred Claire, interview by the author, April 1, 2005.

7. Dan Evans, interview by the author, July 11, 2003.

8. Kris Rone, interview by the author, July 22, 2003.

9. Dan Evans, interview by the author, July 3, 2003.

10. Fred Claire, interview by the author, April 25, 2005.

11. Claire interview, April 1, 2005.

12. Jules Tygiel, *Baseball's Great Experiment: Jackie Robinson and His Legacy* (New York: Oxford University Press, 1983).

13. Ibid., 160.

14. Ibid., 59.

15. Quoted ibid., 110.

16. Ibid., 122.

17. Quoted ibid., 182.

18. *Laredo Times,* August 21, 1935.

19. Quoted in Mark Langill, "Celebrating Fernando," www.Dodgers.com (special report), December 27, 2001.

20. Jane Leavy, *Sandy Koufax: A Lefty's Legacy* (New York: Harper-Collins, 2002), 73.

21. Campanis and Walker quoted ibid., 56.

22. Ibid., 70.

23. Quoted ibid., 72–73.

24. Dan Evans, interview by the author, July 3, 2003.

25. Langill, "Celebrating Fernando."

26. Quoted ibid.

27. Quoted ibid.

28. Quoted ibid.

29. Quoted ibid.

30. Quoted in Steve Delsohn, *True Blue: The Dramatic History of the Los Angeles Dodgers Told by the Men Who Lived It* (New York: William Morrow, 2001), 150.

31. *Fernandomania: The Story of Fernando Valenzuela,* ESPN Classic documentary (2001).

32. Robert Whiting, *The Meaning of Ichiro: The New Wave from Japan and the Transformation of Our National Pastime* (New York: Warner Books, 2004), 98.

33. Quoted in Rod Beaton, "Dodgers' Lineup Reflects Global Approach," *USA Today,* April 19, 1995.

34. Quoted in Associated Press report, February 1, 1995.

35. Quoted in Larry Whiteside, "The Rising Son Returns to Japan," *Boston Globe,* November 17, 1996.

36. Quoted in Mark Langill, "Nomo: A Season to Remember," *Dodger Yearbook Stories,* 1996.

37. Whiting, *Ichiro,* 106, 107.

38. Ibid., 109.

39. Quoted in Kevin Johnson, "Love for Nomo Bridges Pacific and then Some," *USA Today,* October 6, 1995.

40. Paul Sakuma, "Impressive Debut for Nomo," *Chicago Sun-Times,* May 3, 1995.

41. Whiting, *Ichiro,* 111.

42. Quoted in Langill, "Nomo," 75. Nomo did, in fact, understand English much better than he let on. He simply wasn't comfortable with it.

43. Milton Jamail, "Spanning the Globe," *Dodgers Magazine* 7, no. 4 (2000): 33–50; Claire interview, April 1, 2005.

44. Alan M. Klein, *Sugarball: The American Game, The Dominican Dream* (New Haven: Yale University Press, 1991), 98–105.

45. Paul Hagen, "Better Than the Real Thing," *Baseball America*, February 4–17, 2002, 8.

46. Kris Rone, interview by the author, July 11, 2003.

47. Noah Liberman, "Dodgers Score After Taking Spanish Radio In-house," *SportsBusiness Journal*, December 9–15, 2002, 1.

48. Rone interview.

49. Rich Saenz, interview by the author, August 14, 2000.

50. Rone interview.

51. Bonnie Harris and Mark Magnier, "A Big Pitch for Japanese Tourists," *Los Angeles Times*, February 26, 2002.

52. Charles Elmore, "He's a Merchandizer's Dream, a Collector's Target, a Hitter's Nightmare," *Palm Beach Post*, July 20, 1995, 1C.

53. Rone interview.

54. Mariko Sanchanta, "Japan Predicts Bumper Year for Tourists from Overseas," *Financial Times*, January 8, 2004, section 2.

55. Rone interview.

56. Larry Stewart, "Word Is Out on Dodgers, and It's Not Very Good," Los Angeles Times.com, December 12, 2005.

Chapter 4. The Dominican Republic

1. Statistics compiled by author from *Total Baseball*, 7th ed., ed. John Thorn, Pete Palmer, and Michael Gershman (Kingston, N.Y.: Total Sports, 2001).

2. Quoted in Bill Koenig, "Fenway Fiesta: Pedro's Pitching!" *USA Today, Baseball Weekly*, April 15–21, 1998, 8.

3. Quoted in Gordon Edes, "Safe at Home: Martinez Is Still an Island Wonder in Dominican Republic," *Boston Globe*, February 6, 2000.

4. "Baseball: King Sport in Dominican Republic," Associated Press report, March 29, 2001.

5. Quoted ibid.

6. Louie Eljaua, interview by the author, June 11, 2002.

7. Roger Plant, *Sugar and Modern Slavery: A Tale of Two Countries* (London: Zed, 1987), 5–7.

8. We are fortunate to have several Dominican sources covering baseball's origins. Fernando Vicioso and Manuel Alvarez compiled a history of the game in 1967 (*Béisbol Dominicano, 1891–1967* [Santo Domingo, 1967]), and Cuqui Córdova chronicled the history of Dominican baseball for more than twenty years in the country's foremost daily newspaper, *Listín Diario*. The two English-language histories of the game rely heavily upon these sources: Alan Klein, *Sugarball: The American Game, the Dominican Dream* (New Haven: Yale University Press, 1991), and Rob Ruck, *The Tropic of Baseball: Baseball in the Dominican Republic* (Westport, Conn.: Mecklermedia, 1991).

9. Vicioso and Alvarez, *Béisbol Dominicano*, 12; Ruck, *Tropic of Baseball*, 5; Klein, *Sugarball*, 14.

10. Finding the moment of introduction of any cultural artifact is difficult. The scholarship of most sport studies, especially in developing nations, is sketchy at best. See Alan Klein, *Baseball on the Border: A Tale of Two Laredos* (Princeton: Princeton University Press, 1997), chapter 2, for a discussion of the origins of baseball in Mexico.

11. Klein, *Sugarball*, 19.

12. Ruck, *Tropic of Baseball*, 10.

13. Ibid.

14. William H. Beezley, *Judas at the Jockey Club and Other Episodes of Porfirian Mexico* (Lincoln: University of Nebraska Press, 1987).

15. Klein, *Sugarball*, 16–17.

16. Donn Rogosin, *Invisible Men: Life in Baseball's Negro Leagues* (New York: Atheneum, 1985), 166.

17. Cuqui Córdova, interview by the author, January 20, 1989.

18. Klein, *Sugarball*; Marcos Bretón and José Luis Villegas, *Away Games: The Life and Times of a Latin Ballplayer* (New York: Simon and Schuster, 1999).

19. Tim Wendel, *The New Face of Baseball: The One-Hundred-Year Rise and Triumph of Latinos in America's Favorite Sport* (New York: Rayo, 2003).

20. Bretón and Villegas, *Away Games*, 62.

21. Jay Coakley, *Sport in Society: Issues and Controversies*, 7th ed. (New York: McGraw Hill, 2003).

22. Jesse Sanchez, "New Visa Policy in Effect," MLB.com, July 1, 2004.

23. Quoted in Bretón and Villegas, *Away Games*, 71.

24. Quoted in Bill Brubaker, "Caribbean Curve Ball: Baseball's Dominican Pipeline," *Washington Post National Weekly*, March 31, 1986.

25. Internal memorandum, Los Angeles Dodgers.

26. Quoted in Brubaker, "Caribbean Curve Ball."

27. Luis Silverio, interview by the author, February 8, 2002.

28. Louie Eljaua, interview by the author, May 16, 2002.

29. Field interview, Campo Las Palmas, January 5, 1988.

30. Bretón and Villegas, *Away Games*, 74–82.

31. Ibid., 76.

32. Ibid., 172.

33. Quoted ibid., 48.

34. Ruck, *Tropic of Baseball*, 83.

35. Klein, *Sugarball*, 87–93.

36. Jim Salisbury, "Search for Dominican Talent No Longer a Hit-or-Miss Affair," *Philadelphia Inquirer*, July 23, 2002.

37. Jesús Alou, interview by the author, June 11, 2002.

38. Louie Eljaua, interview by the author, June 10, 2002.

39. Luis Silverio, interview by the author, June 12, 2002.

40. Klein, *Sugarball*, 46–47.

41. Juan Forero, "Cultivating a Field of Dreams," *Newark Star-Ledger*, July 5, 1998, section 5, p.1.

42. Silverio interview, June 12, 2002. In May 2005 the exchange rate was approximately twenty-five pesos to a dollar, and estimates of average annual Dominican income in U.S. dollars ranged from $1,800 to $3,200.

43. Steve Fainaru, "The Business of Building Ballplayers," *Washington Post,* June 17, 2001.

44. Samuel Herrera, interview by the author, November 12, 2002.

45. Nelson Gerónimo, interview by the author, November 13, 2002.

46. Silverio interview, June 12, 2002.

47. Ibid.

48. Louie Eljaua, interview by the author, July 31, 2003.

49. Silverio interview, June 12, 2002.

50. Ibid.

51. Alou interview, June 11, 2002.

52. Quoted in Forero, "Cultivating."

53. John Hoberman, *Darwin's Athletes: How Sport Has Damaged Black America and Preserved the Myth of Race* (Boston: Mariner, 1997).

54. José Felipe Rivera, *Población y sociedad* (Santo Domingo, 1983), 327–329.

55. Quoted in Andres Cala, "Poverty in the Dominican Republic Drives Some to Desperate Measures to Play Ball," Associated Press (International News), September 6, 2001.

56. Quoted in Forero, "Cultivating."

57. Ben Cherington, interview by the author, May 23, 2003.

58. Fainaru, "Business."

59. M. Estellie Smith, ed., *Perspectives on the Informal Economy* (Lanham, Md.: University Press of America, 1990); Cathy Rakowski, ed., *Contrapunto: The Informal Sector Debate in Latin America* (Albany, N.Y.: SUNY Press, 1994).

60. Quoted in Michael Knisley, "Everybody Has the Dream," *Sporting News,* February 19, 2001, 3.

61. Rafael Pérez, interview by the author, November 8, 2002. In March 2005 Pérez resigned his position to become head of international player development for the New York Mets.

62. Ibid.

63. Louie Eljaua, interview by the author, August 31, 2002.

64. Jeff Shugel, interview by the author, June 12, 2002.

65. Ibid.

66. Dan Evans, interview by the author, September 3, 2003.

67. Pérez interview, November 8, 2002.

68. Ibid.

69. Ibid.

70. Johnny Díaz, "Dominicans Cast Ballots," *Boston Globe,* May 17, 2004.

71. Gordon Edes, Baseball Notes, *Boston Globe,* May 18, 2004.

72. Rafael Pérez, interview by the author, October 2, 2004.

73. Steve Henson, "Some Players Do Own Thing," *Los Angeles Times,* March 29, 2005.

74. Quoted in Edes, "Safe at Home."

75. Peter Prengaman, "New Dominican Leader Faces Dire Economy," *Boston Globe,* May 18, 2004.

76. Alejandro Portes and Saskia Sassen-Koob, "Making It Underground: Comparative Material on the Informal Sector in Western Market Economics." *American Journal of Sociology* 93 (1987): 30–61.

77. Michael Silverman, "Game Has Empty Feeling," *Boston Herald,* March 12, 2000.

78. Russell Adams, "MLB Signs Richer TV Deal and Official Beer in Baseball-Crazy Dominican Republic," *SportsBusiness Journal,* May 10–16, 2004, 1.

79. Michael McCarthy, "Advertisers Tap into Hispanic Gold Mine," *Boston Globe,* February 21, 2003.

Chapter 5. Japan

This chapter could not have been written without the generosity of Robert Whiting and Marty Kuehnert. They brokered my trip to Tokyo and gave freely of their time and knowledge of Japanese baseball.

1. Robert Whiting has numerous works on Japanese baseball, but the three best known are *The Chrysanthemum and the Bat: Baseball Samurai Style* (New York: Avon, 1983); *You Gotta Have Wa* (New York: Macmillan, 1989); and *The Meaning of Ichiro* (New York: Warner, 2004).

2. In addition to Whiting, the other significant contributor to our knowledge of the game is Marty Kuehnert. Most of his writing has been in Japanese, but his weekly column in English is essential reading on topics of current interest. Most recently Kuehnert briefly served as general manager of the newest team in Nippon Professional Baseball, the Tohoku Rakuten Golden Eagles. The Yale anthropologist William Kelly has also studied the Japanese baseball scene and contributed several articles and chapters. He is currently finishing a book on the Hanshin Tigers, one of Japan's most followed teams.

3. Quoted in Whiting, *You Gotta Have Wa,* 292.

4. Quoted ibid., 300–301.

5. Quoted ibid., 296.

6. Whiting, *You Gotta Have Wa,* 273.

7. Ibid., 303.

8. Quoted ibid., 294.

9. Quoted in Marty Kuehnert, "Matsui and Bass Both Get the Shaft in Voting Process," *Japan Times,* January 14, 2004.

10. Quoted in Whiting, *Meaning of Ichiro,* 76.

11. Ibid., 77, 80.

12. Quoted ibid., 80.

13. Tyler Kepner, "Rediscovering Japan: Yanks Know Ruth and Gehrig Slept There Too," *New York Times,* March 28, 2004.

14. Ray Poitevint, interview by the author, December 3, 2002.

15. Quoted in Marty Kuehnert, "Lasorda Defends Himself, Dodgers Over Deal with Buffaloes," *Japan Times,* July 14, 2004.

16. Marty Kuehnert, interview by the author, July 9, 2004.

17. Jim Allen, interview by the author, July 4, 2004.

18. Derrick Thomas, interview by the author, July 6, 2004.

19. Quoted in Whiting, *Meaning of Ichiro,* 98.

20. Ibid., 101.

21. Quoted ibid., 105.

22. Quoted ibid., 144.

23. Quoted ibid., 25.

24. Kuehnert interview, July 9, 2004.

25. Poitevint interview, December 3, 2002.

26. Kris Rone, interview by the author, September 3, 2002.

27. Jim Allen, interview by the author, July 3, 2004.

28. Shinjo never became the impact player the Giants had banked on, and after two years in the organization, he returned to Japan to play.

29. Allen interview, July 3, 2004.

30. Ibid.

31. Quoted ibid.

32. Ibid.

33. Described in Whiting, *Meaning of Ichiro,* 226.

34. In a little-known Boston "first," it was a Japanese student attending a Boston-area college in the 1870s, and falling for the Red Stockings, as the National League team was then known, who assembled the first Japanese team in Japan. Whiting, *You Gotta Have Wa,* 27.

35. Whiting, *You Gotta Have Wa,* 32.

36. Quoted in Whiting, *Meaning of Ichiro,* 62.

37. Russell Adams, "New Name Deals for Red Sox Firm," *SportsBusiness Journal,* August 9–15, 2004, 1.

38. Kuehnert interview, July 9, 2004.

39. Whiting, *Meaning of Ichiro,* 133.

40. Gary Garland, whose website Japanbaseballdaily.com is a treasure trove of valuable information, was instrumental in helping me to find material on *Yomiuri Shimbun* and Watanabe.

41. Jim Allen, interview by the author, July 6, 2004.

42. Whiting, *Meaning of Ichiro,* 90.

43. Gary Garland, personal communication, August 30, 2003.

44. Allen interview, July 6, 2004.

45. Kuehnert interview, July 9, 2004.

46. Quoted in Makoto Ito, "Baseball Business in a Hole," Japantoday.com, June 16, 2004, 3.

47. Quoted ibid.

48. Marty Kuehnert, "No Name Selling, No-name Commissioner Tells Kintetsu," *Japan Times,* February 11, 2004.

49. Kuehnert interview, July 9, 2004.

50. Quoted in Jim Allen, "Pro Baseball Heads Toward a Single League," *Daily Yomiuri,* July 8, 2004.

51. Merger News, Japanbaseballdailynews.com, July 12, 2004.

52. Ibid.

53. Merger News, Japanbaseballdailynews.com, July 3, 2004.

54. Merger News, Japanbaseballdailynews.com, September 6, 2004.

55. Ibid.

56. Whiting, personal communication, October 12, 2004.

57. Robert Whiting, "Gaijin GM," draft prepared for *Sports Illustrated.*

58. "Popularity of MLB in Japan—Poll and Research Results," internal MLBI document.

59. Quoted in Marc Topkin, "Making MLB Heading to Japan Feel Comfortable," *St. Petersburg Times,* March 23, 2004.

60. "Popularity of MLB in Japan."

61. Quoted in Eijiro Kawada, "Japanese Youngsters Interested in More Than Baseball These Days," *Tacoma News-Tribune,* May 9, 2003.

62. Quoted in Doug Struck, "Japanese Appreciative of Their Exports," *Washington Post,* May 1, 2003.

63. Quoted in "Sadaharu Oh Praises Ichiro as 'Real Thing,'" Associated Press, July 3, 2001.

64. Jim Small, interview by author, July 8, 2004.

65. Kuehnert interview, July 9, 2004.

66. Small interview, July 8, 2004.

67. MLBI, internal document.

68. Small interview, July 8, 2004.

69. Gordon Edes, "MLB's Clout Helped Break Millar Logjam," *Boston Globe,* February 24, 2003.

70. Quoted in Whiting, *Meaning of Ichiro,* 63.

71. Quoted in Kuehnert interview, July 9, 2004.

72. Whiting, *Meaning of Ichiro,* 144.

73. Kuehnert interview, July 9, 2004.

74. Jim Allen, interview with author, July 5, 2004.

75. Charlie Nobles, "Players from Over There Get a Shot Over Here," New York Times.com, May 18, 2005; Ben Bolch, "Whole New Ballgame," LATimes.com, July 28, 2005.

Chapter 6. Italy, Germany, and the United Kingdom

1. Dan Bonanno, "Italian Baseball," unpublished report, MLB properties.

2. Dan Bonanno, interview by the author, June 29, 2002.

3. Clive Russell, interview by the author, July 2, 2002.

4. Bonanno interview.

5. Jim Davenport, interview by the author, July 29, 2001.

6. Bonanno interview.

7. Mauro Mazotti, interview by the author, June 27, 2002.

8. Dan Bonanno, interview by the author, July 7, 2001.

9. Mazotti interview.

10. Dan Newman, interview by the author, July 31, 2001.

11. Bonanno interview, June 29, 2002.

12. Ibid.

13. Ibid.

14. Mazotti interview.

15. Alberto Falzone, interview by the author, June 30, 2002.

16. Mazotti interview.

17. Falzone interview.

18. Bill Holmberg, interview by the author, June 30, 2002.

19. Bonanno interview, June 29, 2002.

20. Quoted in Rick Hummel, "Simontacchi Gains Changeup, Experience in the Italian League," *St. Louis Post-Dispatch,* May 5, 2002.

21. Mark Cherbone, interview by the author, June 28, 2004.

22. Dave Bidini, *Baseballissimo: My Summer in the Italian Minor Leagues* (Toronto: McClelland and Stewart, 2004), 76.

23. David Block, *Baseball Before We Knew It: A Search for the Roots of the Game* (Lincoln: University of Nebraska Press, 2005).

24. Klaus Helmig, interview by the author, October 13, 2001.

25. George Pascal, interview by the author, July 25, 2001.

26. Helmig interview.

27. Ibid.

28. Ibid.

29. Klaus Helmig, interview by the author, October 21, 2001.

30. Ibid.

31. Ibid.

32. Pascal interview.

33. Ibid.

34. Jim Small, interview by the author, July 8, 2004.

35. Pascal interview.

36. I am indebted in this section to Chetwynd's unpublished "Brit Ball," a historical account of the history of the game in the United Kingdom.

37. Josh Chetwynd, "The Day Britain Triumphed Over the United States," *Double Play,* Spring 2002, 30.

38. Clive Russell, interview by the author, September 7, 2004.

39. Clive Russell, interview by the author, July 2, 2002.

40. Ibid.

41. Jim Small, interview by the author, July 25, 2002.
42. Bob Fromer, interview by the author, July 2, 2002.
43. Russell, interview, September 7, 2004.
44. Pat Doyle, interview by the author, July 21, 2001.
45. Small interview, July 8, 2004.
46. Clive Russell, interview by the author, October, 19, 2004.
47. Sandy Alderson, interview by the author, November 30, 2004.
48. Small interview, July 8, 2004.
49. Clive Russell, interview by the author, June 21, 2001.
50. Jim Small, interview by the author, July 5, 2004.
51. Basil Tarasko, interview by the author, July 29, 2001.
52. Basil Tarasko, "Ten Years of Baseball Development in Ukraine Marked by Significant Progress," www.ukrweekly.com.
53. Basil Tarasko, interview by the author, September 1, 2001.
54. Small interview, July 5, 2004.

Chapter 7. South Africa

1. Edwin Bennett, interview by the author, June 27, 2002. Under apartheid the terms Black, White, and Colored (Asians and people of mixed race) were official racial designations, and they remain in common usage, so I have capitalized them in the South African context.
2. Barry Armitage, interview by the author, March 28, 2004.
3. Ibid.
4. My overview in this chapter is informed by Douglas Booth's excellent history of sport and apartheid in South Africa, *The Race Game: Sport and Politics in South Africa* (London: Cass, 1998). See also Hermann Giliomee and Richard Elphick, "The Structure of European Domination on the Cape, 1652–1820," in *The Shaping of South African Society, 1652–1820,* ed. Hermann B. Giliomee and Richard Elphick (London: Cass, 1979), 359–390.
5. Giliomee and Elphick, "Structure of European Domination," 371.
6. Quoted in Dennis Brutus, "Sport and Apartheid," *Current Affairs Bulletin* 46, no. 12 (1970): 179.
7. Booth, *Race Game,* 78.
8. Ibid., 86–88.
9. Ibid., 147.
10. Edwin Bennett, interview by the author, February 19, 2002.
11. Booth, *Race Game,* 179.
12. Republic of South Africa, House of Assembly Debates (Pretoria, 1953), cols. 3576, 3585–3586, quoted in Booth, *Race Game,* 62.
13. Bennett interview, February 19, 2002.
14. Pett Yus, interview by the author, February 16, 2002.
15. Bennett interview, February 19, 2002.

16. Yus interview.
17. Bennett interview, February 19, 2002.
18. Booth, *Race Game*, 138.
19. Bennett interview, February 19, 2002.
20. Ibid.
21. Mike Randall, interview by the author, February 21, 2002.
22. Bill Holmberg, interview by the author, July 3, 2002.
23. Edwin Bennett, interview by the author, February 20, 2002.
24. Randall interview.
25. Mike Randall, interview by the author, February 22, 2002.
26. Ibid.
27. Bennett interview, February 19, 2002.
28. Allard Baird, interview by the author, May 11, 2001.
29. Carol Kyte, interview by the author, July 22, 2002.
30. Baird interview.
31. Ibid.
32. Luis Silverio, interview by the author, February 8, 2002.
33. Baird interview.
34. Ibid.
35. Bennett interview, February 19, 2002.
36. Armitage interview.

Chapter 8. When Will There Be a Real World Series?

1. Quoted in Claire Smith, "Land of Rising Opportunities," *Sporting News*, March 4, 1991, 24.
2. Quoted in Thomas Boswell, "Franchise for the World," *Washington Post*, April 19, 1991.
3. There was, of course, the annual major league exhibition tour of Japan that fall, but even that was at the time being thought of as little more than a goodwill tour and shopping spree.
4. Joseph Maguire, "More Than a Sporting 'Touchdown': The Making of American Football in Britain, 1982–1989," *Sociology of Sport Journal* 7, no. 3 (1990): 213–237.
5. Quoted in Barry Bloom, "Mission Accomplished: The Padres Practice Globalization Without the Help of Major-league Baseball," *Sport*, September 1997, 46.
6. Larry Stone, "MLB's Japan Tour Another Selig Step onto World Stage," *Seattle Times*, April 2, 2000: D10.
7. Jim Allen, interview by the author, July 6, 2004.
8. Ibid.
9. Elizabeth J. Milleker, ed., *The Year One: Art of the Ancient World East and West* (New York: Metropolitan Museum of Art, 2000), 3.

10. David Harvey, *The Condition of Postmodernity* (Oxford: Blackwell, 1989), 29.

11. Thomas L. Friedman, *The Lexus and the Olive Tree* (New York: Anchor, 1999).

12. Harvey, *Conditions*, 293.

13. John Micklethwait and Adrian Wooldridge, *A Future Perfect: The Challenge and Hidden Promise of Globalization* (New York: Crown, 2000), 37.

14. Manuel Castells, *The Rise of the Network Society* (Oxford: Blackwell, 1996), 31.

15. Friedman, *Lexus*, xviii.

16. Paul Hirst and Grahame Thompson, *Globalization in Question: The International Economy and the Possibilities of Governance* (Cambridge: Polity, 1996).

17. David Held, Anthony G. McGrew, David Goldblatt, and Jonathan Perraton, *Global Transformations: Politics, Economics, and Culture* (Palo Alto: Stanford University Press, 1999), 15.

18. Hiawatha Bray, "As Economy Gains, Outsourcing Surges," *Boston Globe*, November 2, 2003.

19. Chris Gaither, "US workers see hard times," *Boston Globe*, November 3, 2003.

20. Quoted ibid.

21. Anna Tsing, "The Global Situation," in *The Anthropology of Globalization: A Reader*, ed. Jonathan Xavier Inda and Renato Rosaldo (London: Blackwell, 2002), 452–482.

22. Joseph Stiglitz, *Globalization and Its Discontents* (New York: Norton, 2002), 22.

23. Tina Rosenberg, "Globalization," *New York Times Magazine*, August 18, 2002, 28–33, 50.

24. See, for instance, Anthony Giddens, *Runaway World: How Globalization is Reshaping Our Lives* (New York: Routledge, 2000), or Rosenberg, "Globalization."

25. Rosenberg, "Globalization," 31.

26. James L. Scott, *Weapons of the Weak: Everyday Forms of Peasant Resistance* (New Haven: Yale University Press, 1985).

27. Mitchell Stephens, "Brave New World: As the World Shrinks, Cultures Blend and Diversity Disappears," *Los Angeles Times Magazine*, January 17, 1993, 21.

28. Ulf Hannerz, "Notes on the Global Ecumene," *Public Culture* 1, no. 2 (1989): 66–75.

29. Some of the most important investigations of sport and globalization include Alan Bairner, *Sport, Nationalism, and Globalization* (Albany: State University of New York Press, 2001); John Bale and Joseph Maguire, eds., *The Global Sports Arena* (London: Frank Cass, 1994); Toby Miller, Geoffrey A. Lawrence, Jim McKay, and David Rowe, *Globalization and Sport: Playing the World* (London: Sage, 2001); Jean Harvey, G. Rail, and L. Thibault, "Globalization and Sport: Sketching a Theoretical Model for Empirical Analysis," *Journal of Sport and Social Issues* 20, no. 3 (1996): 258–277; and David L. Andrews, B. Carrington, Z. Mazur, and S. Jackson, "'Jordanscapes': A Preliminary Analysis of the Global Popular," *Sociology of Sport Journal* 13, no. 4 (1996): 428–457. Though a historian, Walter LaFeber has written a compelling examination of globalization that deserves attention, *Michael Jordan and the New Global Capitalism* (New York: Norton, 1999).

30. John Sugden and Alan Tomlinson, *FIFA and the Contest for World Football: Who Rules the People's Game?* (Cambridge: Blackwell, 1998); John Sugden and Alan Tomlinson, "Power and Resistance in the Governance of World Football: Theorizing FIFA's Transnational Impact," *Journal of Sport and Social Issues* 22, no. 3 (1998): 299–316.

31. Joseph Maguire's most important works in this regard are *Global Sport: Identities, Societies, Civilizations* (Cambridge: Polity, 1999); "Globalization, Sport Development, and the Media/Sport Production Complex," *Sport Science Review* 2, no. 1 (1993): 29–47; "Blade Runners: Canadian Migrants, Ice Hockey, and the Global Sports Process," *Journal of Sport and Social Issues* 20, no. 3 (1996): 335–360; "Sport, Identity Politics, and Globalization: Diminishing Contrasts, Increasing Varieties," *Sociology of Sport Journal* 11, no. 4 (1994): 398–427.

32. See Norbert Elias, *The Civilizing Process* (Oxford: Blackwell, 1982), 251–258.

33. Quoted in John Lombardo, "NBA Imports Talent and Exports the Game," *SportsBusiness Journal,* October 25–31, 2004, 25.

34. Douglas B. Holt, *How Brands Become Icons: The Principles of Cultural Branding* (Boston: Harvard Business School Press, 2004).

35. Clay Risen, "Re-branding America," *Boston Globe,* March 13, 2005. See also Harwood L. Childs, ed., *Propaganda and Dictatorship* (Princeton: Princeton University Press, 1936).

36. Simon Anholt and Jeremy Hildreth, *Brand America: The Mother of All Brands* (London: Cyan, 2005).

37. Robert Whiting, personal communication, October 31, 2004.

38. Jim Small, interview by the author, December 2, 2004.

39. Ibid.

40. Jim Small, interview by the author, July 26, 2002.

41. Edwin Bennett, interview by the author, February 20, 2002.

42. Eric Hobsbawm and Terence Ranger, eds., *The Invention of Tradition* (Cambridge: Cambridge University Press, 1983).

43. Janet Lever, *Soccer Madness* (Chicago: University of Chicago Press, 1983).

44. Ron Koffman, "Time to Tackle the Hooligans," www.Haaretz.com, November 2, 2004.

45. Steven Erlanger, "A National Hero One Day, an Enemy to Some the Next," New York Times.com, April 22, 2005.

46. Barry Armitage, interview by the author, March 20, 2004.

47. Quoted in Barry Bloom, "Mission Accomplished: The San Diego Padres Have Practiced Globalization Without the Help of MLB," *Sport,* September 1997, 46–50.

48. Daniel Kaplan and John Rofe, "MLB Building Record Loan Pool," *SportsBusiness Journal,* August 28–September 3, 2000, 1.

49. Bill King, "MLB Tops Leagues in Lobbying Efforts," *SportsBusiness Journal,* October 11–17, 1999, 6.

50. Alan Schwarz, "First Dominican Draft Proved Chaotic," *Baseball America,* January 22–February 4, 2001, 7.

51. Ralph Avila, interview by the author, March 26, 2003.

52. Quoted in Tom Singer, "Should There Be a Worldwide Draft?" MLB.com, May 9, 2002.

53. Quoted ibid.

54. Dean Taylor, interview by the author, December 4, 2002.

55. Interview by the author, August 3, 2002.

56. Quoted in Lawrence Rocca, "World Draft Could Ease Inequities in Baseball Signing," Newhouse News Service, July 29, 2002.

57. Ben Cherington, interview by the author, August 18, 2002.

58. Michael Knisley, "Dodging the Draft," *Sporting News,* February 19, 2001, 11.

59. Jesús Alou, interview by the author, June 11, 2003.

60. Sandy Alderson, interview by the author, December 9, 2004.

61. Quoted in David Rawnsley, "An Argument Against the Worldwide Draft," *Baseball America,* February 19–March 4, 2001, 17.

62. Baseball had been played as a demonstration sport as early as the 1912 Olympics in Stockholm, Sweden, and a number of times thereafter.

63. Quoted in John Powers, "US Baseball Is Stunned, Fails to Make Olympics," *Boston Globe,* November 8, 2003.

64. Quoted in Will Longo, "Building a Winner, They Hope," *Baseball America,* September 18–October 1, 2000, 8.

65. Stephen Wilson, "IOC May Drop Baseball from Olympics," Association Press Online, August 29, 2002.

66. Amy Shipley, "Baseball's International Stage: MLB Is Planning a World Cup, While IOC Wants Deeper Commitment," *Washington Post,* May 21, 2003.

67. Quoted in John Manuel, "Big Leaguers Could Save Olympic Baseball," *Baseball America,* November 11–24, 2002, 3.

68. Quoted in Shipley, "Baseball's International Stage."

69. Alderson interview.

70. Quoted in William C. Rhoden, "Olympic Softball a Victim of U.S. Supremacy," New York Times.com, July 9, 2005.

71. Quoted in Associated Press, "Secret Ballot Eliminates Baseball, Softball," espn.com, July 8, 2005.

72. Quoted in Tim Brown and David Wharton, "Out of Olympics, Baseball Plans a Real World Series," LATimes.com July 12, 2005.

73. Quoted in Associated Press, "Secret Ballot."

74. Barry Bloom, "Baseball Could Return to Olympics," MLB.com, October 28, 2005.

75. Robert Whiting, *The Chrysanthemum and the Bat: Baseball Samurai Style* (New York: Avon, 1983), 222.

76. Small interview, December 2, 2004.

77. Ibid.

78. "Estrada's Diary: Oh What a Meeting," MLB.com, November 9, 2004.

79. Small interview, December 2, 2004.

80. Quoted in John Manuel, "World Cup Proceeds, but Questions Remain," *Baseball America*, November 12–25, 2001, 3.

81. Quoted in Alan Schwarz, "World Baseball Classic Becomes Reality," *Baseball America*, June 6–19, 2005, 7.

82. Rafael Hermoso, "Baseball: Today It's Puerto Rico, Tomorrow It's the World," *New York Times*, April 15, 2003.

83. Quoted in Murray Chass, "Problems with Proposed MLB 2005 World Cup," www.sportsbusinessnews.com (The Daily Dose), February 11, 2004 (originally published as "MLB Needs to Play Tough for World Cup" in *New York Times*, February 10, 2004).

84. Quoted in Amy Chozick, "Global Pitch" *Wall Street Journal*, October 18, 2004, 1.

85. Quoted in Barry Bloom, "World Cup Given Owners' Blessing," www.sportsbusinessnews.com (The Daily Dose), August 20, 2004 (originally published at MLB.com).

86. Barry M. Bloom, "MLB Close on WBC Venues, Japan," MLB.com, August 17, 2005.

87. These revenue distribution figures were taken from the Liga de béisbol profesional de la República Dominicana website, in a detailed description of the World Baseball Classic, dated April 2005 contributed by Aldo Notari, head of the International Baseball Federation, and Gene Orza, head of the MLB Players Association.

88. Quoted in Jack Gallagher, "Playing World Baseball Classic in Spring or Fall Makes No Sense At All," *Japan Times*, June 8, 2005.

89. Quoted in Bloom, "MLB Close on WBC Venues."

90. Quoted in Gallagher, "Playing World Baseball Classic."

91. Quoted in Bruce Wallace, "Japan Might Balk at This Brand-New Ballgame," LATimes.com, June 13, 2005.

92. Ken Davidoff, "Is Japan About to Pull Out of the World Baseball Classic?" www.sportsbusinessnews.com (The Daily Dose), May 30, 2005 (originally published as "Culture Shock Shakes Japan-MLB Plan" in *New York Newsday*, May 29, 2005).

93. Jim Small, interview by the author, July 8, 2004.

94. Quoted in Schwarz, "World Baseball Classic."

95. Wayne Graczyk, "MLB Japan Tries to Reassure NPB on World Baseball Classic," *Japan Times*, June 5, 2005.

96. "Barring Cuba from Baseball Tourney Embarrasses US, III," www.sportsbusinessnews.com (The Daily Dose), December 17, 2005 (originally published by the Associated Press, December 16, 2005).

97. Paul Archey, interview by the author, January 14, 2005.

98. Cody Holt, "Major League Video," www.looksmart.com, April 1, 2004.

99. Matthew Futterman, "Baseball's MLB.com Is a Hit, Poised For an IPO," newhousenews.com, August 2, 2004.

100. Quoted in Holt, "Major League Video."

101. Futterman, "Baseball's MLB.com."

102. Alderson interview.

103. Alan Klein, "Old Pride, New Prejudice: Dominican Baseball and the Twenty-First Century," manuscript in progress.

104. Sandy Alderson, interview by the author, November 30, 2004.

105. Alderson interview, November 30, 2004.

106. Dan Duguette, interview by the author, November 1, 2001.

107. Quoted in Tom Krasovic, "Club's Finances Pass MLB Inspection—'We're very pleased,'" *San Diego Union-Tribune,* May 10, 2003.

INDEX

Made in the USA
Middletown, DE
12 January 2020